Social work and sexual conduct

Library of Social Work

General Editor:
Noel Timms
Professor of Social Work Studies
University of Newcastle upon Tyne

Social work and sexual conduct

John Hart

Department of Applied Social Studies
Sheffield City Polytechnic

Routledge & Kegan Paul
London, Boston and Henley

First published in 1979
by Routledge & Kegan Paul Ltd
39 Store Street,
London WC1E 7DD,
Broadway House,
Newtown Road,
Henley-on-Thames,
Oxon RG9 1EN and
9 Park Street,
Boston, Mass. 02108, USA
Set in 10/11pt English
and printed in Great Britain by
The Lavenham Press Ltd,
Lavenham, Suffolk

British Library Cataloguing in Publication Data

Hart, John

Social work and sexual conduct. - (Library
of Social Work ISSN 0305-4381).
1. Social Service and Sex.
I. Title II. Series
301.41'7'02436   HV41   79-40160

ISBN 0 7100 0217 3

For Richard Pinder

Contents

Contents

Acknowledgments

To the people in England and Scotland who participated in the study my thanks and I hope they find the book has done them justice. I am very fortunate in my friends. Those who have been particularly helpful have been Jack Porter, Maureen Blyth, and the Gay Social Workers and Probation Officers Group. Especial thanks to Judith Crocker for her toleration if not encouragement of my handwriting and to three friends: Colin Raban, sociologist, Diane Richardson, psychologist, and Eric Sainsbury, Professor of Social Administration.

J.H.

Introduction

This book is divided into three parts. The first locates social work within discussions about sexuality. Part 2 contains a study of some aspects of sexual conduct, particularly that which has become public deviance. It consists of extensive excerpts from transcripted interviews with a small number of probation officers, social workers and clients. The views of about forty people form the basis of the reports in the study which illustrate the ways in which social workers and clients handle sexual conduct when it concerns them both. Conclusions and implications are drawn in Part 3.

Why are so few people quoted at such length without extensive conceptualization? I believe that the approach adopted presents the reader with unusually rich and frank discussions in an area which the emerging profession of social work often finds is fraught with 'moral panics'. To illustrate the uniqueness of the material, perhaps I need only mention some of the areas: the social workers' own sexual experience; the clients' view of their workers; sexual conduct in residential work; the ways in which social workers cope with paedophilia. I hope this will encourage the reader to tolerate the open-ended nature of the presentation, although it is important to read the interviews in conjunction with the orientation in Part 1. Of particular importance is the moral rather than technical view of the subject, for which I gather material in Chapter 3. This process is continued in the interim conclusions after each section of the interviews. From these tentative findings, a normative view of social work and sexual conduct is developed in Part 3 where I attempt to balance 'the need for further research' with the problems of sexual conduct with which workers and clients are, I am very aware, struggling today. The book should begin to provide a way of assessing and dealing with sexual conduct which cannot be 'the last word' on the subject because of the ambivalences in the position held by social work in our society.

1

Introduction

It is also possible to argue that a unified social work view is impossible, given the diversity of workers' ideologies. This makes it even more important to present the interviews in as much detail as possible. This will also, I hope, allow readers to form alternative assessments and strategies. Certainly if social work is as 'individualized' as is sometimes suggested, then we should study in great detail the views of individual workers. Throughout this book for convenience social work is described as a 'profession'. I am aware of the controversial nature of such a label. My preference would be for a term such as anti-profession or semi-profession.

The book is not about such matters as techniques of counselling in sexual dysfunctioning, family planning, sex education. These important matters are referred to in the 'Further sources' chapter. What the book is about is where social work has a unique claim for developing expertise—at the moral interface between society and the sexual problem person. There are not many cheap thrills in the book because it is my experience that such things are too expensive for our customers.

Part one

Sexual conduct

Chapter 1

Ways of
understanding sex

This chapter contains a definition of sexual conduct and goes on to
look at the ways in which social work has to both rely on and apply
knowledge from physiology, biology, psychology, sociology and
morality in order to understand its role in relation to sexual conduct.
The presentation of the contributions of these areas of knowledge is
very selective, critical and multi-disciplinary. It emphasizes the
importance of interaction: between and within disciplines; theory
and practice; society and its agents of control and change; individual
behaviour and social structure. The *uses* of knowledge are highlighted. Therefore the presentation is also practice orientated and
provides an outline for the discussion in Chapters 2 and 3 of the past
and present status of social work and sexual conduct and the
presentation of the study.

Richan (1972) identifies three distinct language systems in social
work: (1) the clinical; (2) the analytical; (3) the ideological. In
looking at sexual conduct we will use all three, but perhaps the first
question to be considered *is* ideological—why study sexual conduct,
for what use is the knowledge gained? The answer to this will help
readers evaluate this presentation in the light of their own experience.
    The personal politics of liberation movements are accessible to
view in the growth of writings in the area of women's studies and
studies of homosexuals where authors may acknowledge political
allegiance and/or personal orientation (for example, Wilson, 1977;
Babuscio, 1976). The present study is within a similar context. In
deciding to report on sexual conduct and social work, I believe this
to be a useful empirical study of a neglected area. Having been
witness to, and a participant in, the profession's past reliance on
personal pathological explanations, or moral prohibition of diverse
sexual expression, I hope to provide alternative ways of understanding such conduct. I recognize that historically the demands of

the economy have dictated anti-feminist measures (Wilson, 1977) and expressions of 'taboo morality' (Ryan, 1975) in social policy. In hoping to change such matters as they are represented by and affect social work, I will present and argue for the legitimacy of the client's view and the worker's response in order to increase society's tolerance of certain behaviours.

What is sexual conduct?

From an operational viewpoint, in recognition of social work's individualized commitment in society, we need a definition which will be inclusive enough to allow for such very special kinds of behaviour. Our definition should also be obviously 'of this world'.

A definition: 'The expression of the physical and psychological experience of sexual desire and/or sexual usage, for physical and/or social ends.'

Having produced one such definition to use as a basis for describing the area of our interest, we have to say something about the ways in which we understand the human behaviour which the definition attempts to contain. This is a mammoth task, and a word is necessary about the quest for holistic description in social work before we succumb to the inevitable reductionist exercise. Too often 'text books to the trade' in social work seem to take place outside one's day-by-day experience both as a professional and as a person outside that role. Although audio and visual recording of social work encounters are becoming familiar in training, the felt ambiguities in the workers' role are hard to convey in the written word. Perhaps years of self-delusion producing process records has not helped the profession achieve the synthesis of political and personal awareness which is necessary to convey the value and technical components of social work in action. A style is needed which demands accuracy of reportage and technique within a framework of blatant values and commitments. If a technique is useful in this it is in the service of making the easy things look difficult and the difficult easy! (See Appendix.) The conventions of the social sciences need to be respected: methodology should be made explicit and thereby replicable. From the social sciences we have knowledge and also a critical stance to 'findings' informed by a sociology of knowledge. As Leonard (1976, p. 252) emphasizes, 'social facts have a dual nature, that they exist both in themselves and in the conceptualizations of those who observe them'. Social work needs all these inputs and yet more—what is missing is the poetry of, say, meeting a client in Tesco, or the time you were at a disco and started pondering why it was that X was so elated or depressed that day. Or perhaps the recognition after having had a sexual experience yourself that it was a client's face which appeared on your screen of images. Of course all this can be referred to as 'professional distance/role', 'commitment to welfare', 'personal politics' and 'double dose communications'. What is needed is a professional ideology which insists that these experiences with implicit costs and rewards are woven into a theoretical base for social work which will thereby be worthy of the *valuable* clients and practitioners it serves.

We have the wide definition of our subject allowing for the specific and the general. For an understanding of both we will need to turn to physiology, biology, psychology, sociology and morality. We cannot evaluate comprehensively the enormous contribution each has made to the understanding of sexuality but rather note the main areas of interest of workers in each area. The *interdependence* of disciplines will be stressed and their connection with social policy and social work practice. We will also provide some examples of 'theories in action' as they may affect social workers' understanding of sexual conduct. The search is for the way sex is seen and understood by the professional and by the participant observer.

To return to the definition: to make this *practically* useful we have to describe what is meant by sexual desire/usage, physical and psychological experience, and to account for the social environment. It should be noted that in the definition, sexual desire and sexual usage are seen as possibly separate. The reason for this is that sexual acts may not of themselves be related to sexual desire. The sexual expression may be of subsidiary importance, for example, in a struggle for power or as a means of expressing aggression in rape or 'queer bashing'. Some of the behaviours in our study may be judged in origin and purpose as only marginally sited in the sexual arena. They may, however, be perceived by society in general and its representatives as being sexual conduct and therefore presented to the social worker as such a problem. Hence even when any erotic component may be questionable, we will discuss the behaviour as sexual because for all its cognizance of non-verbal communications, social work is primarily concerned with visible gestures.

Physiological and biological understanding

Before it is assumed that the understanding of sex is located 'in the head' or 'in social structure', we will refer to Masters and Johnson (1966) who made available a picture of the cycle of physiological reactions in the human male and female. Their work normalized the idea of wide-ranging possibilities in sexual response. It legitimized demands for sexual equality and later provided a basis for a clear-headed behavioural approach to what is now described as

7

Sexual conduct

dysfunctioning. For a helpful discussion of the physiology of sex, see Paintin (1976, p. 13), although this example of behaviour may have less than universal applicability: 'Prior to ejaculation, penile erection may subside if sexual activity is interrupted by some disturbing factor such as a telephone bell.' Rutter (1971) describes physical sexual development, hormonal changes, and clearly divides psycho-sexual development into, (1) sexual activity and interests, (2) concepts of sexual differences and the creation of babies, and (3) sex role differentiation. He also evaluates biological, psychoanalytic and psychosexual theories of sexual development.

We have immediately to recognize Freud (1917, p. 137) as both inheriting and also passing on the biological tradition in accounts of human conduct, 'The force by which the sexual instinct is represented in the mind we call "libido"—sexual desire—and we regard it as something analogous to hunger, the will to power, and so on, where the ego-instincts are concerned.' Jones (1955) notes that Freud believed the libido had an organic base—a chemical nature. Freud thought the sexual instinct found expression in different parts of the body as the child developed. He viewed the growth of character and personality as occurring through these developmental stages—oral, anal, phallic. This instinctual life of the individual had to be mediated by social experience in order to be channelled into socially harmonious expression. As Rieff (1960, p. 167) puts it, for Freud 'Sexuality is prefigurative, the clue to the meaning of later conduct and appetite; if a patient manifests some moral or gestural abnormality the analyst assumes he will find a premonition of it in the early sexual life during the course of treatment.' As we shall note, Freud's views are still debated today and his influence is observable in explanations of how both sexual and social conformity and non-conformity are related to 'man's instinct'. See for example Keith Joseph's famous 1974 Birmingham speech:

'The worship of instinct, of spontaneity, the rejection of self-discipline, is not progress; it is degeneration. It was Freud who argued that repression of instincts is the price we pay for civilisation. He considered the price well paid. So can we, now.'

See also Chapter 2 for a discussion of the development of Freud's theories and social work.

Debate continues about the primacy of a biological base or determination of human sexual behaviour. A useful review of the evidence, with different conclusions, is provided by Hardy (1971) and Whalin (1971). Hardy, writing in the 1960s, claimed that some type of biological drive theory still predominated in discussion of human sexual motivation. He argued that theories of this type do not account for either the diversity or the variability of cross-cultural

8

human behaviour. He concluded 'that the overwhelming proportion of the variance in human sexual motivation and behaviour is not explicable in terms of some biologic need or tension, however conceived' (p. 64). He then expounded an alternative theory of learning and reinforcement in sexual behaviour from various degrees of pleasurable experience. He allowed that such experience might not always be pleasurable with the consequence of ambivalence about a particular aspect of sexuality. This in itself represents a rather 'pure' view of the dominance of cognitive processes in learning about sexual behaviour and it is disputed by Whalin. He does not have an exclusive preference for biological explanations but sees behaviour as resulting from both motivation and habit. He separates sexual motivation into two components, *sexual arousal*, which is managed by experience much in the way that Hardy concludes. Whalin sees sexual *arousability* as being determined by a hormonal state in association with the effects of experience. He concludes, 'that hormones affect arousability by altering the threshold for erotic stimulation, regardless of whether the threshold in question is one of peripheral tissue sensitivity or of central neural sensitivity' (pp. 83-4). He states there is another physiological consideration in the feedback effect of sexual stimulation on subsequent arousability. He cites orgasm in the male resulting in zero arousability, whilst for females a second orgasm is possible within a very short time. Alongside this physiologically based sexual arousability comes the importance of learned experience in that arousal occurs with an increasing number of stimuli.

Lloyd (1976, p. 10) considers that the academic interest in biological contributions to human behaviour can be understood in this way, 'Behaviourism has been under strong attack for over a decade and during this period psychologists have rediscovered biology.' She discusses the contributions of theorists such as Hutt (1972) righting 'a balance of biological and experiential factors which had in the past swung too heavily to the nurture side by taking advantage of considerable strides which have been made in the biological sciences, (p. 12). The most interesting aspect of the continuing debate about nature/nurture as it affects our understanding is the 'social reception' of such concepts in understanding what constitutes a 'sexual drive'.

The sex instinct is seen as male, animal-based, dangerous, and once aroused, difficult to deny. Carol Maggs (reported in *Guardian Women*, 28 June 1977) had been very brutally attacked by a man who was released later on appeal:

One minute he was talking civilly—next minute he pushed me to the ground and held me with his knees and tried to force

9

me. I think it was because I had rejected him. I shouted 'Get off, I don't want you', but he wouldn't stop. I have heard about pure animal instinct, but if a bitch is not interested a dog will stop.

She has the perspective of victim, adherent and critic of the theory.

In any discussion of the nature of sexual drive, it may be considered that a chemical agent can change behaviour by suppressing the sexual urge. Bancroft (1974, p. 213) warns that the use of drugs such as oestrogens involves serious side effects and that in relation to other drugs such as cyproterone acetate, 'Only very recently have adequate attempts been made to evaluate these drugs and it is clear that we still know very little about their real effects on sexual behaviour' (references given).

Laschet (1973) is not so guarded in her enthusiasm for cyproterone acetate. She describes treatment with this drug, used to reduce or inhibit the sexual reactions of a wide range of sexual delinquents in West Germany, involving homosexual and heterosexual paedophilia, exhibitionism, indecent assault, sex murder, incest, fetishism and sodomy. She reports on satisfactory adjustment and complete social integration only for exhibitionists, hypersexuals and states that some paedophiles proved resistant.

Eysenck (1976, pp. 10-11) published an extension of his personality theory—with its cluster of traits labelled Neuroticism, Extraversion and Psychoticism. He sees these as 'innate physiological structures, differences in which are responsible, in interaction with environmental determinants, for producing the phenotypic behaviour patterns that we observe, rate and measure.' He does this in the area of sexual behaviour. One of his conclusions (p. 232) is,

We thus have two patterns of behaviour that are acceptable because they lead to personal satisfaction and happiness—the introvertive traditional one of monogamy and family life, the extraverted one of wine, women and song. Either pattern may lead to dissatisfaction and unhappiness, however, when there is an admixture in the personality of psychiatric, abnormal, pathological characteristics, whether of the quasi-neurotic, or the quasi-psychotic, quasi-psychopathic variety.

North and Toates (1977) believe that, 'the sex drive, and its need for novelty, is part of man's animal inheritance and may be attributable to identifiable nervous system properties. Why some go in for promiscuity more than others may be due to the nervous system they were born with.'

Social workers may be involved in treatments which rely on biological theories of sexual behaviour. Probation Officer 1 in this study (see p. 189) describes a middle-aged man, in a skilled job, apparently with a satisfactory matrimonial situation who looked at and fondled little girls; to save him from a long prison sentence and the collapse of his social stability the officer arranges the possibility of drug treatment: 'If you are injected with this, all libido will disappear. . . . "Please, that's what I want, can I have this . . .?" It was virtually a chemical castration of the chap.' For an example of a theory held in practice in relation to 'innate sex drive' see Probation Officer 3 (p. 71-2).

From a practitioner's stance, a biological viewpoint about origins of sexual expression may be held whilst change in the area of sexual behaviour is sought by chemical means as cited above, or by psychodynamic investigation, or by means of behaviour therapy. The theory itself does, however, have consequences for the decisions made by professionals encountering manifestations of sexual interest. Wilson and Davison (1974) provide a very useful review of the assessment and treatment of homosexuality by behaviour therapy:

the traditional viewpoint about sexual development being the successive manifestations of a largely fixed biological drive (libido!) influences therapeutic decisions. If the sex drive is biologically determined and relatively fixed in amount, then it follows logically that the prevailing expression (e.g. homosexuality) has to be blocked so that it can be channelled elsewhere (e.g. heterosexuality).

These authors conclude,

There is still little compelling evidence showing that homosexuality is either genetically determined or hormonally based. Money (1970) has concluded that a biological predisposition toward homosexuality might exist, but 'not in the ordained sense, only if the social conditions are right'.

These approaches separate discussion of theories of sexual motivation from questions of gender role and sexual identification which are seen as subjects for separate sociological and cultural enquiry. This is not the view of other writers. There has been a renewal of interest in the biological/societal basis of gender role as well as a continuing debate about the hormonal determinants of certain types of sexual behaviours.

We should return to Freud in considering the explanations of sex differences. As Rieff (1960, p. 175) argues, 'Freud sees sexuality as women's problem in a special sense beyond the general sense in which it is a problem for any person, male or female.' Some understanding of the expansion in women's studies in psychology and sociology can be gained from Rieff's (p. 182) assertion 'That the great critical

11

figures in modern philosophy, literature, psychology—Nietzsche, Lawrence, Freud—were mysogynists.' Certainly psychoanalytical theory assumes that some sort of predetermined relationship exists between physiological and psychological sexual characteristics in men and women. Undoubtedly account must be taken of physiology and biology, both in terms of sexual drive and sexual differentiation, but this does not provide an adequate explanation of specific manifestations of sexuality. Archer (1976, p. 252) points to the animal experimentation at the basis of many biological conclusions about human sexuality, and specifies the question to be asked: 'how a genetically-influenced trait is expressed in the range of environmental conditions in which it may develop. Even in the rodents, which have featured prominently in animal-based theories, hormonally-produced sex differences are environmentally labile.'

Lloyd (1976, p. 16) in accounting for male/female differences suggests an *interactionist perspective*:

> I believe that only through an analysis of the interaction of biological and social variables can we begin to approach an adequate understanding of the few reliable differences in the intellectual and temperamental behaviour of men and women which have been reported. Equally, we need to consider both the impact of society on science and the reaction of society to scientific findings.

She usefully looks beyond 'questions of fact' to the values and motivations behind the decision to study and emphasize certain explanations of human conduct:

> As a psychologist, I think that the illusion of normlessness and lack of boundaries which popular discussion of the 'permissive society' creates also furnish impetus to a search for universal, immutable verities, which biologically-based explanations appears to supply.

We may then conclude this brief view of biological contributions to the understanding of sexual conduct by stating the obvious that these explanations as they refer to sexual behaviour, including sex-role differences, do not in themselves provide more than a single-sided view of causation and behaviour. Referring again to the Freudian view of the sexual instinct analogous to hunger—this does not equip us with a way of understanding the popularity of T.V. snacks! The impact of the theory is probably much greater than its scientific status would warrant. However, we should note the importance of studies in reproductive biology having provided an alternative to psychoanalytic formulations by enabling us to separate discussions of reproductive from sexual behaviours. We can note that amongst many psychologists the interdependence of theories is already taken seriously in study of the physiological, biological, psychological and the environmental.

Psychological understanding and therapy

It was predictable that following the plethora of myths and archetypes of the psychoanalyst, psychology should have been motivated to seek out large representative samples of the population and get down to measuring the occurrences and frequencies of certain behaviours rather than search for 'meaning' with an individual patient. For some, this concern with precision and surface behaviour has gone too far. As Mackay (1976, pp. 86-7) writes,

> It is regrettable, in my view, that in their endeavour to attain scientific respectability, many of the foremost behaviour therapists have felt it necessary to design experiments which bear a closer resemblance to drug trials in clinical pharmacology than to investigations of subtle psychological changes.

It is in the area of behavioural analysis and therapy that psychology has made an impact on the way that professionals in the 1960s and 1970s have understood sexual conduct. There is a frequently heard joke about the homosexual who, having had successful aversion therapy, shook hands with a male nurse and then threw up! I first heard this from a client in 1968 and it may point to how the idea of aversion therapy has also become accepted into the popular view of sexual expression and disapproval. Wilson and Davison (1974) ask why has 'behaviour therapy been so wedded to the use of aversion therapy in the treatment of homosexuals? We believe that homosexual behaviour has been viewed by client, therapist and society alike as undesirable at best, and pathological at worst.' They go on to discuss the possibility of therapists adjusting individuals to a more satisfactory permanent homosexual identity. It is also worth describing at some length the technical expertise developed by Quinn et al. (1970). A 28-year-old man with a long history of homosexuality, of superior intelligence and 'relatively normal personality' received 35 anticipatory avoidance conditioning sessions, 10 sessions of desensitization to relieve anxiety connected with heterosexual interest after his homosexual interest had declined. After eighteen months he reported increasing homosexual interest with heterosexual fantasy or behaviour involving anxiety and depression. A further 20 sessions were then embarked upon: prior to treatment, he was deprived of water for eighteen hours, and given

13

salt and an oral diuretic to ingest in order to sensitize him to liquid reinforcers. Then he was presented with a female slide he found attractive and was encouraged to fantasize. An increase in his phallic blood flow, as measured by the plethysmograph, was reinforced by a drink of chilled lime. Some phallic response was recorded. The patient reported a marked reduction in tension and increased vividness of heterosexual fantasy. This treatment, described as a 'Pilot-study', took place in Belfast, where of course all homosexual behaviour was illegal.

Mackay (1976, p. 126) presents an excellent review of the types of therapy available based on a behavioural analysis of the individual. He states that these procedures 'should not be regarded as a mindless technology based on a questionable assumption of homogeneity regarding diagnostic groups, but as a therapeutic approach which can be adapted to the requirements of the individual.' Here we see the emphasis swinging back to the individual and also incidentally away from the 1960s polarity between psychotherapy and behaviour therapy as the treatment of choice.

The area of behaviour which we have already touched upon in discussing sexual differences is one of some importance for the professional involved in assessing and dealing with sexual expression. Here the precision of the psychologist is important in moving beyond a Freudian assumption of sex roles and sexual behaviour being *normally* related to genetic sexual gender. Writers such as Money and Ehrhardt (1972) make distinctions between biological sex and gender identity, which they see as a self-concept, the way individuals perceive their sex. A sex-role or gender-role they regard as the public expression of this particular self-concept. This moves the discussion from the psychoanalytic 'psychosexual development' to the concept of psychosexual differentiation. With this perspective there can be a distinction between maleness, femaleness, and the way that at a certain time in any given culture individuals express their self-concepts in behaviour which are ascribed as 'feminine' or 'masculine'. This framework now provides us with ways to distinguish a number of semi-independent variables in observable sexual conduct: sexual arousal, sexual arousability, sexual preferences, sexual gratification, sexual activity. To parody a past popular song—you *can* have one without the other!

There now follow some operational examples illustrating some aspects of sex-role stereotyping. Storr's at one time popular 'guide book' for social workers on *Sexual Deviation* (1964, p. 89) stated

One reason why homosexual relationships tend to be unstable is that the couple are so often more competitive with each other than man and wife. The marriages which are most emotionally satisfying and most stable are those in which the male and female roles are clearly demarcated, so that competitive striving is eliminated and each member of the couple can be a complement to the other, rather than a competitor. Few wives enjoy a husband's interference in the kitchen; most husbands prefer to keep their wives out of the office: and there can be little doubt that one of the reasons for the prevalence of divorce is that since the emancipation and higher education of women, marriage has become a more difficult relationship.

Storr is helpfully obvious for us in his own confusion concerning the content of sexual preference (homosexual, heterosexual) and sex-role behaviours (male, female). His view of 'healthy' sex-role expression involved conforming to masculine and feminine stereotypes—whatever the individuals' sexual preference.

American research often quoted is the longitudinal study by Kagan and Moss (1962) started between 1929 and 1937. Early passivity in boys was found to relate to a similar personality in adolescence and adulthood, non-masculine interests resulted in later anxiety about sexuality and less heterosexual activity. Zuger (1966) studied sixteen boys referred to psychiatric clinics in America for effeminate behaviour. He concluded that on follow-up the majority were homosexual, but his methodology leaves something to be desired—for example, his comment on one boy who appeared to be heterosexual on follow-up but on testing drew a figure with 'large eyes with prominent eyelashes, a sign considered by some [reference given] to be indicative of homosexuality'. Bakwin (1968) also looked at gender-role behaviour and its relation to homosexuality. An example of what he considers deviant gender-role behaviour is as follows:

mothers state that the boys are gentle, helpful about the house, obedient, and neat to an unusual degree. They show a marked preference for their mothers and often comment admiringly on their clothes and general appearance. They show a precocious interest in art, beautiful materials and dancing, and often voice a desire to be dancers or actors.

Bakwin does recognize a difference in homosexuals whose deviation is limited to erotic behaviour and those whose gender-role behaviour can be detected in childhood as being deviant. Green (1969, p. 34) surveyed his own and others' work in this area and soberly concluded, 'Not until there is a series of treated cross-gender-orientated children matched against a control, non-treated group can it be said with assurance that psychologic treatment instituted at any age is of definite value in gender-role re-orientation.' He stated that we do

15

not know whether the boys in this study with apparent cross-gender identification 'will grow up to be transsexuals, transvestites, fetishists, homosexuals, or without significant sexual anomaly, nor can it be judged what childhood behaviour may be considered a harbinger of any of these sexual anomalies.' However, in Green and Fuller (1973) in a paper reporting on group treatment of feminine boys and their parents it is stated, 'Boys who behave as girls appear to be at high risk for the adult emergence of homosexuality and transsexualism.' This association was still not proven and the research was still continuing. Meantime the boys aged from 4 to 9 years whose parents expressed concern about their feminine behaviour were, 'reinforced for activities using large muscles or for bravery, such as climbing high on the monkey bars'. Feminine gestures/role-taking were disapproved of by the male therapist, *viz.* 'you don't *look* much like a stewardess, you look more like a *pilot*'.

A number of important issues are raised by this kind of approach: (1) the theoretical foundation of the treatment; (2) how much masculine and feminine behaviour is related to (a) sex roles, (b) gender-identity, and cross-gender behaviour (not necessarily the same), and (c) sexual preferences; (3) the concerns of the wider society and the way these are expressed by and through the individual parents; (4) the historical nature of the judgments about what is masculine/feminine behaviour, remembering the age of the boys and the pace of social change; (5) the moral nature of the therapy. (But see Green (1978).)

Broverman *et al.* (1970) showed that some American social workers, psychologists and psychiatrists shared the views of those academics and practitioners who equate 'mental healthiness' with sex-role stereotyped behaviour. Rogers (1976, p. 176) provides a warning for us all here:

Naive extrapolation is, I am afraid, far too common, particularly when subsequent workers latch on to and quote previous work without reading it carefully or without enough knowledge in the area to properly assess it. One fears for the psychiatric profession in this respect.

In a survey (Elstein *et al.*, 1977) of the sexual knowledge of GPs attending a post-graduate teaching programme in the Wessex region, it was found that only half of them responded correctly to the false statement, 'transvestism . . . is usually linked with homosexual behaviour'. Another response to the statement 'the body build of most homosexuals lacks any distinguishing features' varied from 90.4 per cent correct replies from GPs of less than 10 years' experience to 58.3 per cent correct replies from those with over 20 years' experience. A general finding was that those GPs in practice for the longest length of time generally had more conservative attitudes to sexual matters than shorter-serving GPs.

We do not know in any comparable way about the state of knowledge and attitudes among British social workers. As we are illustrating, they are dependent on other disciplines' 'findings'. There is then the act of applying that 'knowledge' through their own experience and values and the interaction with the individual client. These encounters with the client may be an important educative experience for the social worker. A probation officer (no. 2 in the study) answered my question about holding stereotypes thus:

'This homosexual blew my stereotypes of homosexuals wide open, because I had him on probation or after-care five years before I knew he was a homosexual. He works very often on building sites, is quite rugged in appearance; to me he's a very masculine sort of bloke. . . . It's one of my great professional disasters. I should have known after five years of knowing him. Another officer found out. By that stage he was living with another bloke and it arose during a social inquiry.' (See also p. 158.)

In concluding this section we can note that the debate about the origins and functions of sex-roles will continue. Indeed, Goldberg (1974) has argued that anthropology observes that all societies are organized into male hierarchies. Male power is achieved by a hormonal determinant related to aggression, which is specific to the male animal. Hence the inevitability of social relationships which we find with male dominance over the female. This is disputed by Reed (1975, p. 44) from a perspective stretching back to the beginning of humankind where matriarchy existed as evidence of women being the biologically advantaged sex: 'far from being handicapped by their maternal functions, [women] acquired from them the very traits conducive to advancing from animality to human life and cooperative labour.'

It is obvious that we require a critical awareness of the psychologists' way of understanding sexual conduct. If in addition to the physiological or biological variables and the understanding of sex-role behaviour involved in sexual conduct we are to study the *meanings* of these expressions, then we will, like some of the writers on psychology, need to turn to other disciplines. Indeed, Wilson and Davison (1974) acknowledge a similar debt as ourselves to Gagnon and Simon (1974):

It must be reiterated that more than genital arousal is inherent in what Gagnon and Simon call the 'scripting' of psychosexual identity, such that modes of dress, courtship, speech patterns,

17

and other social factors become the necessary concern of the behaviour therapist. (There is more to sexuality than genital secretions.)

Sociological understanding

Gagnon and Simon (1974) see themselves as heirs to a century of increasing freedom to observe and discuss sexual behaviour. They look back to Freud (pp. 55-6):

> a world dominated by the search for motivation . . . sexual arousal lies in nature; the social world responds and shapes but does not initiate. In Freud, sex itself seems disembodied and we are left with a world full of ideas and psychic structures only tangentially related to the bodies that are performing the acts.

They contrast this view with that of the 'other giant' Kinsey—'the bodies arrange themselves, orgasm occurs, one counts it seeking a continuation of rates where normalcy is a function of location on a distribution scale' (p. 6). The contribution of Gagnon and Simon is to place sexual acts, or more correctly, sexual actors, within a context of the meanings people ascribe to behaviour whether it is biologically or socially derived. An illustration may help where the observable behaviour appears erotic but the participants classify it quite differently: a newspaper photograph shows two scantily dressed men in a passionate embrace—in the context of a football match both participants and some spectators would understand this as non-erotic behaviour.

In Britain, Schofield (1965b) has provided information about sexual knowledge, attitudes, problems and activities. He first studied a representative sample of 18-year-olds and then traced as many of them as he could seven years later (Schofield, 1973, p. 11): 'The objectives were to obtain descriptive information about residence, schooling, occupation, leisure, group activities, marital situation, sex education, knowledge of sex, attitudes towards sex, sexual behaviour, incidence of venereal diseases and use of contraceptives.' The volumes contain a vast amount of useful information for the academic and the practitioner alike. For example, only 43 per cent of the 25-year-olds said they had enjoyed their first experience of intercourse, and being married to the partner made no difference to this. Also of concern is that 57 per cent of the group had sex problems and 24 per cent had a sex problem which they had not discussed with anyone. No one mentioned discussing a sex problem with a social worker. Nine per cent of men and 21 per cent of women having intercourse had never used contraception; another 12 per cent of men and 4 per cent of women had hardly ever used contraception (Schofield, 1973). This sort of data is useful as 'background noise' indicative of general trends but its validity is as culture and time-capsuled as Freud's. It is to the interactionist we must be drawn. In addition to Gagnon and Simon (1974) other important contributors to an interactionist account of sexual conduct are Humphreys (1970), Weinberg and Williams (1974) and Plummer (1975). All these are concerned with male homosexuality, but the insights they provide can illuminate other kinds of sexual conduct in society, as well as the behaviour of other minority groups. Weinberg and Williams (pp. 274-5) see 'homosexual' as a

> social status and the role expectations surrounding it account for the types of homosexuality that any society produces. . . . This status is not inherent in the individuals associated with it, but it influences them by organising other persons' reaction to them and giving those persons who occupy the status a stereotyped set of traits to orient their own behaviours and attitudes toward themselves.

With this perspective they present a view across three societies—the USA, Netherlands and Denmark—of societal responses to the homosexual and the returned response of such persons to their society. This data enables them to challenge a number of stereotypes about such matters as psychological adjustment. Although European homosexuals experienced greater societal rejection, this did not lead to greater psychological problems. 'We may conclude that *for many homosexuals*, problems of self-acceptance and psychosomatic symptoms may not be any more prevalent than for the population at large' (p. 149). In relation to aging, 'We find no age-related differences in self-acceptance, anxiety, depression, or loneliness. . . . Older respondents' worry less about exposure of their homosexuality, have more stable self-concepts, and are less effeminate' (p. 217).

Plummer provides a British interactionist perspective on achieving the status of a homosexual. Even more interesting for our understanding is his question 'why, when so many people are potentially available for homosexual experiences and identification, do so few enter stable homosexual roles?' (p. 137). He suggests that the reason is the ways in which homosexual sensitivity is weakened in society and heterosexual sensitivity strengthened. We have only to think of alcohol advertisements, the portrayal of homosexuals in comedy, the choice of television camera shots in dance routines, to feel the truth of the assertion. In our search for precise descriptions of phenomena alongside an elegant methodological approach with obvious value commitment, we turn to Humphreys. He describes casual sex in American public conveniences (1970, p. 154):

19

What the covert deviant needs is a sexual machine—collapsible to hip pocket size, silent in operation—plus the excitement of a risk-taking encounter. In tearoom sex he has the closest thing to such a device. This encounter functions, for the sex market, as does the automat for the culinary, providing a low cost, impersonal, democratic means of commodity distribution.

Humphreys found that the largest group of participants in such encounters were married men.

Davis (1971) looks at the way in which a woman is labelled as possessing certain traits as she 'becomes' a prostitute, and the way in which this process is internalized by the woman and leads in turn to further progress in a deviant criminal career. Prostitutes and homosexuals share the public rejection society expresses in laws forbidding their public acts. They therefore often become the 'clients' of social agencies because of their way of expressing sexual behaviour. According to interactionist sociological understanding, this process amplifies the 'outsider' image of the individual—the process of stigmatization. A woman probation officer (no. 3 in the Study) shows awareness of the stereotyping which occurs with prostitutes:

'She presents very well. A judge once said the equivalent to her of "What's a nice girl like you doing here?" and said the probation officer should have asked for psychiatric reports, because he believed she must be mad and because she didn't fit the image. My reaction was sort of to swear quietly because I know she doesn't need any psychiatric treatment. She has aged considerably. . . . Other officers, particularly men, comment on the physical change in her. I think that it's something I heard; prostitutes age fast. I didn't really believe this and I don't think it's the prostitution but the whole life-style. It's the all-night parties and moving around and not eating regularly, meeting a hell of a lot of hard people. She encounters enough of the sordid side of life—people who are screwed up—to have made her a pretty hard sort of person, but at the same time there is a lot about her that is likeable.' (See also p. 138.)

In a search for understanding of the content of our definition of sexual conduct there is an obvious tendency to rely on interactionist perspectives whether in the field of physiology, biology, psychology or sociology. If in our operational concerns we are involved as social workers or probation officers with the individual at the point where sexual interest has become public, then that person is not just there because s/he decided or was impelled to commit a sexual misdemeanour or crime. It seems likely that as sex crimes each year amount to such a small percentage of all offences charged (McGrath, 1976) that the majority of 'sexual offenders' are never the subject of official concern. This under-reporting is likely to apply to other types of sexual behaviour, including sexual problems in or out of a marital relationship (Schofield, 1973). In understanding sexual conduct, therefore, we can only do so adequately by adopting an approach which considers the effects on the person of interactions between themselves and significant others—their family, community, social help and control agencies. Such a perspective says little about the choices which are available to be made about the focus of intervention. We might decide that our way of understanding sexual conduct led us to think that the right way for social workers was to cease working with individuals and concentrate on acting as change agents to decriminalize prostitution or to prevent a proposed restriction on legal abortion from becoming law. This would be a moral choice. As our review of some of the literature on sexual conduct has already both involved so many unacknowledged moral choices and given rise to even more, it is time we considered a moral approach to understanding sexual conduct.

Moral understanding

Certain expressions of sexual conduct are regarded as immoral by society. We 'know' this because society expresses its rejection by use of the criminal law. If it is decided that we want to decriminalize certain sexual behaviour, then this should also be for moral reasons. This kind of argument was used by the Church of England evidence to the Wolfenden Committee (Bailey, 1956). 'For a human act to be susceptible of moral evaluation it must be free from external compulsion—though it may be internally compelled by good, neutral or bad motives, conscious or unconscious.' Here the criminal law is seen as not having a function in private sexual behaviours—although clergy, social workers, teachers, psychiatrists, etc. most certainly would have a mandate. The assumption is that moral choice is the concern of the adult. When a person reaches that status is very uncertain. Of course Piaget (1932) saw moral development in stages of maturity with adolescence as a position from which mature judgments could begin to be made. This is only of minimal help if we are to understand such problems as the age at which an individual can *choose* to perform certain sexual acts. The helping professions could, however, take more note of the moral status of the individual actor rather than form a deterministic view that the client was 'immature', or accept as Taylor (1972) puts it, 'that a large section of our society is subject to sudden blackouts and irresistible urges over which they lack any control'.

21

In understanding the way in which sexual conduct is viewed morally, we have the parameters of the criminal law, but within this can we detect a universal moral view of sexual matters? Douglas (1970) argues that (American) society is so complex, so diverse, that there has to be a split between private and public morality. The latter is an assumption of an absolute morality, not subject to interpretation between the individual and his social situation. In any society there may not be much support for absolute morality but the existence of small fundamentalist pressure groups within that society ensures the continuance of public morality through show trials and 'moral panics'. To give a cross-cultural example, 'Then the high priest rent his clothes, saying, "He hath spoken blasphemy. What think ye?" They answered and said, "He is guilty of death"' (Matthew 27: 65-66). *Gay News* and its editor, Denis Lemon, were convicted of publishing a blasphemous libel in 1977. The prosecution stated, 'You can say, as a Bishop did, that Christ may have been a homosexual, provided you say it in reasonably restrained and measured tones.' The essence of the crime consisted of the publication of words about the Christian religion, 'so scurrilous as to pass the limits of decent controversy' (reported in the *Guardian*, Tuesday 5 June 1977). In these two examples it is the public nature of the threat to absolute morality which condemns the moral entrepreneur. In a situation of social change, with the challenges to absolute morality becoming more vociferous, it seems likely that those who hold absolute views will feel threatened and will react accordingly (see, for example, Zurcher and Kirkpatrick, 1976). In our society these people will often be Christians because of a traditional association between Christian virtues and chastity. (For many examples see *Pornography. The Longford Report*, 1972, Coronet Books/Hodder Paperbacks edn, London, 1972.)

Although, as we have noted, social work is in receipt of knowledge from a number of disciplines, social work can also be included here as being a moral activity, for in its use of knowledge it contributes to a moral view of sexual conduct. The fact that the moral views on display are ambiguous is to be expected given the diverse pressures on the social worker in our society. A probation officer in the initial study (see p. 70) is describing his aims in working with a married man in his 50s, on probation for gross indecency with a teenage boy:

'Principally it was to help him keep his place in society and have a relationship with a male under 21 without breaking the law. This is how I saw it at the outset.

'Things became rather complicated when he stated quite openly that he would pursue relationships with males under the age of 21 and get into a position in which he might find himself compromised. And also I came under attack from his wife, because she would sit there and say, "Well, why aren't you doing something? You're not supposed to tell him he can go out with guys who are under 21." And then you realise that the marriage is breaking up because of this. And it was very difficult for her to accept the fact that, OK, I appreciate that he had broken the law, but on the other hand I've got to try and help him move around without being in breach of the law.'

Chapter 2

Social work and
sexual conduct

This chapter comments on the interest taken in matters of sexuality
in British and North American social work. It suggests that the
American emphasis on techniques, education and advocacy and the
comparative under-development of such concerns in Britain can be
seen in the latter's traditional and expanding relationship with
public welfare services and therefore with questions of 'right' moral
conduct.

An attempt is made to link British social work within a context of
social change, both in the wider society and in the visibility and
education of social workers. A theme of uncertainty emerges in
which the moral role of social work is again introduced and the way
is prepared for a lengthy discussion of this in Chapter 3.

Social work literature in Britain on sexual behaviour is sparse in
comparison with North American publications. In 1972 a reader on
(American) social work and human sexuality was produced (Gochros
and Schultz, 1972). American journals such as *Social Casework* and
Social Work now carry frequent articles on such topics as sexism,
rape counselling, gay clients. Indeed in 1975 in *Social Work* Schultz
asked 'Does sexual intimacy always retard the worker's professional
objectivity?' He is specifically referring to treating sexual dysfunction
in a country where 3,500-5,000 professionals, clinics or agencies
were involved in such treatments, and these include social workers.
He concluded that no ethical guidelines were available and asked
questions which both separate our two cultures and equally point to
identical future concerns, 'How should state statutes that licence
social workers define who "merits the public trust" and good
"moral" character of professionals treating sexual dysfunctioning?
Will insurance companies accept the new techniques and thus
protect professionals against malpractice suits?'

Professional cultural differences do result in a different emphasis
on issues of apparent mutual concern. British social work has grown

up as part of the provision of statutory social services and has thus been closely related to government-sponsored social policies. At first this was a marginal contribution, but more recently social work has become an important purveyor of public welfare. American social work is on the fringe of social policy. Although affected by social policy factors such as funding, legislation, political climate, it remains more concerned with the *techniques* rather than the *purposes* of intervention. This is a generalization, but the point is nicely made in an American book *Therapy with Families of Sexually Acting-out Girls* (Friedman *et al.*, 1971), 'we as family therapists generally adopt a neutral position in regard to these sociological issues in delinquency. Similarly, we are generally neutral as to whether the sexual "acting-out" behaviour of an unmarried girl is "delinquent", morally "bad" or "deviant".'

To discover reasons for the past relative neglect in Britain of the sexual dimensions involved in the methods of social work, we have to glance backwards into social policy and social work history Geoffrey Pearson (1975, p. 164) has attempted to supply a sociological imagination to its history and he comments on the nineteenth-century concern with *contagion*:

> The sewer speaks to the nineteenth century about its dangerous moral and material conditions. . . . A common image of the poor, for example, was that they were licentious and enjoyed a sexual freedom (and a sexual corruption) not available to the middle classes.

The early 'founding mothers' of social work in the second half of the nineteenth century were very concerned with sexual behaviour. This was seen in terms of the sexual 'depravity' widespread in the towns of this era. Social workers and reformers like Josephine Butler saw the costs of the industrial revolution in terms of the social conditions which Petrie (1971, p. 249) vividly describes in his account of Butler's campaign for the cause of women's liberation and against *organized* prostitution. He discusses recruitment to brothels:

> Unwanted babies were acquired, often from day-nurses in slum areas, and from baby-farmers. They were kept until they were old enough to practise fellatio; at four or five they were deemed to be sufficiently developed for penetration, after which they were discarded.

These first social workers, faced with what they experienced as the breakdown of the family unit, diagnosed the results in terms of a lack of moral stability, which included specific sexual behaviours— incest, promiscuity, paederasty, prostitution. Both the latter were frequently accompanied by 'the English vice' of sado-masochism.

25

In this climate what constituted sexual depravity or perversion must be seen in terms of the exploitation of women and children. Social work theorists tended to be indiscriminate in their concerns about sexual expression. In America around 1917, Mary Richmond instructed her students to make very detailed notes about sexual matters. For example, in discussing the 'Feeble Minded' (Richmond, 1917, p. 445), question 50 under the heading 'Morality' was 'Is child sexually promiscuous? Does he show any sexual perversion in practice? By telling vulgar stories?'

The fact that this concern, although perhaps with its benevolent characteristics uppermost, extended to the (female) workers themselves is illustrated in Timms's (1964, p. 19) account of the origins of psychiatric social work training in Britain. Before setting off for America in 1927 to study at the New York Child Guidance Clinic, one woman was asked 'If she felt that going to America was likely to interfere with her religious or sex life.'

There are then some grounds for assuming that social workers' first concern with sexual conduct was of a very *moral* kind in the sense that they were, like the nineteenth-century and early twentieth-century Police Court Missionaries, attempting to reclaim offenders from the evils of vice—which would have involved all the human weakness to which they were witness—drunkenness, unemployment, marital conflict, child abuse, poverty, appalling living conditions and undoubtedly the results of many aspects of sexual behaviour. Before dismissing such concerns as merely proof of 'pre-professional' attitudes or a lack of political awareness, we should remember these workers were faced with the results of gross deprivation, financial, medical and educational. In these circumstances and in the absence of a welfare state, perhaps the only strategy available was to preach abstinence, from drink or gambling or sex.

The influence of psychoanalysis in the first half of the twentieth century was extremely potent and the importance which Freud attached to sexual drives provided for social workers among others a legitimate intellectual way of discussing human behaviour which acknowledged from infancy onwards the pervasiveness of sexual interest. The apparent shift from a moral code was regretted by some social workers; as late as 1960 in the *British Journal of Venereal Diseases* a welfare officer expressed it thus (O'Hare, 1960):

Promiscuity is undoubtedly widespread in England since the narrow code of Victorian morality by which 'sex' and 'sin' were synonymous was replaced by the popular press evangelisation of psychiatry for the masses—the cult of the libido and the decline of self-control as a virtue. Youth has been freed from the fear of the devil.

She goes on to discuss '100 girls who, whilst under the age of 20, became habitually promiscuous and for whom promiscuity was a way of life.' However, this confident moral tone was from something of a lone voice. At a 1959 Association of Social Workers' Conference, Russell (1960, p. 42) acknowledged moral dilemmas in the selection of students for social work training: 'A certain number of problems obviously centre around sex, and we are faced with having to think out our views about accepting girls with illegitimate babies; those we know to be living with, but not married to, a man; and people who have been through divorce and separation.' She later referred (p. 43) to homosexuality and 'the very difficult question of whether the student should embark on a social work career and, if so, what branches might be all right to enter'.

Throughout the 1960s in the leading British social work journal *Case Conference* there is little mention of sexual conduct. In terms of direct discussion of sexuality, a sort of 'latency period' seems to occur during which such matters were seen in the perspective of social work's by then well-established participation in psychodynamic explanations of human ills. The implication for sexual conduct and social work was both technical and moral. The psychoanalysts postulated that at some point during the infant's early years s/he experienced a heightened libidinous interest in a number of areas of the body. These were at first related to stages of intra-psychic development and were called the oral and anal stages. Later the infant developed through phallic urethral to genital stages where the mental development had also an inter-psychic component. Freud's use of specific body areas to describe character and personality development was taken up and developed by social workers both in America and later in Britain. An influential text book in the 1960s in both countries was Reiner and Kaufman (1959). This was concerned with the 'acting-out', hard-to-reach clients familiar to many agencies. They were categorized as having 'character disorders' which meant they were fixated at a pre-Oedipal phase of development. Clients were further subdivided into such types as, for example, 'oral erotic', 'anal aggressive'. Caseworkers were enjoined to treat such clients with responses appropriate to their level of psychosexual functioning. Although the terms used are allied with Freudian stages of the development of the libido the purpose of the prescribed relationship with the caseworkers was seen primarily not in order to develop 'insight' but rather in terms of corrective mothering of an infant. An illustration from my own experience may make this point clear. During a period of three years whilst undergoing training very influenced by neo-Freudian ego psychology, I was working with a woman in her late 40s who had lived through a number of stormy relationships with men. After a short-lived marriage, she had later given birth to four illegitimate children, one of whom had been adopted. At the time she was living with the father of the two youngest. He was mostly unemployed, drank heavily, hinted he belonged to the IRA, broke up the home and frequently beat her up. My client felt very ashamed of her past and in this her Roman Catholicism was important. She spoke of being rejected by her parents and being brought up by her grandmother until she was 12 when her grandmother also became unable to care for her. On my course, I was encouraged to diagnose this woman as having a character disorder and to develop a consequential close 'oral feeding' corrective relationship with her, to help her develop more ego strength. The violence which she suffered was seen as part evidence of her masochistic traits, although the eventual result was the police prosecuting her husband for assault and the woman being admitted to temporary hostel accommodation with her daughter. During the period she was visiting the office there were many crises and she became seriously depressed. She cried a lot and was obviously subjected to frequent physical abuse. In supervision I was guided to see this latter condition as something which could be alleviated by concentrating on the woman's ability to identify her own provoking behaviour towards her cohabitee. At the termination interview she said, 'I think that if I had met you years ago maybe I wouldn't have had to go through all I have.' I interpreted this (to myself) as the client's recognition that she had been provided with some of the early mothering she had missed. Two years later I was very surprised to hear news of this ex-client from a woman friend who organized a self-help group; 'The things she said about you, she really fancied you!' I had been totally unaware in my treatment strategies of this aspect of the client's response to me despite being supervised on a course entitled 'Advanced Casework'. For this learning it had been necessary to have a knowledge of infantile sexuality, but at an intellectualized level of appreciation; seen as a manifestation of some earlier developmental or relationship problem.

Marriage: Studies in Emotional Conflict and Growth (Pincus, 1960) predictably contains a large number of references to sexual problems in the marriages described. The overall impression, however, is not one of sexual power and expression but of a 'clinical' report rooted in the client's unconscious, devoid of body language (p. 173, original in italics):

Mr. Cooper still needs to test out his worker's acceptance of his aggressive, dirty sexuality, divorced from feeling, and the sexual relationship with his wife must still be on his omnipotent terms. The hate and anger which he experienced as a child when he imagined his parents' intercourse, seem to be rekindled by his own sexual feelings.

Despite references to intense feelings, the overall picture seems homely, domestic (p. 232):

Once they are married, neither may have much opportunity to continue to engage in activities with his own sex . . . as for instance, sport may both reassure a young man of his masculinity and also satisfy his unconscious need for homosexual involvement; and time at the hairdresser's and the baby clinic, or intimate gossip with her neighbours or workmates, may do the same for a woman.

We learn very little directly about the caseworkers involved, although there are references to their conscious and unconscious processes.

The influence of Freudian and neo-Freudian psychology with psychic structures hierarchically ordered continued to influence social work even in the late 1960s. It was through such a lens that sexual conduct was both viewed technically and evaluated morally. Munro and McCulloch (1969, pp. 153, 157) say,

Since it is generally believed that homosexuality is a result of a failure to complete development in one aspect of an individual's emotional field, it seems wrong to us to glamorise or unduly publicise the condition as desirable. . . . Most lesbian woman are content to keep their homosexual inclinations hidden from general view and it is only the most psychopathic among them who make a show of their abnormality.

These authors have some advice (p. 156):

In offering help the social worker must be friendly and non-moralistic, but at the same time she can still strive in most cases to present the view that normal standards of sexual behaviour are a desirable goal for the individual to attain.

If these reflections on some social work writing about sex now appear dated, this is due to changes in the society in which such an aspiring profession operates (however, see also Munro and McCulloch's revised 2nd edition (1975) of their textbook for social workers which still contains these statements about homosexuality). Included in these changes are the greater availability of birth control, indeed the growing separation of reproduction from sexual behaviours, the medical control of venereal disease, the importance of women in the economy, the decline in the birth rate and the lessening of gender-role rigidities. There is also the educational input of the media and the close relationship between consumption, eroticism and advertising. These strands have all contributed to create a climate where sexuality is likely to be the subject of daily discussion. This is well described by Gagnon and Simon (1974, p. 291) as 'The eroticization of the social backdrop'. Social work is no longer dominated by single women who were assumed not to know about things sexual (indeed the work could be seen as a 'sublimation'). Allowances are made now that social work's men and women can and do have a sex life. The implications of these cultural changes cannot be adequately discussed from the social work viewpoint without some reference to the legislation involved. It is within a statutory framework that British social work carries out many of its tasks and duties. Examples would be the Street Offences Act, 1959, which made soliciting a statutory concern for probation officers, and the Sexual Offences Act, 1967, which relieved those same workers of another client group (at least those who were fortunate enough to be over the age of 21 and kept their sexual expression strictly private and didn't go on holiday to Scotland or Northern Ireland). Of general applicability to social work's women clients was the Sexual Offences (Amendment) Act of 1976 (in relation to rape victims), the Sex Discrimination Act and the Equal Pay Act of 1975, and the Domestic Violence and Matrimonial Proceedings Act, 1976. In their underlying attitudes to sexual conduct these examples of legislation are not unambiguously liberal but social workers may detect a *trend* towards more open acknowledgment both of the diversity of sexual preference and the rights of the individual to equal protection irrespective of marital status or sexual gender.

The pace of societal change in the past twenty years has been chronicled by Toffler (1971); a simple example may illustrate the speed of these changes. In the 1960s Bob Dylan was, as the writer and performer of songs of social criticism like 'The Times They Are A-Changing', a folk hero of the young. Now his songs are attacked by the Women's Movement for having lyrics as in 'Lay Lady Lay' and 'Just Like A Woman'.

Certainly social work in Britain has yet to work out a relationship with self-help groups like those inspired by women's or gay liberation movements and we shall return to this question later in the book.

How deeply surface criticism of traditional sex roles and behaviour extends is a question we could legitimately ask of the social workers placed between social institutions of great power—the law, medicine, education, and people whose place in the social structure is rarely where they would have chosen to be and who feel themselves to have few choices about their own life-style. We can turn to the social worker as a thermometer of the effects of social change. The results obtained are likely to reflect the ambivalence which discussion of sexual behaviour still causes. This may be glimpsed by reviewing some newspaper reports:

DEATH PENALTY FOR SEX OFFENDERS

Dr. Bowers also calls for heavy penalties on those who abuse the hospital and ambulance services by, for example, dialling 999 when they are drunk. All injuries caused by violence should be notifiable, as are gunshot wounds. All drunken drivers should be banned from driving for life, he says, and adds that the birch should be restored for acts of violence and the death penalty not only for terrorism but also for drug-pushing and sexual offences against children (*Guardian*, 7 June 1976).

REINSTATEMENT UPSETS POLICE

Council lawyers in . . . have been told to investigate whether their Chief Constable can legally defy an order from the Home Secretary telling him to reinstate a policeman who was dismissed after being convicted of sex offences.

The constable, a 36 year old married man with two children was dismissed after being convicted at . . . early last year of a gross indecency. He admitted paying boys £1 to beat him with a cane which he hid down his trouser leg while waiting outside a youth club. The court gave him a conditional discharge for 3 years after being told he was receiving medical treatment (*Guardian*, 7 June 1976).

ATTACK ON BID TO EASE SEX LAWS

Probation officers who suggested there should be more permissiveness in the laws on sexual offenders ought to be ashamed of themselves, members of the South Yorkshire Police Committee were told yesterday (*Sheffield Morning Telegraph*, 9 July 1976).

These are examples of some of the mixed messages which are received by social workers (and others). They have to take account of the demands of the liberationists as well as those of powerful groups in society who wish for a limiting of what they see as sexual licence. It is often implied that 'high' standards of morals and behaviour are required from social workers as public servants. In searching for their mandate in this confusion, social workers no doubt will still retain enough of the weapons of Freudian psychology to be suspicious of the motives of those who demand repressive measures against people who threaten a consensus view of society. Indeed, psychodynamic explanations may still be used both to justify liberation or to advocate the control or treatment of certain expressions of sexual interest. Faced with such an uncertain moral mandate, the social worker may fall back on his or her own personal or religious views about good and bad behaviour. We have to include in this listing of attitudinal influences what has become, at least in the literature and in training institutions, the dominant theme of the 1970s.

31

Sociological deluge or the rise of deviancy theory

To understand the reaction of an élite group such as social workers to social phenomena, we have to continue tracing the filters through which their own perceptions are mediated. Increasingly this has been neither through work experience, moral or religious certainty, nor derivations from psychiatry. Social work has in the 1960s and 1970s looked to the social sciences for help and has there found what Cohen (1976, p. 78) calls

The promise of deviancy theory. . . . The basic premises of this perspective are simple enough and involve little more than recognising the deviants' right to present their own definition of the situation, a humanisation of their supposed process of becoming deviant and a sensitivity to the undesirable and stigmatising effects of intervention by control agents.

For social work as an aspiring profession the implications of the sociology of deviance have been with their general concerns involving delinquency, mental illness, poverty, and of course sexual behaviour. Although as we shall see the practical effects of such teaching are as yet little known, the perspective has provided a legitimate alternative view of certain behaviours not as residing in individual badness or psychopathology but as part of a time-honoured political process whereby some acts are labelled as 'sick', 'disturbed', 'immature'. The fact that those who attach the label have often been social workers is something with which the profession is still visibly struggling. The vulnerability of social workers to criticism of their interventions is interesting to observe and highlights the insecurities involved in the process of professionalization. More established professions involved with similar clientele do not appear to have been rocked with such force by academic criticism. To return to the example from Friedman (1971, p. 3), the challenge is not so powerful in American social work where the social worker is seen as therapist. It is now possible in Britain for social workers to leave courses qualified and soon authorized as having authority under the 1959 Mental Health Act to deprive a citizen of all civil liberties, with no right of appeal, the person having been diagnosed as suffering from a mental disorder—without necessarily seeing a psychiatrist. Yet the social worker may have acquired from courses on the sociology of deviancy an active disbelief in the concept of mental illness. Discussion of sexual behaviour is usually included on CQSW courses under Psychiatry or Human Growth and Behaviour teaching. This is, however, often alongside what Cohen (1976, p. 85) has (slightly) caricatured: 'In some quarters prisoners were seen as being in the vanguard of the revolutionary struggle, homosexuals as precursors of the destruction of the bourgeois capitalist family, and schizophrenics as visionary prophets of man's alienation.' The impact of deviancy theory must be assessed with the changed recruitment, education and employment of social workers.

There has therefore been an increase in the influence on CQSW courses of disciplines taught with a deviancy perspective—criminology, sociology, social administration—and graduates may arrive at social work teaching already or concurrently exposed to deviancy theory and critical of any explanations of conduct which neglects the social dimension. Not only has deviancy theory provided a challenge to social work's individualistic explanations of human behaviour, it has also enabled social workers to bring their personal politics into theory and practice. Although only a beginning has been made, the effects of personal and political liberation movements are beginning to show: social workers themselves assert the right of personal ideology to govern their study and practice. An example can be seen in welfare rights interest and advocacy with a consequential implied narrowing of the distance between professional and client. The implications of this ideological visibility for other areas such as sexual conduct are at present generally only theoretically or academically obvious in this country. Perhaps some new recruits could not have been attracted to social work, however, were it not for changes which have taken place in the career prospects, especially of local authority employed social workers.

The changes in the visibility of social work since 1971

Prior to the creation of local authority social service departments social work may have been as Pearson (1975) alleges, primarily an agent of social control, but it was not a very important one. As probation officer, medical or psychiatric social worker, child care officer, welfare worker, or family caseworker, the individual's allegiance was to his/her own small occupational group, and unity did not always exist between these. In addition to the workers' lack of corporate identity, even qualified social work was diluted by placement with more prestigious professions—for probation it was the law, for medical and psychiatric social work it was medicine. Training until the late 1960s was very influenced by the Diploma or Certificate in Psychiatric Social Work first developed at the London School of Economics and the idea of a Bachelor's or Master's degree in Applied Social Studies containing also a professional qualification was still developing. Social work both in its training and its location of practice had little power as a social institution. Seen in this light, 1971 was a year of consolidating a change which was inevitable if social work was to be in the mainstream as a respected agent in the control of social problems; the expectations of other helping professions and of the general public were thereby increased. Consequently the actions of social workers have become newsworthy and inevitably most media interest is likely to be recorded when social work has failed in its implicit promise to deliver the social goods—or bads! On these occasions, when social work has appeared to fail to cope with the social problems with which it has been (appropriately or not) entrusted, then the failure is seen as being that of an agent of social control. These 'failures' are likely to be most visible in the area of sex and violence. Since the reorganization of social work into single local authority departments, there have been a number of public issues related to social work and sexual conduct. These have included disputes about the suitability for employment of workers convicted of sexual offences, the placement of a child with a known prostitute, and the apparent connivance of social workers in under-age sexual relations. The implication is that in reviewing sexuality and social work, we have to account not only for the attitudes of social workers to client sexual conduct, but also examine the place that their own sexual behaviour and preferences have in the expectations held out by their employers, the general public, and perhaps even their clients.

The implications for social work

These appear at first to be ominous, for in the last decade, alongside an increase in political power, awareness and responsibility, we can observe a decline in reliance on formerly avowed and often borrowed treatment technology. Structural factors in society are now seen as being of at least as much the legitimate concern of social work as the problems expressed by individuals, but the prescription for practice remains vague beyond some acknowledgment of the dangers of iatrogenic intervention (still to borrow medical terminology). Here Cohen (1976, p. 84) has warned that 'Non-intervention can become a euphemism for benign neglect, for simply doing nothing.' At the individual level the interventions of social workers have long been under attack as Bean (1976, p. 105) points out: 'The difficulty confronting probation officers is that they believe themselves to be primarily concerned with personality assessment when they are more likely to be involved in moral evaluations.' Clearly there exists an implication that the basis of the moral operations of social workers has to be re-thought. My observation in working with CQSW students in two different settings—in videotaped role-play and in joint interviews with social service clients—highlights what I believe to be a felt discrepancy between the values taught on qualifying courses, especially in relation to the sociology of deviance, and the encounters of the students with a client presenting personal diffi-culties. In the role-play the students act as almost totally unco-operative, sometimes militant, usually hostile clients, whilst in 'real life' their sincere wish to help is greeted usually with a kind of shy welcome by their clients. (Some research by Sainsbury (1977) seems to confirm this latter observation also to be true of qualified social workers.)

Sexual conduct is an area where 'respect for privacy' is an accepted social value. When social workers become involved this is often because someone else other than the person, or the person and their sexual partner, are concerned. Private behaviour has become public demonstration whether because of the violation of community mores, law enforcement or personal distress. Evaluations are being made by a number of actors about the acceptability of these individuals' conduct. Gagnon and Simon (1974, pp. 3-4) describe the nature of societal response to sexuality:

> At no point is the belief in the national and universal more
> entrenched than in the study of sexuality. The critical
> significance of reproduction in species survival is made central
> to a model of man and woman in which biological arrangements
> are translated into sociocultural imperatives.

Social work, among other helping professions, is charged by society to help relieve personal distress. It also has the dual responsibility for inspecting, controlling, preventing or treating deviant behaviour.

Evidence, hypothesis or theory must be evaluated in the light of its relevance to the moral and technical role of the social worker. The uniqueness of social work is something which has frequently been forgotten in the past when enthusiasm for the insights gained and treatments applied by other disciplines has resulted in their uncritical application, with little cognizance of differences like the cultural setting of the helping encounters or the power relationship of the client and worker. This danger is clearly to be seen in social work's interest in the psychologists' behavioural techniques. The take-over by psychologists of many of the treatment functions of psychiatrists both in the mental hospital and the community is a subject for separate study (see, for example, *The Role of Psychologists in the Health Service*, HMSO, 1977). Given our discussion of the decline of interest in psychodynamic casework and a concern with destigma-tizing the client, the attraction for social workers of a behavioural approach can be briefly noted. We should not fall into the waiting trap of becoming 'sexual technicians'. We will only do this if we forget that a dual role of help and control is always held by the social worker, often with a client who is not self-referred. This will become clear if we look at Bancroft's comprehensive review of behavioural techniques applied to what he calls *Deviant Sexual Behaviour* (1974, p. 20). He refers to sociological views of deviance and the 'expert's' role in the modification of such behaviour, concluding,

> there will continue to be individuals who are severely distressed by the consequences of their deviance, whether of 'individual' or 'subcultural' type. It is of little help to such individuals to point out that social attitudes are gradually changing, however desirable change may be. They will continue to seek help in becoming less deviant.

Mackay (1976, p. 129) in his review of the treatment of sexual behaviour goes so far as to state, 'It has also been stressed in this chapter that behaviour therapy is just a set of principles and techniques which is independent of any value system.'

Whilst such 'neutral stances' towards behavioural change are a dubious basis for any professional group, the position of the social worker is explicitly different. Outside certain quasi-private practice situations, s/he has a specific dimension of control over the client. The consequential responsibility in such a power relationship requires a consideration of both the political and personal implications of sexual conduct in each case. Then we need to go beyond that point, proceeding as Whittaker (1976, p. 14) advocates (in mental health practice), 'inductively to build an overall theory or practice which is based upon case experience rather than to deduct one from any existing body of theory'. The importance of now considering in some detail social work and sexual conduct is that there will be symbolized in these discussions much broader professional dilemmas. Again as Gagnon and Simon (1974, p. 14) put it,

> our laws embody our *felt margin* [author's italics] between those acts that are natural and those that are crimes against nature, delineating a narrow domain of *de-jure* legitimacy by constraining the age, gender, legal and kin relationships between sexual actors, as well as setting limits on the sites of behaviour and the connections between organs.

It is in this *felt margin* that social work operates, facing always legal and moral rules, sometimes constrained by them, sometimes enforcing them and sometimes bending them or trying to change them. Hence our question as the title of Chapter 3.

Whose moral tutor?

Before going on to the study we will discuss the role of the social worker in a number of important areas where sexual conduct is encountered: in Serious Crimes; the probation service; residential work; paedophilia cases. The chapter concludes with some account of the conflicts and personal costs for clients and workers and a discussion of the models of sexuality in society held or expressed by social workers in their attitudes to clients' sexual conduct.

PLACARD 'SHAMED' MAN IN PROBATION HOSTEL
Social workers hung a placard around a child molester's neck which said: 'I am a sex offender, don't trust what I say', Winchester Crown Court was told yesterday.
   Mr. Percy Russell, Hampshire's chief probation officer confirmed last night that the 24 residents at the Culverlands hostel frequently have placards hung round their necks.
   'This is a form of treatment devised in America where it is known as the Phoenix System. The idea is to make people face themselves as they really are . . . sometimes by being harsh to them', he said (*Guardian,* 9 February 1978).

The result of the changes in social work's self-perception is that it has become legitimate to discuss structural factors in society as being of as much concern as the problems of individuals (Bailey and Brake, 1975). Individualistic psychodynamic certainties have been felt to be on the wane. It has been suggested that this trend would be supported by social work's consumers (Mayer and Timms, 1970). The *content* of the social work which is replacing an emphasis on the psychological problems of the individual is hard to gauge. Certainly welfare rights play some part in the prescription but if we are presently concerned with sexual behaviours, then this type of training input may not provide an adequate interventive skill. In the area of social work and sexuality we are often involved with criminal behaviour. To guide us in such circumstances we have Bean's (1976) rejection of the 'therapeutic ethic' or at the opposite extreme Foren and Bailey (1968, pp. 18-19), 'In social work, as in the parental situation, the *Oxford Dictionary* ingredients of authority—the "power or right to enforce obedience" and "personal or practical influence"—combine to provide the opportunity for constructive help.' If neither of these stances is sufficient for our purpose then we have to take some account of the variety of ways in which social workers assess, treat and acknowledge sexual conduct as agents of both social control and help. Here we will not assume as did Bean that the interventions of the worker will always be on the side of social control, nor on the other hand do we share Foren and Bailey's confidence in social work's identification with 'the good authority'.

In seeking to identify some of the *choices* made by workers in confronting clients' sexual behaviour, we should not forget that social work is an instrument of social policy. With a decrease in the rate of expansion in the social services, criticism of the social worker as 'soft policeman', and disappointment with the performance of political parties, there may be a temptation to turn inwards and focus only on the production of efficient therapists to individuals, groups, families or communities. It was my brief impression on a visit to North America in 1977 that something of this process had happened there in social work schools (Hart, 1978). In Britain there is some evidence of a renewed interest in the interpersonal trans- actions between worker and client. Brown (1977) emphasizes the necessity of allowing for 'personal style' of the worker and Whittington (1977) goes beyond a consideration of bureaucratic or professional allegiance to list eight ideal typologies of social workers' orientations, ranging from 'control' through 'economistic' to 'service'. However, none of these possible stances can be seen in isolation from the particular problem behaviour of the client, the impact on cultural norms, and the rules within which the worker meets the client in his/her situation. How, why and when a particular attitude is taken or a response made by a social worker to a client is as yet little known. Hardiker (1977) looked at probation officers' social inquiry report recommendations and found a mixture of treatment and justice orientations: 'Treatment orientations tended to be held when the offender had a relatively serious criminal record, severe personal/social problems, the recommendation was for either probation or custody.' It appeared that younger graduate officers were less treatment orientated than older Home Office trained, experienced probation officers. However, these orientations were used very much in relation to what the officer estimated would be the court's response to a certain recommendation. Hardiker suggests that rather than discuss ideologies, we should consider 'operational philosophy'. These findings are of course restricted to social inquiry practices. We have yet to learn how these initial public stances relate to the later encounters between the social worker and client.

In Chapter 1 we chose some academic theories concerning sexual behaviour and attempted to use these to understand the way in which social workers and the more general public view sexual conduct. The process of two-way reflection involved in academic and popular cultural images is a matter of controversy. Here we are beginning to locate social work as being at the moral interface between society and the problem person or problem behaviour. If we are to describe and even to codify such an activity, we have to understand more of the moral choices which social workers make. Halmos (1965) was an important writer in the 1960s seeing the activities of social workers, counsellors, psychiatrists as being composed of moral tutorage. A flavour of the social work scene, reflected and affected by this stance, can be glimpsed in this quotation (p. 178):

> The counsellor—vaccinated as he is now against political fever—has certain sobered suggestions to make about the provision of mental health services, . . . about illegitimacy, divorce laws. . . . As yet today no simple political-ideological formula will attract the counsellor *qua* counsellor as a most appropriate, congenial and relevant system of doctrines to bring him his counselling goals; and perhaps, in an important sense, he is predestined to remain politically reserved or wholly uncommitted.

Given this view, Halmos (p. 7) is able to describe ways in which the counsellor operates, 'The counsellor applies himself in a way which suggests a set of convictions, a powerful mood, a moral stance, a *faith*.' This faith is in the continual improvement of human personality and the 'means of faith' is love—the increasing tolerance for others in society. This description of social work's 'applied values' may still seem in tune with the times (Jordan, 1977):

> The potential value of social work lies in the possibility of social workers having sufficient moral integrity and autonomy to see in the most disadvantaged or disabled of people, some potential for enhanced humanity or citizenship. Hope lies in the possibility of the social worker committing himself to a client as a person and as a citizen.

However, the 1960s Halmos view of the 'politically uncommitted' now appears at best naive. Halmos had something of importance to observe implicitly about the social control functions of the counselling

39

ethic (1965, p. 188): 'the sanctions provided by the counselling ideology *in lieu* of the other worldly deterrents . . . must be viewed as reinforcements of conventional sexual morality'. This shows how *The Faith of the Counsellors* rested on the assumption of an age of consensus. Social workers now operate in and with a consciousness of a society composed of many diverse, competing and unequal groups. If moral tutorage is still a valid aim, then we have to answer the questions, whom are we tutoring, and from what ideological standpoint, and what are the values contained in that enterprise?

Until recently it has been difficult to make any professionally discrete statement about ethical standards in social work. In 1975 the British Association of Social Workers produced a code of ethics. These were revised in 1976 to read:

Paragraph 6. Statement of Principles.
Basic to the profession of social work is the recognition of the the value and dignity of every human being irrespective of origin, status, sex, sexual orientation, age, belief or contribution to society. The profession accepts a responsibility to encourage and facilitate the self-realisation of the individual person with due regard for the interest of others.

The problem here is what constitutes 'self-realisation' and how is this achieved 'with due regard for the interest of others'. Complicating, if not diluting this professional declaration is social work's relationship with absolute, taboo, or traditional morality. This ebbs and flows in society in response to many factors which may be unrelated to sexual conduct. In this state, we could understand if the social worker sent 'an urgent tickertape'—from limbo. We will now deal with some specific examples where these conflicts are visible in social work practice in order to throw into relief the social worker's unique position as agent of both control and liberation.

Serious crimes

At this point our definition is at once relevant in containing the possibility of 'sexual usage'—and apparently also unhelpful in that it enables us to discuss for example, rape, as being part of sexual conduct. Many people would prefer to see such acts as aggressive. However, we shall use rape as a focus for illustrating the moral tutoring role of social work. (See p. 6 for definition.)

Many liberals regard rape as outside their usual moral evaluations and demand punishments which stand as evidence of society's condemnation of such acts—with apparently nothing to say about the *humanity* of the offender. This is partly a public response to the accusation of male chauvinism which saw women as having few rights to demur at the violation of their bodies by men and, therefore, it proved difficult to declare abuse of what man at least subconsciously saw as his own property. Soothill and Jack (1975) looked at the way the British press in 1951, 1961 and 1971 covered rape cases, and considered its treatment of the victim. Although they found an increase in reportage over the years, this reflected the higher number of cases coming before the courts. Their findings are open to alternative conclusions to the ones they draw:

> What is clear from our research is that no victim need fear 'abominations of the body' being revealed to the world through press publicity. On the contrary newspapers tend to be particularly flattering to the victims: from newspaper reports it would appear that only tall and attractive blondes and brunettes get raped!

Geis (1977) attempted to place the crime of rape in an interesting historical context. He studied the records of witch trials in England. He stated that these mainly finished around 1670, were usually directed towards women (although a study of male witches is a fascinating prospect) and, says Geis, were part of the power struggle between men and women in a society where the formers' economic status was under threat. In the trials the evidence allowable to secure conviction amounted to an assessment of the accused's previous moral character. Such evidence included an examination of the women for 'the marks of the devil'—these might include warts especially in the genital area. A parallel situation occurs in the way raped women have been treated in our modern society which is experiencing economic change and women's increased political awareness alongside an increase in the reporting and perhaps the incidence of rape. The occurrence of rape, as with other serious sexual crimes, is impossible to measure. Reasons include the legal protection of husbands within marriage against charges of intercourse without consent and the fears of the victim about the prosecution process including the way medics, police, solicitors, and the press would treat her accusation (see for example reports of the Rape Crisis Centre who make the point that men also get raped).

If we return to the social workers' ethics, 'the value and dignity of every human being' will not allow us to neglect the rapist as do many contemporary writers in their concern for the victim. The known facts about those who are convicted of rape also point us back to the need to retain individualized evaluations of even such serious crimes. Gibbens (1977) traced 200 convictions for rape in England and Wales in 1961. He found that 36 per cent of the total group were in fact convicted of attempted rape and a few of aiding and abetting rape. Thirty per cent involved 'paedophiliac' rape of girls under 14.

41

The paedophiliac group include most of the few rapists who were manifestly psychiatrically disordered and in need of hospital treatment. Twenty per cent were 'aggressive rapists'—in that they had previous convictions for aggressive non-sexual offences. The 50 per cent remaining had not had previous aggressive offence convictions. Over half of these had no previous convictions of any kind and three-quarters were not convicted of anything in the next twelve years. These included young men who were described as previously socially or sexually very inhibited. Between 15 and 20 per cent of all these cases involved two or more others convicted with the rapist. Where it was the rape of a child, a 'rather high proportion' was of 13-year-old girls by groups of boys aged 16 to 18. Gibbens notes that 82 out of a 1951 and 1961 total of 368 charged in rape cases had been acquitted and that 'subsequent violent and sex offences are roughly similar in both acquitted and convicted'.

Emerging from this helpful study is a picture of use to the social worker who may be involved with the rapist especially those dealing with parole or in child care decisions (See for example DHSS Circular LAC(77)8, Welsh Office Circular WOC 65/77 *Release of prisoners convicted of offences against children in the home.* Incest and sexual assault are included as cases where the Home Office will notify Directors of Social Services of the release on licence of such offenders.) The nature of the offence, alone or with a group, the social and sexual skills of the men, are all of relevance as is his previous criminal record. Age is an important consideration and not just for social workers, but also for those who determine the appropriate sentence for rapists who are at either end of the age range:

JUDGE WARNS RAPIST, 68
A Judge at Leeds Crown Court yesterday gave a warning to a 68 year old pensioner who pleaded guilty to raping a 70 year old widow.
    Mr. Justice Thesiger said, 'With your state of health, with your high blood pressure, I warn you not to behave like this. You may overtire your heart and die in most unfortunate circumstances.' Then he gave Mr. X., a widower, a two year suspended sentence (*Guardian*, 29 March 1977).

As Denzin (1970, p. 149) suggests:

As a person moves through the life cycle, we can expect to observe varying moments of high and low public deviancy potential. In fact, the structure of our society's social control and treatment agencies directly corresponds to variations in the life cycle.

To move back to the victim and quote again Carol Maggs (see p. 9), 'It's alright being angry but who wants to know an angry person? The hardest thing is to get back to being emotional. You're not the same person any more. It's hard to lose your youth at 17 and be offered £150 in compensation.' There is not just the possibility of anger, physical and emotional hurt to be considered but also the fact that the victim may be distressed by the fate of the attacker. A woman wrote to the *Guardian* (4 July 1977) recalling that her daughter had been raped two years earlier when she was 8. The man, with a history of mental illness, who was drunk at the time of the offence, was given 12 years' imprisonment:

> When you are only eight years old, twelve years is more than a lifetime. I don't mean that she was not even more shaken by being raped, but the long sentence certainly did nothing to help her return to normal. She still looks very troubled when she sees prison scenes on television and asks if his bed will be uncomfortable and if he will have enough blankets, if his meals will be worse than school dinners, if he will have friends there and so on. She worries about him. As far as she is concerned, he is just an ordinary sort of person who was a bit mad at the time.

If we now consider in more detail the social work role, the moral ambiguities and choices become apparent. The rapist's crime specifically offends against the principles of social work and a possible political allegiance with the women's movement. It may also be offensive to more generally held attitudes to sexuality. Any moral tutoring here would consequently take the form of ensuring that older, established professions such as the police, medicine and the law, were more sensitized to the seriousness of the crime. From such a position is there room to increase society's tolerance for the perpetrator, 'to encourage and facilitate [clients'] self-realisation . . . with due regard for the interest of others'? Should the endeavour be in the direction of trying to control the future behaviour of the rapist, or to change his attitudes to sexuality? There are a number of moral and technical problems here. First, as Gibbens (1977) concludes, the likelihood of further aggressive sexual offences is small and any view of this behaviour would have to stretch further than a decade. Second, such a 'treatment perspective' is contrary to the principles of justice. Third, we have no proven way of preventing the behaviour in any given case. Fourth, even if such a method of control existed, presumably ethical judgments would prevent its use. The behaviour would be seen as specifically *sexual* aggression and a chemical or physical castration applied to the rapist.

With this framework, let us look at individual cases. In the study

Probation Officer 4 conveyed his attitude of moral outrage both at his client's offence and his subsequent attitude to the crime:

'one day he grabbed a 3-year-old girl in the street as he had come out of a pub, dragged her into the lavatories at the back, attempted to choke her, attempted to rape her and left her there and walked away . . . the child was horribly injured, I think that cost him eight years that one. . . . In our conversations [in prison] he simply says he hasn't done it . . . but then he tells my why and how it happened. . . . [Client gave reason as being the sexual problems in the marriage.] Everyone that I've talked to about this seems to share this feeling of horror and I think he has got that as well. I think that's what's in the way. It's difficult to acknowledge something horrible in one breath and then talk about it calmly in another. But that's roughly where I think he's got to go . . . to come out at the end with some idea of himself that isn't altogether horrible.'

'What were your aims in this case?'

'The first preoccupation that most people have is to prevent him doing it again. In most people's minds, and in mine, is the thought of some other 3-year-old child being—well, that child was lucky to live—that's the over-riding anxiety which I share with everybody else. . . .'

In this excerpt from a case discussion, we can observe a moral response in terms of evaluating the behaviour and the man's attitude, and also in the idea of eventual reconciliation—of the client's own self-image and presumably in his re-entering normal community life.

Probation Officer 5 talks of helping the rapist, not in direct work but by trying to increase community tolerance of the client when he is released back into that community. Here the officer is attempting to work as a kind of advocate between the client and his community. The client in prison denies to his wife and to the probation officer that he committed rape, because he was not able to get an erection. The officer goes along with this denial:

'My aim would be to get him to rehabilitate with his family now his sexual offence in my eyes would be finished when he was out—whether it would be finished with his neighbours because he tried to rape his next-door neighbour approximately at the same time as this other rape offence took place [which had occurred during an armed robbery of a petrol station] . . . the next-door neighbour quickly spreads the word round to any newcomers in the area and continues the pattern of harassment of the family in such a way as now the wife has let the hedge round the home grow to nine feet. . . . I have on one occasion tried to talk to the next-door neighbour but the husband became rather aggressive at this point and wanted nothing to do with it, he didn't want his wife involved with the probation service and that family next door so that avenue might be closed, but in a future date it might again open in fact when my client comes out.'

Some social workers would not see the treatment of the individual rapist as separate from day-by-day work to change prevailing ideologies in society:

'I feel very mixed up about it . . . the call of the women's movement for much stiffer penalties. What we are talking about in fact is a re-emphasis on what is regarded as serious and what isn't. Rape is not regarded as being a very serious crime and thus an insult to all the women who have been assaulted' (Social Worker A in the study).

'It's no use saying, well the rapes happened and we have to give the rapist a good dose for his money, and be very, very punitive in a society which condones all sorts of other types of rape which go on, and until you can recognize that rape is very much a product of how people see sex and sexuality, even in their own lives, then I don't think one can punish a man for committing rape when he comes from a situation which probably has incited him to commit rape in a lot of ways, certainly that has transformed him into a being capable of rape. The contradiction to that is I feel very strongly about the crime against that individual woman. . . . It is the sexual factor which brings the punitive morality of society as well, not only on the rapist but on the raped . . . it's not just seen as a serious assault, it's seen as a serious *sexual* assault. A woman should be accorded very firm human rights . . . people who rape have to be dealt with in this society in the way that people are actually asking they are dealt with. There are some sections of the women's movement who are getting to the point now where they are asking that rapists should be treated psychiatrically which is utter absurdity. I don't think we should lose sight of the type of society which produces rape. . . . I think the rapist should be dealt with like anyone else who commits a serious physical assault—at the moment' (Social Worker B).

The problem for social work considering a serious crime such as rape is that it may be seen as 'different', i.e. beyond moral evaluation. Morris (1976, p. 97) reminds us of the importance of

45

allowing the possibility of moral choice. 'Any theory which assumes that deviance is the product of things outside the deviant's immediate control, be they biological or sociological, denies the relevance of his moral status.' However, an emphasis on the *choice* of the rapist in committing the act may also further complicate the response of the social worker. Social reform groups may be tempted to take a punitive line with such offenders and this may well be transmitted to social workers. In the study, female Probation Officer 3 speaks of her contact with a 19-year-old:

'I have a physical reaction to him which tells me he is weird. . . . I found [later] that he was charged with murder of a woman whom he had never seen before who he assaulted out of the blue—the assault was in a public place. He had injured this woman very seriously indeed, had taken some money and gone away, had come back, had sexually assaulted her whilst she lay there, sort of dying, and then went off again and she died about three hours later in hospital. My reaction to that was quite powerful—I felt for the first time since I came into the service that I'd been in a dangerous situation myself because my assessment of that lad was that it was a flick of a coin who he decided to assault and it would have been as easy to get me—going down to my car at night—as to get that woman, in fact there was probably more provocation because he did know me and I almost felt I walked in the shadow of something for a time. It really worked on me. . . . It wasn't the murder, it wasn't the violence, it was the fact that he went back and assaulted her when she was in that state which I felt to be pretty sick. I was then faced with having to make contact with him, the first time was when he was in the cells . . . there was a policeman sitting there 'cos they wouldn't leave me alone and I went down thinking, I don't know what I'm going to say, and I walked in and just sat and looked at him and part of me just didn't want to know him and there was part of me which had a job to do . . . I almost went on to auto-pilot if you know what I mean. I sat there and said "Well how are you love?" [laughs] . . . he said he wasn't worried about anything except whether he was going to get a job when he came out. And my reaction to that was anger, which I had to control. . . . I'm going to have a hell of a lot of repulsion certainly for the offence and it just associates itself too much with him.'

Pressure groups may, in attempting to legitimize their own means of sexual expression, make punitive moral judgments about other types of expression. The Campaign for Homosexual Equality's proposed Sexual Offences Bill made provision (in its Fourth

Schedule) for a punishment of life imprisonment for sexual intercourse with a boy aged under 13. Of course moral evaluations must
exist in dealing with sexual expression as Probation Officer 6 said,

'Do I have a ladder on a sort of "nasty scale"? . . . I think
society—or women especially—I think are prepared to condone
heavy breathers on phones. If a man indecently exposes
himself, they are far more likely to laugh at it than be petrified
and I would go along, and act it out, by placing far more time
and energy on those who I thought were worrying from their
own safety's point of view and probably the standards of
society. I would be very anxious about sexual offences on
children; but not necessarily in an incest situation where vast
amounts are said to go on but never come to court because of
the nature of the people involved. I couldn't get terribly
frightened by an incestuous relationship, unless of course the
girl was 11 or 12 and the man was sort of a nasty piece of
work.'
'Where do your evaluations come from?'
'Well I try to link myself in there with society's values in that I
tend to go along with them, I think. My attitude to indecent
exposure is more tolerant and so are society's becoming I *think*.
I would be more worried and would try to control those where
society would have least toleration. If you like, I do mirror, I
do reflect what goes on. I am not worried about seeing my role
as having elements of social control in it.'

These workers' evaluations find some support in the literature.
The most comprehensive research on sex offenders in America came
from Gebhard *et al.* (1965). It was based on sexual case histories of
white males: 1,356 convicted and usually in penal institutions for
one or more sex offences, 188 comprising a prison group without
convictions for sex offences, and a control group of 477 who had no
criminal convictions. The interviewing was completed between 1940
and 1960 and the study was begun and directed by Kinsey until his
death in 1956. They divided sex offenders into nine types ('child' is
under 12 years, 'minor' is 12-15 years):

1 Heterosexual, consensual, with a child
2 Heterosexual, consensual, with a minor
3 Heterosexual, consensual, with an adult
4 Heterosexual, forced, with a child
5 Heterosexual, forced, with a minor
6 Heterosexual, forced, with an adult
7 Homosexual, consensual, with a child
8 Homosexual, consensual, with a minor
9 Homosexual, consensual, with an adult

In addition they included peepers and exhibitionists. In terms of compared results the following details emerged. Type 4 was described as suffering from several serious handicaps in early life, most importantly intellectual dullness and a background of parental friction and broken homes. Their adult relationships with females were stormy. In many respects they held a rather split view of women as good, i.e. virgin brides, and bad i.e. prostitutes. They 'combined dullness, alcoholism and an asocial attitude into a life style that brought them the distinction of being the most criminal and recidivistic of all the groups under consideration' (p. 154).

Type 5 are described as having had disturbed backgrounds, periods of institutional life, 'irresponsible, aggressive and amoral young men seeking the gratification of today with little concern for the future . . . an unenviable record of serious offences, violence and recidivism' (pp. 175 and 176). Type 6 are described in this way: 'The majority of aggressors versus adults may be succinctly described as criminally inclined men who take what they want, whether money, material or women, and their sex offences are by-products of their general criminality' (p. 205).

This evidence's applicability for social work has to be judged in the light of its categorizing and its cultural, time-capsuled state and the experience of the offending behaviour, arrest and penal measures being an interactive one for the sexual offender. Given these important provisos, the Gebhard research does give further credence to the idea that rapists are a group apart in considerations of the morality of sexual conduct. Compare for example the above comments with the conclusions made about Type 9: 'The homosexual offenders vs. adults, as a group, do not appear particularly criminal or dangerous. They do not damage society, they merely do not fit into it' (p. 357).

In social work and serious crimes we can observe the case for making explicit the moral role chosen by the worker. Here ethical standards—respect for the self-actualization of the individual and the rights of others have to be balanced within a known-about ideological framework. The question is not simply are we acting as agent of social control but how much control/influence on the client can we permit (outside of a legal process) and how much pressure can be placed on the community to act more tolerantly towards a serious offender? We see an interactive process with the offender, society and the worker engaged in communications, each of whose limits of tolerance are unknown by the other. It is this unpredictable state which divides us from the kind of comfortable counselling world described by Halmos. It is the condition of a faith-less generation of social workers. If we are to move on to other more clearly sexual conduct matters, it should not be at the cost of denying our functions in respect of the 'intolerable' in personal behaviour. In situations where clients are unable to grant others value and dignity, a reciprocity may ensue. We should be very anxious to define our moral role for these clients who may be labelled as psychopaths and have the least power in any clash with society and its appointed agents of control and change.

The probation service

'But in the mass of their daily work they choose not to invoke or attempt to enforce most legal rules, both because it is impossible to do so and because doing so would not advance their taken-for-granted purpose in life—maintaining social order.' Actually Douglas (1971, p. 311) was referring to the police but he could equally well have been concerned to describe the activities of the probation service except, of couse, 'maintaining social order' would have to be weighted against/alongside 'Advise, assist and befriend' the offender. The result is still the non-enforcement of many legal rules in the interests of both society and the individual. However, the published accounts of the probation service's success in preventing further offences, or even on its own terms, bringing about a better personal adjustment of the offender, is at best unproven. (See Davies (1977) for example.) It could be further argued that social work should not *primarily* be concerned with preventing further offences. Despite this, Glastonbury (1972) found that the public appeared (prior to the creation of local authority social services departments) to express understanding of what was the job of probation officers, rather than that of apparently 'less directive' social workers. This confirms my impression that there is a general respect for the probation service but really in terms of its role as a humane, individualized upholder of public morality. Confirmation of this can be observed in the case of a probation officer who declared, 'My salesmanship for Post Office forgery was very simply an attempt to find the best alternative to his current villainous preoccupations' (Parkinson, 1977). When this was reported in the popular press his managers suspended the writer from probation duties. Here the public image of the probation service was seen to be at risk. The difficulties of actually preventing delinquent behaviour were recognized by all probation officers in my study. The resultant *accommodations* that all made illustrate the dilemmas of social work in the probation setting but these should not all be seen negatively. The probation order is made during a 'theatrical ritual of the positive' in court. The wrongdoer agrees to be placed under the supervision of the do-gooder. The court then gives the client permission to remain part of the community. Legal constraints are involved but if these were to be actively and immediately exercised, then presumably the offender would have been more severely rejected by removal from the community. The officer is expected to use personal influence in order to prevent the offender from again challenging public morality. My observation is that the officer is given a good deal of discretion in his work with the offender. Denzin (1970) would see this type of activity as being a way of maintaining social order by means of interactional ritual. This may, in the course of a probation relationship, involve the possibility of continued law-breaking. The comparative lack of a hierarchical structure in the management of the probation service emphasizes and encourages the idea of the personal mandate and responsibility of the officer. The costs and opportunities of such a position are available for observation in such a publicly sensitive area as work concerned with sexual conduct. As Read and Millard stated (1977) in relation to the Parkinson case, 'how vulnerable they [probation officers] are when the rules which circumscribe their behaviour are vague, and their values and knowledge are uncertain'.

The extract below from the study shows Probation Officer 3 in one such accommodation—using her relationship with an offender to try and ensure he is able to continue to live in the community without public demonstration of his deviance. In order to achieve this she does technically break the criminal law and also encourages behaviour which can be seen as contravening conventional sexual moral codes. Kenneth is in his mid-40s, a previously institutionalized subnormal. He was charged on a couple of occasions with indecent assaults on minors and placed on probation:

'My attitude towards Ken's offences—it seems to me that it was very much horseplay amongst the kids. The sort of thing that goes on in showers in any school and I felt that the lads involved were wide enough to know what was going on. I feel Ken's always at risk and I tend to go through patches of saying to him, "Ken, leave little boys alone". I constantly tell him not to have little boys in the house but that is an ongoing hassle. He denies that he encourages them but I know that he does. But as far as his homosexuality, if you can call it that because it's much more a juvenile sexuality and therefore I can't take these offences seriously because no one has been hurt by them I feel. I quite like having Ken on probation because I feel he needs looking after in the open society because of his low intelligence and it helps him to survive. He has contact with one of these subnormality hospitals in the area. I know the staff there very well because it's quite a small establishment and a few months ago we had complaints from a new member of staff that Ken was having a homosexual relationship with another man there. The general attitudes of the staff was that this man could buy and sell Ken. He's a lot craftier. They know that a certain amount of homosexuality goes on on the wards and they take a very sensible attitude towards it. They don't like someone who is very naive or unable to defend themselves being used by other patients but if they think they are equals and they are getting something out of it and no harm is coming from it, then they play it very sensibly. Because of an incident that happened there, Ken was banned from the hospital but I contacted the psychiatrist involved about it and I've diplomatically talked to various members of staff and I have an understanding with them that if Ken starts visiting there again it will be all right. I know that before long I've got to start dropping some hints to Ken that he might be spending some summer weekends going out there and I suppose a lot of people would say that I was colluding with him. To me, I think that it is the right thing to do, I think he has a right to his sexual life. He has a sexual drive and if he exercises it there, it isn't going to do anybody any harm. It will be controlled to a certain extent in there, the staff will know what's going on. I also think that youngsters that live around will be less at risk.'

'From what you are saying this has been reasonably conflict-free for you?'

'Completely so.'

'You haven't felt bound by expectations from society or other people that this isn't the role you should be pursuing as a PO?'

'Not at all, if anyone challenged me on it, I would be quite happy to defend it. I wouldn't expect everybody to understand it but I am confident of it.'

'What makes you confident?'

'I suppose it is a responsibility and authority that goes with the job. I would possibly begin to get quite angry if I was criticized from outside the service. A criticism from inside the service I would have to think about. I wouldn't expect to get any. From outside the service I think my reaction would be as it is in other cases. I think society is inclined to land us or to leave us the responsibility for lots of problems and expect us to do the impossible. It is very easy to criticize from the outside when you don't have to take the problem on. Perhaps a bit impatient too because I was perhaps a bit more educated in the problem than other people are.'

'By virtue of being a PO?'

'By virtue of experience now, which has come from being a PO.'

For the probation officer, the possibility of further offences is always a factor in the relationship and Probation Officer 5 describes how this in fact curtails his discussing certain sexual matters with clients:

'I'm always afraid of what damage I might do, especially with younger people, when I talk about sexual matters . . . —not getting across one's point fully—especially in ages of 15-16-17 you get to homosexual thoughts and the explanation on my part or the understanding on the client's part is not fully developed and they go away with a half opinion of what's been said. A young boy, nearly 16, was a bit feministic, he looked feminine, one or two of his habits seemed a bit feministic to me and it had been commented upon by child guidance when he went there on one occasion. I was trying to bolster up his own image of masculinity and when discussing it with him he froze a bit and I think I foolishly pressed on in this case, thinking I might overcome that freezing by talking more about the subject. And that boy went out and committed an offence directly on leaving my office, and the following week he did the same and the following week he did the same. Now I felt very guilty about that boy committing offences and he's now in borstal. It really upset me at the time and my handling of that situation—may have had nothing to do with it—but may have caused him to commit offences in some way. . . . I really felt guilty about that lad being in borstal.'

The discretion available to the probation officer may be the envy of workers in other organizational structures. The responsibilities implied by public and professional trust are very onerous. When faced with serious crimes, having begun to disregard 'psychiatric' explanations of deviant behaviour, the probation officer is left with alternatives which may involve deterministic accounts—'I get this urge I can't control', or 'Incest seems to flourish in mining villages, it's culturally accepted.' Frequently there is a denial by the offender that the proven behaviour actually occurred, 'Sure, I would have raped her but I couldn't get a hard on.'

Little wonder that the worker will be tempted to look around for other technicians to fill the gap left by the psychoanalyst and s/he may find some of the views of the behaviourists immediately attractive. Even if both technically and ideologically these methods of control are unacceptable for the individual, the setting may make for extreme dilemmas for the probation officer. Take the case of the officer working in a prison where behaviour therapy and drug treatment is used on his or her clients. With whom is the role of the moral tutor there? Does social work as a profession provide in such circumstances a legitimate framework for the worker as moral entrepreneur in relation to other professionals?

Within these wider system conflicts are the day-by-day meetings where the probation officer is working with those to whom are ascribed high public deviance. Entrusted with the task of making their sexual conduct less a public threat s/he has an armoury consisting of relationship skills and public trust. The moral choices made in each case is always with these two elements somewhere in mind. The discretion implied here as we are seeing can involve a lot of personal conflict for the social worker. There is equal concern for the client, for as Morris (1976) notes, we may know the prejudice of judges but those of administrators may be concealed within a bureaucracy.

Residential social work

A Personal Social Services Council Report (1977) contained a chapter on 'Residential Care Reviewed. Daily Living: Questions for Staff'. No. 58 (p. 57) read:

Do staff feel that residents should not be allowed to form intimate relationships or be allowed sexual freedom? . . . Do they understand that handicap of any form does not necessarily diminish the need for sexual relationships?

No. 66 (p. 58) read:

There is special need for counselling in the handling of sexual problems, bereavement and terminal care, and for open discussion linked with the counselling. There are many personal and administrative problems raised by freer attitudes to sexual relationships and these need careful consideration by both staff and management. It is significant that no comments were received from residents and staff in residential homes on matters related to sex or death.

The obvious problem of sexual conduct in residential care is the public aspect of such behaviour where so often there is no privacy for the client. In the past with the concept of total institutions going unchallenged, sexual behaviour was furtive, illicit and often part of unequal power relationships which developed in the subculture. A concern with sexual needs can be seen as part of the improvement in standards of sexual care of those living in some types of institution. 'Prisoners who are cold and hungry are scarcely concerned with sex, but when these same men are given well-balanced meals, comfortable clothing and other creature comforts, they become predictably vulnerable to sexual frustrations' (Kirkham, 1971, p. 328). Institutions have also to be seen in the context of the wider society from which they offer shelter. Also their residents are already socialized into cultural mores in relation to sexual conduct which in our society means increasing freedom of sexual expression. These attitudes are likely to be taken along with the younger resident, although amongst the old there are cultural differences.

In 1976 I was involved in the admission of a woman in her 80s to a home for the elderly. She did not really want to leave the house of her son and daughter-in-law but the tension between them was so great as to involve 'granny battering'. The old woman had been descended from gypsies and had always been 'outspoken'. After her admission, a distressing occasion with the old woman in tears begging not to be left, the matron telephoned on a number of occasions complaining to me that my client would have to return home as she was using words like 'cunt' to describe her feelings about the home and its staff and this was upsetting the other residents.

One of the problems in relation to sexual conduct in residential care is that entry to such facilities stigmatizes the person by an evaluation that s/he is unfit to live within the mainstream of society. People are judged less than fit to manage their own affairs. The announcement of building a hostel or prison in a residential area often brings fears about the safety of children from sexual molestation. The implication is that the inmates of such establishments are somehow more dangerous than the average stranger—if they were not a threat to the public then surely they would not need to be locked up! Allied with such views is the belief that young people are in institutions to protect them from themselves. Girls being 'in moral danger' is an obvious example. Certainly this is a reason why social workers place children in institutions. As Social Worker A in the study said:

'I was dealing with a girl aged 15 who was very sexually promiscuous. It was a classic case of where a girl's delinquency was defined in terms of promiscuity and where she was totally beyond the control of her parent, and spent a lot of time staying with some other people in a house which was nothing more than a knocking shop. I very much acted as an agent of social control to help her get out of the place . . . to be honest it was to try to disentangle my feelings about her having sex for one thing, but I had strong feelings about her being exploited in a situation where she just didn't have the emotional resources to cope, there was no way this girl could make a decision for herself so I went along with providing alternative resources for her which weren't as it turned out very suitable.'

When the young person is in residential care how far do limits on the expression of their sexuality curtail their rights to express their sexual needs? This dilemma is not faced up to by the PSSC document. Age or sexual discrimination may be very important factors in determining the action of a social worker. This may not always be in expected ways, for example, in the study Social Worker C described how his agency policy in relation to young people affected his handling of an emergency night duty call. This was to a city hotel where a 17-year-old boy had been detained by the police in suspicious circumstances in the room of some Arabs. He discussed with the boy the alternatives to his half-admitted life style and took him to a voluntary hostel. The worker concluded that had the boy been under 17 then he would have been 'impelled' by departmental policy to instigate care proceedings. It is girls who are usually seen as being in moral danger and removed to a home or hostel whilst boys may be implicitly encouraged by their workers to explore their sexuality in the wider community. Righton (1977) in considering the need to nurture positive emotions in residential care, wrote,

> Provided there is no question of exploitation, sexual relationships freely entered into by residents—including adolescents—should not be a matter for automatic inquiry; nor should a sexual relationship between a resident and a worker be grounds for automatic dismissal. Such guarantees—minimal as they are—could do much to free staff from anxiety in developing more adventurous caring.

Amongst the responses to this stance was a letter published in *Community Care*, 23 March 1977, from a residential worker about his relationship with an adolescent girl, 'We were in a love relationship that recognised no bounds except those agreed between us and has remained to this day our private business.' Later in the letter he states, 'I look back and feel no shame for the natural development of our relationship and for feeling more responsibility to my rare friend than to my profession.' A few weeks later the letters column of the magazine (5 May 1977) gave another perspective. A woman wrote that she believed her husband was the writer of the original letter 'We had been married for nine years with two children, then aged seven and four years. Whilst my husband was caring for and loving a 14-year-old girl in care, he was treating me in such a way that our marriage is over.' She ended by asking, 'In his letter he said he felt more responsibility to his friend than to his profession—where do we fit into that responsibility?'

This is an eloquent example of the complexity of the issue of sexuality in residential care once the absolute prohibitions of sexual expression between residents and/or residents and staff are removed (see also Davis, 1975). The inequalities of power within an institution may not disappear when a sexual relationship is entered into, either between residents or staff.

Harris (1977) describes seven models of residential care ranging from the 'Dustbin' model to the 'Therapeutic'. During the study I visited a children's home where the atmosphere was very relaxed and the staff professional and the morale obviously high among children and adults. The officer in charge described what Harris calls the 'Family substitute' model which was in operation. I had asked if this worker wanted to add anything at the end of over an hour's discussion on sexual problems within residential work:

'Yes, very definitely. A lot of this is dependent on the general attitudes, the general patterns of behaviour that are exhibited by your staff—example is a very very powerful element in this. If you have got a marriage which is rocky or abnormal or if there are elements which are by social standards undesirable within your staff, you will find these reflect . . . these do have very considerable repercussions with the children who see this as normality. If you start to produce aberrations of it, your children will reasonably pick these up as abnormalities. I can think of several instances where the marital relationships or co-habitee situations are abnormal by socially accepted standards and I have little doubt that these have an effect on children in care.'

Previously I had asked how the staff coped with children getting crushes on each other or staff members:

'Blimey, I can think of several girls who tried to seduce me. . . . I have a lot of sympathy for staff who fall into this trap. I can very easily understand their feelings. We take certain precautions. My deputy and I have agreed that we never go into girls' rooms at inappropriate times. I would not personally go and get teenage girls up in the morning unless there was somebody there.'

His wife added:

'I was brought up in residential life [her parents were in child care] and so was pretty aware of it but let's face it it certainly isn't pointed out to you at interview and it isn't on any sort of job description.'

The officer in charge: 'This is one area where we shadow students very closely.'

They did allow female staff to go into the boys' bedrooms. The female worker answered her own question as to this apparent discrepancy, 'The quickest answer is that it is the male member of staff who makes a girl pregnant . . . it isn't the answer but. . . .' The couple then went on to talk about being affected by the special problems of the children, possible criticisms from the children's parents and the importance of good staff/children ratios in handling such situations.

Paedophilia

'Speaking abstractly we may hypothesize that the greater the involvement in a relational social structure, the lower the possibility of deviance abscription by members of social control agencies' (Denzin, 1970, p. 148).

A most interesting aspect of the declared or expressed sexual interest/love of pre- and post-pubertal children is crystallized in the above quotation. That is the view of the paedophile as being completely 'different'. During 1977 a great deal of public interest was created by the attempts of a self-help organization—the Paedophile Information Exchange—to change the definition of their sexual interests by public debate about a proposal that 'the law should no longer define ages below which consent to sexual activity cannot be given'. (See their evidence to the Criminal Law Revision Committee 1975.) The group may be seen as untypical of paedophiles in that they are politically active (see their Survey of Members, 1976). They also had members who were interested in children past puberty and into the teens. They distinguish between love of children and liberation of their rights of sexual expression—paedophilia—and the exploitation of the children's sexuality—paederasty. They would also distinguish between paedophiles and those who are apprehended for having sexual relations with children. In PIE's *Childhood Rights* (1977) Brongersma is reported and quotes Gebhard *et al.* (1965) as finding that for an overwhelming majority of those sentenced for having sexual relations with a child, it was situational events or a psychological state which caused this choice rather than personal preference. Brongersma believes the real 'child-lover' is a rare and seldom public person. There is here a problem about the meaning of 'paedophile' in the interpretation of the Gebhard findings (p. 74). In relation to Type 1—girls—(see p. 47 of this book):

> The pedophiles are the commonest variety and constitute from perhaps one quarter to one third of the offenders vs. children. . . . The term 'pedophile' is somewhat unfortunate since these men evidently did not consciously prefer children as sexual partners, but simply found them acceptable.

In relation to Type 7—boys—(p. 294; see also p. 47 of this book):

By far the commonest variety of offender, comprising slightly over half of all our cases, is the pedophile. We include under this term not only males who prefer children, but also those who, while preferring older persons, nevertheless find children sexually desirable.

They also report that the group of aggressors (Type 4) does also contain a few paedophiles but an overlay of alcohol and psychiatric problems prevented more being recognized.

The response of even the serious press to their demands was shown by Polly Toynbee (*Guardian Women* 12 September 1977): 'Disgust, aversion and even anger is what most of us think of the age of consent being lowered to four. I also had the sinking feelings that in five years or so their aims would be acceptable.'

In the study all the gay group of social workers expressed some conflict about their attitudes to paedophile clients. Their attitudes ranged from wishing for more societal tolerance, through not wanting to know of such activities, to considering the possibility of informing the police (see Section A, p. 107). Some people in the gay movement have been very concerned to define gay people as being separate from paedophiles. In order to change both their own private and public image towards respectability, a number of helping professionals who have 'known about' different sexual orientations may well feel it necessary to separate themselves off from any suggestion of being 'child molesters'. This is influenced by a historical connection between paedophilia and homosexuality, at least in the minds of those who make pronouncements on sexual matters. The *Guardian* of 3 April 1976 reported the words of Mr Justice Ackner who was gaoling a teacher for indecent assault on his 10- or 11-year-old pupils:

One reads again and again in histories of young men involved in homosexual activity, that at an early age they were subject to some homosexual attack. There is no medical evidence I have heard to suggest that that cannot but have in some cases, a very serious effect and may well have done in this case.

Likewise feminist social workers may feel strongly that sex with children is intolerable as it is not consensual but part of the rape syndrome in its asymmetrical relationship between child and adult (see Connell and Wilson (1974) and the findings of Gibbens (1977) on paedophiliac rape; see pp. 41-2). For some paedophiles this asymmetry would be seen as part of a love relationship.

The paedophiliac man or woman, then, can expect little support from other sexual liberation movements. Obviously some jobs connected with social work or teaching do give opportunities for men and women with such interests to pursue them but at a covert level and with some danger of discovery and total social collapse. Other avenues exist on the 'open commercial market' to buy the sexual involvement of a child but no doubt this is unsatisfactory for many people. In this situation there has emerged, since October of 1974, the PIE which claims to have many helping professionals in its membership. I had a letter published in the organization's magazine which asked for consumers of the social services to get in touch with me to discuss their experiences. It is not really surprising that no one responded from the general membership, given the likely experience of many in prison or treatment institutions. Neither is the absence of 'public paedophiles' in social work surprising. Few other organizations are apparently so much at odds with one of the foundations of social welfare—i.e. the integrity of the family with its possessive attitude to children and the rights of parents over them. Even when this is recognized to be a wrong emphasis in social policy—and the Children Act of 1975 in some ways reflects this—the change is in the area of concern for the welfare of the child and the expression of this in the power to make decisions being vested in social workers and the courts rather than parents. There is little evidence of a social policy designed in effect to recognize the rights of children and anonymous strangers to form loving and sexual relationships. The legislation is becoming increasingly *protective* of children from adults. At present there is no way of defining a cut-off point on a continuum which at one end denies children sexuality whilst at the other exploits it in barbaric prostitution (see Petrie, 1971; Pearson, 1972; DeMause, 1975).

For social workers attempting to locate such a point in their moral judgments, probably the consideration involved, apart from legal and agency functioning, is the physical and emotional damage to the child. Schofield (1965a) and Burton (1968) present some evidence which relates to the questions. Schofield points to the separateness of paedophiles from homosexuals, reporting that paedophiles were more likely to be heterosexual and did not usually have intercourse with the children. Burton followed up a group of 41 children who had been involved in some kind of sexual offence. She concluded (p. 161):

the underlying personality needs of the children were such that relationships with adults would have been acceptable, rather than frightening and no considerable degree of trauma was sustained. As a group these children showed a significantly greater need for affection, both in phantasy and behaviour than a comparable group of control children.

Further (p. 168):

Most children so involved make an adequate personality adjustment: only a few of the more disturbed children, for whom the sexual acting out was undoubtedly symptomatic of a general disintegration of personality, make a poor adjustment.

Beyond such evidence, however, must be the social worker's evaluation of legal and agency response in the form of how much discretion will s/he be allowed in dealing with such a case, and in that judged margin will operate the worker's evaluation of the composition of good human relationships. To quote again from Burton (1968, p. 88):

What on the surface appears to be an example of aberrant sexual acting out, may then be thought of as a means of wresting the satisfactions necessary for personality growth from an indifferent environment.

Should we and can we as social workers allow that where the environment has failed a child and a loving and sexual relationship exists with a man or woman we should not automatically strive to destroy such a liaison?

Conflicts and personal costs for clients and workers

We believe that the basic unit of society is the family which is founded on marriage. A lasting and happy marriage forms the best environment in which a child can develop the uniquely human capacities for affection, generosity and creative imagination (The Responsible Society, 28 Portland Place, London W1).

It would be reasonable to assume that the social workers who are members of this organization 'For Research and Education in matters affecting the family and youth', would have few personal conflicts in dealing with many of the situations illustrated here. Their overall aim would be the maintenance of family life and deviations from this would be tackled as 'suitable cases for treatment' or prayer. Although arguments about technique might ensue, these could be overridden by the belief in the superiority of a certain life-style reflecting absolute values. It is not just what might be viewed 'right-wing' organizations who hold absolute beliefs about what constitutes the good society, but for our purposes, the Responsible Society can serve as an example that social work has an ongoing relationship with fundamentalist beliefs. As we have discussed, social work has generally lost its faith in the treatment ethic and discovered a personal politics with which a daily struggle continues in its teaching and writing. However necessary this may be for academic respectability and a rightful place in centres for higher education, what seems less certain is how these conflicts are resolved in operational situations. Sexuality provides a dramatic representation of many aspects of an inescapable reality for social work as an emerging profession. This is simply that the workers are both a manifestation of and an influence on social policy and that social work and social policy are in a relationship of reciprocity. Discretion within legal and administrative frameworks must exist otherwise there would be no individual grounding for social welfare. Given this discretion, how do the workers decide to use their influence? Their training may not equip them for the task either because of lack of information or they may find 'professional ethics' to be contradictory or too simple to apply in any given situation. Perhaps for social workers the new awareness of working in a society with many differing and conflicting moral stances complicates their decision-making. It seems reasonable to assume that among the workers themselves, there will be held, in addition to fundamentalist beliefs, at least some of these different moral stances.

If we return to the view that the family is the chosen unit to promote social health and that many of our laws and social institutions and welfare provisions reflect these beliefs, we can see at once a problem for the social worker. S/he is usually dealing with those for whom this model has not been lasting or successful, and who have generally not found a socially sanctioned or tolerated alternative. For example, the 1971 census revealed that 3,320,000 people were living in one-person households out of 18,317,000 households; 18.1 per cent of all households were single person households; 22.2 per cent of all households were non-family households; 6.7 per cent of all households were single-parent households (sources: *Annual Abstract of Statistics,* 1975; *Social Trends,* 1975). We could add to these figures those people who are living emotionally separate lives and those couples whe are deciding to remain childless.

In dealing with matters of sexual conduct, is it therefore always appropriate for social workers to apply judgments and treatments related to a uniform family life model? If it is not, then what alternatives are available and can these embrace a fuller range of sexual expression and life-style including that which is now outlawed? Clearly in the present state of knowledge and feeling, we cannot answer positively for all of the possible alternatives. There is urgent need to consider such implications for the social work endeavour, if for no other reason than the almost certain varying degrees of personal stress for an individual who must make an individual response to a client's situation. Here the worker's total personality will be of utmost importance. Many of us may at times be very

61

disturbed by the way in which a client's plight—perhaps in a state of desolation after loss, for example—reflects on our own. We can relate this to our own past and hopefully see the reflection of what it is and respond again freely to the client's need. In matters of sexuality, personal response is not so contained because sexual feelings and orientation are always around in the encounter with the client. This, we may hypothesize, will result in varying degrees of stress according to the worker's ability to hold and use her/his own sexuality in response to what the client is presenting. An example from the study may clarify this process. The female residential social worker previously mentioned is describing her discussion with an 11-year-old whose mother is a lesbian:

'One of the questions she did ask was "Does it make you cross?" or "Does it make you disagree with what mummy does?" My answer to it was that I couldn't understand why mummy did what she did as I was perfectly happy with, and being married to, a man. But if I was her mummy and I hadn't been happy with a man and found that I was happy with another woman, then perhaps I might have done the same so I wasn't in any way to judge her mummy. I wasn't fit to be able to judge her mummy for what she was doing; no matter what she felt, even if she felt angry with mummy for the way in which she lived.'

At that point her husband the officer-in-charge interrupted: 'Can I ask the obvious question, that is what you tell her, and what you think is different!'

'As a female I am [interrupted again by husband] I had to be honest and say I didn't understand why her mother did it because I had never had the feeling myself so how could I understand? I think that as she gets older, I can discuss with her that I find it very difficult to accept that another lady is living with another woman or two ladies are living together, but I don't find homosexuality repulsive. Let's face it, we [the staff group] have talked about this and without exception everyone feels that males cannot tolerate homosexuality, females cannot accept lesbianism. You feel it's a weakness in your own sex. But she is not ready to accept that yet, she is not old enough I don't think, to take that yet but I think at the moment the important thing is to get across to her that no matter what she feels, her mother is not going to change so if she wants to retain a relationship with her mother, she has got to accept her as she is—my feelings are that she will later on seek her father.'

In this thought-out, caring response we can see indications of the anxiety involved for the workers, and their value judgments. What is the message being conveyed to the child about her mother, and what does the child or client *expect* to hear from the worker? One of the most influential writings of the 1970s in social work education has been that of Mayer and Timms (1970, pp. 129-30): 'Those seeking interpersonal help expected the worker to base his actions on a unicausal-moralistic-suppressive approach to problem solving.'

Social workers, in addition to coping with the stresses of decision-making (or failing to make a decision) from their own personal/ political position, may well have their tensions increased if they apply such a client-conservative perspective to matters of sexual conduct. The potential confusion for those on the receiving end is easy to imagine.

If there are inevitable problems in coping with the range of sexual conduct observed in social work, these difficulties are likely closely to affect the workers themselves. We would observe that this is likely to be true no matter what the worker's life-style or sexual interest. If, however, the worker is gay, then there are certain additional concerns which involve not just professional practice but the right of that woman or man to be a social worker. Although the BASW Code of Ethics was amended in October of 1976 to condemn discrimination on the grounds of sexual orientation, the employers of social workers have no such unanimous views. In 1975 the National Council for Civil Liberties (NCCL) conducted a survey of local authority social service committees' attitudes to gay social workers. A range of attitudes emerged. In Lambeth the Chairman stated (NCCL, 1977, p. 9):

> Race, colour, religion, sex or sexual orientation all play a part in determining or reflecting the personality, attitude and aptitude of an individual and thus all to varying degrees influence or affect recruitment and selection situations. Nevertheless, may I assure you that not one of these attributes or options is used by us to discriminate.

However, the Director of Social Services for Hampshire stated (*ibid.*, p. 18) he would not 'be prepared to condone the employment of homosexual women and men in posts in this Department which carry a responsibility for the care of people and especially the care of children'. Probably one of the most interesting replies, from the viewpoint of social work as an emerging profession, came from the Director at Wakefield who stated that (pp. 24-5) 'a caseworker who did not conceal her or his homosexuality would be subject to discipline or dismissal "not because it was homosexuality but because it would be unprofessional practice"'.

The homosexual individual will, therefore, be subjected to varying degrees of acceptance and rejection by her or his employing authority and may get little support in cases where the sexual conduct of a client is involved. Here of course the supervisory relationship has an inbuilt requirement of a complete openness. This may be difficult enough to achieve when the worker has a *similar* sexual orientation. The gay social workers may well decide to seek support themselves in self-help groups where their life-style is seen as a legitimate alternative to the main stream and a political awareness of the position of minority groups will replace an image of sickness, immaturity or deviance. The interesting element here is that being gay may well have involved the worker 'at the receiving end' of professional help. It is my impression that a large number of homosexual people in the helping professions have been clients or patients in relation to some aspect of their own sexuality (see p. 95). This, as we shall note, does have important implications for the image social workers may have of what constitutes a helping relationship. Although most openly gay people would reject the idea of therapy, of whatever kind, which aimed to change people from their sexual preferences, the experience of such an endeavour may stay with someone long after a conversion process has been undergone during which a political analysis of their situation has been achieved. Social Worker D in the study discussed the effect of her training in Freudian psychology and how it still affected her view of sexuality. She said that she tried at an intellectual level to make a political analysis of the position of women and the possibility of sexual choice, but her background still caused her to make assessments of normal functioning on a hierarchical basis with genital sexuality as the goal. I pointed to the implied assessment of the immaturity of her own way of life. 'Yes, I know, I constantly try to change the evaluation but it's still there.'

Whilst preparing ourselves for the individual case descriptions in the study we do need a tentative framework within which to try to understand the range of the possible moral tutorage in social work. This chapter has highlighted some areas where a role prescription for the social worker could be seen as ambiguous. It may be that the idea of categories of behaviour could be helpful here. We could divide social work's experience of sexual conduct into Ideal Types as shown in Figure 1. In this figure three assumptions are made: (1) that the social worker wishes to be client-centred; (2) that the social worker is working in a setting where statutory responsibilities are a part of his/her duties; (3) that the social worker holds a consensus view of sexuality in society. By this I mean that the worker has views similar to those expressed by the Responsible Society concerning the 'basic unit' of society being the family, founded on marriage. It would follow that a heterosexual married relationship would be seen

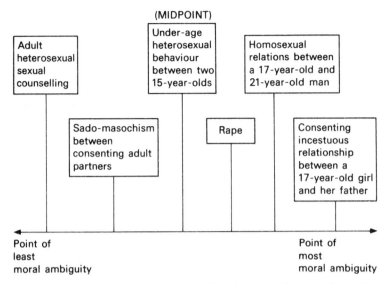

Figure 1. Examples of moral ambiguity for the social worker working at the moral interface of society and the sexual actor

as the most desirable life-style for the client to achieve. Any deviance from this, for example paedophilia, is regarded as evidence of individual maladjustment, immaturity or misbehaviour.

Already in the excerpts from the study we have seen examples of evaluations of behaviour which do not conform to the above. It may be that there is in operation among social workers, whether or not fully articulated and expressed, a conflict model of society. In this model is the notion of groups with unequal power struggling to maintain or achieve a life-style which threatens the others' equilibrium. In the case of sexual conduct, the most powerful would, through control of law enforcement, education, religion, ensure that a valued life-style, 'the family', was preserved. With such a view, for example, it would be possible to see rape as the results of certain structural contradictions within society. This might lead to more or less moral ambiguity for the social worker according to his/her response to the sexual outlaw created by that society. Other kinds of behaviour such as illegal homosexual relations would cause the worker increased or decreased tension according to the way s/he accommodated an ideological position within their day-by-day tasks and duties as a social worker. At this point we are wondering how much a worker's deviant sexual orientation might cause them to link a personal view of their own sexual behaviour/life-style with the client's situation. Alternatively, do the pressures on social workers ensure that they act 'as if' a consensus model is their own in practice? Enough has by now been said to indicate a view of the social workers' activities as possibly unique. All professional groups are granted discretion in what they do with their clients—the priest is given the absolute confidence of the confessional, the psychiatrist of the consultation. As illustrated in this chapter, the social worker has no such public mandate. This is because the psychiatrist is presumably treating medical problems in order to make an individual less maladjusted, whilst the priest is dealing with sins, which in the sexual area is assumed to be in a way which reinforces conventional morality. On the other hand, some social workers, in the view of Sir Keith Joseph (1974):

> abuse their power and authority to urge or condone anti-social behaviour either on political grounds—against an 'unjust society', against 'authority'—or as 'liberation from the trammels of the outmoded family'. But what has been the result? Drugs, drunkenness, teenage pregnancies, vandalism.

The discretion or 'public trust' held by social work is ambivalently given. Some of the reasons for this have already been illustrated. In retreat from both absolute moral standards—'do gooding'—and giving up individualistic explanations of behaviour, the social worker still has to face dealing with public sexual acts which cause alarm bells to ring. But the social worker encounters the deviant individual as a person with needs and maybe even rights to self-expression which may involve illegal behaviour. Without retreating, into absolute morality, a denial of their responsibilities, or into the therapy role, there is nowhere for the worker to go—except to face being moral tutors in a society in conflict. Hence the title of Part 2 where we look in great detail at such encounters.

Part two

The policy and politics of social work

Chapter 4

Description of
the study

'Well I suppose the general moral outlook of the social work
profession ought to be more widely known but until you have
actually discovered what this is—you see we know the general
moral outlook of parsons and doctors, not through them
pasting them up or writing codes of ethics but through
generations of experience; that a Catholic consultant will not do
a termination for example, perhaps that our GP will be
judgmental if we tell him we've got anal VD, and indeed we
will expect our vicar to throw up his hands in horror if we tell
him we are already pregnant before we get married. We have
no means I think, as members of the public, of telling what
social workers stand for, especially as they very often preface
their actions, harsh or easy going, with some variations upon
the expression "I'm trying to help you"' (Social Worker E, one
of the social worker group in the study).

In this thoughtful statement, we may observe the questions which we
are presently engaged upon answering. What is the content of the
package labelled 'Social Work, the Helping Profession'? The idea of
tasks and contracts will aid this search, but in entering into such
agreements the social worker has yet to ask a prior question before
even the problem is presented, and this is, 'What do I stand for?'—
meaning equally, 'What do I represent and wish to promote?' and
'What will I tolerate?' The public has no way of knowing except by
entering into an individual relationship with the social worker. What
does happen in practice is difficult to monitor. Sexual conduct, as
we have noted, is an obviously useful particular area to study for it is
a subject of continual public debate. Most people would see
themselves as having opinions about, and many would regard
themselves as experts on, such matters. If asked about social work's
contribution, public and private, to areas concerned with sexuality,

it seems likely that the general population would assume workers were aiding in the presentation of standards of public morality to those who were likely to be victims or perpetrators of deviance. The strongest case for these assumptions might be expected to be found in the probation service, working with designated sexual offenders.

In 1977 a probation and after-care service invited me to present six lectures/seminars to a group of about twenty probation officers who signified they were interested in discussing 'working with sexual offenders'. As I regarded this topic as a neglected one in training, I accepted the invitation and gained prior permission of the group members to tape-record the sessions with a view to later publication of some of the material. The areas covered were dictated by the case examples which they produced. The range of cases was formidable and included rape, indecent assault, gross indecency, incest. Many of the offenders had long histories of criminal sexual behaviour. My response to this was to discuss with a colleague who was a clinical psychologist the available treatments. In some instances behavioural treatments could be tried when social skills were an apparent cause of the problem behaviour. However, such an approach was of limited value in dealing with the sexually under-inhibited. Bancroft (1974) points to the considerable problems involved in the treatment of people with a 'strong sexual drive'. I wished also to try and locate for the officers their position in the social framework. This was to enable them to choose how to handle the confrontation of the sexual outlaw or deviant and his/her society. Some kind of evaluation of reasons for intervention and non-intervention was needed which placed at its base respect for persons which as Plant (1970, p. 20) puts it, 'is not just a moral principle; on the contrary it is a presupposition of having the concept of a moral principle at all'.

As the course proceeded it became clear that some of the probation officers felt that I was not taking sufficient account of the importance of the impact of the offender upon themselves. One example will illustrate this point: during a discussion of a case of indecent assault, a man in his 20s with a long history of non-violent assaults on women, the woman probation officer had described how her client climbed into women's rooms, just touched the person and left quickly. A psychiatrist had discussed group therapy and given libido-suppressing drugs but had not persisted in his treatment efforts. I had suggested using video to improve the client's self-image. Then the group began asking the officer how the client affected her; she had described his appearance in a very negative way: 'he just seems creepy, I don't know how you technically describe someone who is creepy?'—author—'creepy!' She had described how he had been sexually flirtatious and the group went on to discuss how her personal negative reactions could be used to help them both understand how each saw the other and then to transfer this understanding to the client's situation outside the probation relationship.

Personal response seemed of great importance to the officers in other cases of sexual conduct. The one unqualified officer expressed very directly his views about offences against children:

> 'It's the psychological effect on the children—that's what hurts me more than the actual offence . . . it's a question of rearing up another generation, the fact that some offence against a child may prevent them from having children themselves . . . it's a thing you can't evaluate—the damage to somebody, you can't say "Oh, that's £20,000 the child should be awarded because of the emotional state the offence has caused". They do it if it's a motor accident, I honestly believe they ought to do it for a sexual offence—but I don't know how it would put anybody right. But I think *that* penalty is far better in actual fact than prison.'

Towards the end of the course there was a group discussion of the sexual responses of the officers to their clients. As one woman officer (who was also Probation Officer 3 in the study) said: 'I certainly have found clients attractive and I have sat and looked at them and thought, "My God, you look awful and I know just what you are like and I know what a sod you are so why the hell do I feel like this!".' She turned to another female colleague, 'You must have felt like this sometimes?' 'Very rarely, I don't seem to get that kind of client.' (Laughter from all the group.)

The 'special nature' of work with the sexual offender was articulated by Probation Officer 3. She employs a framework which Taylor (1972) cited as the use of deterministic explanations of and by sex offenders:

> 'It's very difficult to do anything else [but go along with the client's view] which would be saying "What you did was normal and right for you—your sex drive is in that direction". If you say that to somebody then you either say "and I accept you like that" which puts you completely at odds with society—"your sex drive which perhaps you can't do anything about is normal to you, is OK with me". But that's the two of you against the rest of society or you say "there is something basically, radically wrong with you and I think you have got to stay outside the pale or you have got to change" and how do you say to somebody you must change something as innate as the direction of their sex drive when we haven't the first notion of how to do it?'

71

She contrasted this dilemma with dealing with other types of offenders who had different cultural norms in relation to their delinquency:

'I got into an argument with one very intelligent, delinquent lad who said, "You are the minority, I am part of the majority and you live in a very precious sort of society with an extremely precious code of ethics . . .". But at least I feel that there is some slight hope that by logic he might alter . . . that is completely different from talking about somebody's sex drive which is much more innate, much more difficult to get at.'

I decided to try and find out how these sort of dilemmas were faced in respect of all clients on a probation officer's caseload where not just sexual offenders but sexual conduct had been or could have been an area for concern and/or discussion.

In attempting to find out the answers to these questions, I was faced with a group of social workers who were intent on emphasizing the importance of *individual* case situations. These workers were valuing the uniqueness of the meeting with each client more highly than theoretical, legal or organizational consideration. This, one might tentatively conclude, emphasized the broadness, vagueness and diversity of social work's aims, treatment methods and moral code(s) when individual responses are raised to almost the status of a fetish. When one considers social workers as a total group, half of whom even in fieldwork are unqualified, then as a group they could appear as very diverse without a unifying professional culture. Indeed they might see 'individualization' as their major contribution to welfare. However, we cannot regard this as a satisfactory conclusion, even from the viewpoint of the individual client, for we need to know what are the factors which do influence the responses of each worker.

Thus, in addition to the questions above, I sought to ascertain the importance of certain personal influences on a particular area of social work intervention. The next step therefore was, given that a sexual element is present in all encounters, to ascertain how influential are such intimate factors as gender and personal sexual experience and orientation in creating a social work response?

The implications for further study

I considered that it might be very useful to compare the responses of two groups: heterosexual probation officers and social workers and homosexual probation officers and social workers. To study the latter might be especially illuminating as their own conduct is often seen as close to that of the sexual outlaw or outcast.

It was then hoped to broaden the perspective to include as many clients as possible who had been at the receiving end of social workers' attention to their sexual conduct.

In deciding upon this focus, in addition to personal choice factors already discussed in Chapter 1, I had the trust of a probation and after-care service which enabled me to discuss areas of conduct normally regarded as private and to have access to workers and clients who were willing to co-operate. To choose sexual orientation as an area of special interest in a social work encounter is to risk missing other more important factors which may be operating. Again, I would justify this by virtue of the unique access I was able to gain to people willing freely to discuss these topics. I remain open to the point that what might emerge from transcripts of the recorded interviews is that personal sexual characteristics or behaviour in either client or workers is not more important than other factors. Indeed during the research I found myself criticized by gay local authority Social Worker C in the study, who considered that by concentrating on sexuality in social work, I was 'Eroticising Bathrails'. Also as gay Social Worker E in the study observed,

'I don't think that one can erect one's own minority as an example of a particularly sensitive or open or aware, unprejudiced group of people. I'm afraid I think we share the prejudices of other people except on this particular score where conformity, if it is conformity, breaks down because we have discovered we just can't live with a particular conformist attitude when it affects ourselves so very closely.'

Although this excerpt does provide a warning about concentrating on one aspect of a person, it also hints at a very important possibility. That is, of having both a private and a political analysis of one's own behaviour. If the attitude is taken that 'what I do in my private life is my own concern', then the possibility of conscious effects on professional decisions is minimal, even though such private matters may be influential. However, if private behaviour is seen also as a valid way of life which should be publicly recognized, allowed for, and (even) encouraged, then private behaviour is a contemporaneously political act and will be automatically seen by the worker as also influential in professional decision-making. Hence the importance of studying those workers for whom sexuality may of necessity have become the subject of political as well as personal analysis.

Kinsey *et al.* (1948) noted that in absolute terms 'homosexual' or 'heterosexual' is a meaningless category. However, my respondents' self-definition was heterosexual or homosexual with some important other perspectives which are included in individual cases. It is important to recognize that the two groups may not be strictly comparable as the homosexual group were generally committed to a gay life-style with certain political and personal consequences. No such identification unifies the heterosexual group.

We must take into account the differences in work setting. I am assuming that social work is a unity in terms of its activities which are carried out through common knowledge and skills, although the application of these may vary in accordance with duties and tasks in settings such as residential, social services, probation, intermediate treatment.

Outside the two groups I considered it important to extend the study to ask similar questions in a residential setting. I was fortunate in finding one where the staff were enthusiastic in their co-operation and were able to discuss a wide range of sexual conduct management within their home during the two visits I made. I was also able to discuss the consumer's viewpoint in an interview with a boy then aged 18 who had been in care for three years from the age of 14. His two primary care-givers in the home were married to each other, in their early 40s, both had completed in-service training and the officer-in-charge was also qualified in residential social work. They lived with their teenage children in a home for twelve children. It was well staffed, very well provided for materially, and because of high professional standards received a large percentage of kids with chronic behavioural, physical and emotional problems.

I was able to interview 9 men and 4 women who had been the clients of helping professionals. Six of them were clients of the probation officers in the study, 1 had been the patient of a psychiatrist, 2 had been in residential care, 1 had been involved with social workers because of his relationship with his girlfriend and 1 had been in residential care with residential workers who were part of the study. Two women were the clients of probation officers not in the study. Because of the need to respect the people involved (clients and workers) the range of 'case' is limited to those people who were willing and able to be articulate about their sexual conduct with someone outside the helping or statutory relationship. This has resulted in, for example, no rapists being included in the consumer's viewpoint.

The clients of gay social workers and probation officers were not approached because of my intention to avoid situations which might inappropriately identify these colleagues within their organizations.

The Appendix should be consulted for further details of people in the groups and the interviews I conducted.

Chapter 5

The study

The cases

Those discussed ranged from what might be seen as ordinary, e.g.
under-aged sexual relations, to what might be seen as bizarre, e.g. a
woman in her 50s and her son in his 20s who had been charged with
incestuous behaviour. A sexual relationship had existed between the
pair since the boy had been 14.

To achieve some ordering of approximately 40 hours of tape-
recordings, the responses of these two groups of gay and 'straight'
social workers and the clients will be classified according to the type
of sexual conduct being discussed. An analysis of the responses
revealed that individuals did discuss cases in what might be seen as
categories, although there is overlap—for instance, incest might also
be rape, prostitution may also be under-age sex (especially in the
case of a male prostitute—see case with local authority Social
Worker C, p. 55). It will be convenient to discuss the findings
classified according to the type of case or situation primarily under
discussion. These categories are:

A Sexual conduct involving children and young people under
   the age of 21 and the way that social workers accommodated
   such conduct.
B Sex in the family.
C Prostitution.
D Other manifestations of sexual conduct: exhibitionism,
   fetishism, transvestism, transsexualism.
E Where sexual conduct is apparently a secondary issue, i.e.
   where sex is important but not the main focus, for example,
   where the workers are conscious of their own sexuality, or
   when a client happens to be homosexual but this is not the
   primary reason for the person becoming a client of the
   social worker.

75

F   A discussion of the worker's training in the area of sexuality.

(N. B. See pp. 40-9 for cases involving sex and violence.)

Fairly extensive quotations will be made from the tapes judged appropriate and useful to the discussion, especially where it may be possible later to examine some of the congruences and incongruences between the aims/beliefs and attitudes of worker and client. (N.B. These cases will be denoted by the prefix 'C').

A   Sexual conduct involving children and young people under the age of 21 and the way that social workers accommodated such conduct

Probation Officer 7

'C'   Fred, aged 50, is oh probation for shoplifting, although there is a history of indecency and gross indecency with boys aged between 10 and 14, the record of such offences stretching back to 1950. The probation officer described how, since Fred's last release from prison, he had tried to help Fred in a practical way—finding him a flat, arranging social security:

'The probation order had just started and we were seeing a lot of each other, and I thought it was quite good contact really and I read quite carefully what the previous probation officer had done with Fred, but I found that as soon as I started to move into this area of his behaviour with the youngsters that he backed away, which was a pity because I thought we had the foundation of doing something and actually looking at what happened. He claimed that his behaviour is in the past and it is no longer a problem for him. I was then able to say that this was what he had said to his previous probation officer and yet he had committed an offence and gone to prison for it. He is staying with a family which he says he has known for a long time and they have a teenage boy who has recently been in detention centre. Fred had got himself a job with a company car, in a garage, was able to run the parents of this lad over to the detention centre to visit the boy and they were quite grateful for this. When the boy came out Fred was able to set on him in the garage. So, there is this relationship with this lad and I know the lad's supervising officer is wondering what Fred's involvement is and they come to the office together. When I say to Fred what sort of relationship have you got with this lad, he sort of denies any involvement sexually and yet it seems to me that there probably is. A colleague of mine also

said that she saw him coming out of an amusement arcade and
apparently this is a famous "pick up" place. Fred was seen sort
of leering round looking to see the local talent.'
*'Obviously in this case you felt you ought to take a greater
interest in who he came to the office with. Now, why was that?'*
'I'm not sure whether the pressures and tensions were from
outside on to me. You know you've got to do something because
he's coming to the office with a younger bloke because his
record is such that he's got into trouble with a younger guy or
he's been up for indecent assault, or whether it was something
that I felt was wrong and had to intervene, I couldn't tell. My
rationalization was that if there had been a court case and it
emerged that they were associating together and the probation
service knew of this, a magistrate might wonder why we hadn't
acted although I don't know what the hell we could have done.
The lad is under 18 so technically he is committing an offence.
I have to live with that tension, having stated to Fred that I
wondered about the nature of his involvement with this young
boy.'
[This officer is mistaking the age of consent for male
homosexuals, which is 21.]
*'Given that he's not giving you a mandate, do you feel
reasonably happy to leave it at that?'*
'At the moment, there are practical issues that Fred brings to
light. Hopefully we are going to clear these out of the way and
then I hope to have some re-assessment on why we've got
contact, why Fred sees me, so that I can throw the onus on to
him a bit more. It is obvious that he sees me as useful in
getting the local authority flat, that seems a quite identifiable
point of contact. When that is out of the way he's going to have
accommodation and employment and he's still going to have to
see me and at that point, I think we can say, right, what is this
all about and I think it might be worth having some sort of
re-assessment.'
'Therefore your long-term aims will be to do what?'
'I'd like him to look at the implication of his behaviour. I feel
as if he's quite self-destructive about it. It seems that he does
have homosexual interests in younger boys. I am sort of
wondering whether or not he can't reconcile himself to being
homosexual and trying to develop some sort of relationship in
another area. I cannot see Fred as being content with the
present situation.'
*'You really feel you are making an assessment of his own life
situation and wanting to do something about that rather than
stop his sexual behaviour at the moment. Do you feel in general*

77

*that your employers and society are happy for you to be taking
that kind of line?'*
'Yes, because the ultimate objective [stopping his offending
behaviour] is one with which I agree.'
*'In dealing with him, I wonder, do you feel that previous
training or life in general would help or not?'*
'I wouldn't have thought that training could have helped.
Possibly experience in the job of meeting people, going into
crisis situations, fairly tense, finding it difficult to talk, that
sort of experience dealing with those type of people might have
helped me, had there been any willingness to talk on the part
of Fred.'

'C' I interviewed Fred in the probation offices. He was small,
tense, with a somewhat ingratiating manner during the interview,
and I did not feel able to tape-record the discussion but was confined
to note-taking. Overall I felt that Fred was very concerned to
impress upon me that he had a very good relationship with his
probation officer and that he no longer was at risk in relation to
young boys.
He said that he had not been convicted of a sexual offence since
1970 and that he had achieved this 'on my own two feet'. His view of
prison was that the sentencers did not know that for sex offenders
they were sentencing to 'a life of hell':

'We live in a dark world, I was on my last non-sexual offence
still categorized as a sexual offender. I think that's where the
system is wrong—the governor told me that I would never go to
an open prison, I would always be treated as if in prison for a
sex offence.'

I asked Fred what he thought was the origin of his sexual interests:

'It was when I was 13, at approved school. I saw a lot of
homosexuality there. I like talking to younger people, it might
be that I wasn't allowed to mix when I was a kid—now I don't
mix well. I'm a loner. There is a lot of homosexuality in prison
but I didn't get involved with it because I didn't want people to
know. My last sexual offence didn't get any publicity and I was
lucky not to be on Rule 43 [being separated from the rest of
the prisoners].'

I asked if Fred thought his behaviour should be punished:

'Yes, but not in prison, it wasn't rape of a 4-year-old—it was a
lad of 13 or 14 who had quite a lot of sexual experience. I
should have gone to hospital. If there is something wrong with

you the doctor is there to cure it. I think it's the same with
what I did. Not all sex offenders are the same, that's why
probation officers have to understand people. They are
employed to help people irrespective of if you have robbed the
Bank of England or whatever. I have had a number of sexual
offences but the probation officers have not been any use, I've
continued to get into trouble.'

I asked how the probation officer could have stopped Fred: 'That's
difficult because I don't know why I did it in the first place. There
must be a reason why.' I asked, 'How would a probation officer find
out?' 'I think a doctor or psychiatrist should have been able to find
out and do something about it.'

I asked Fred if the law changed and his behaviour was decriminalized, would he still have a problem? His response to this question
was to show a lot of anxiety and state flatly, 'Now I try not to get into
a position of being alone with a boy although I sleep in the same
room as this boy but I don't do anything.' Did Fred think he was
alone in his sexual interests?

'No, it's permissive now, not like in my day—it's not natural
behaviour though, it's an illness. I am interested in teenage
boys. I can't understand those who go for 4- or 5-year-olds.
Girls don't interest me of any age. I always wanted a lad of me
own although I can understand the way that the parents feel
but it wasn't the boy's first time.'

I attempted to obtain Fred's views about his probation officer:

'I think he is trying to help me with getting a flat, but his
hands are tied. I get on all right with him. The officer I had
before, I couldn't get on with him. I think he was prejudiced.
When my wife wanted a clothing allowance for our daughter he
wouldn't get us one. He wasn't bothered, he couldn't or
wouldn't discuss things and I couldn't discuss things with him.
I think he is a lecturer now. On probation it all depends on
who you get. He may have been all right as a probation officer
but he was no good to me.'

I then asked about the relevance of the sex of the probation officer:
'A female probation officer would be all right because I would put it
down to her being trained for that sort of thing.'
I finally asked Fred to imagine a situation where a friend had a
sexual problem. Who would he recommend he contacted? 'I would
tell him to go and see a doctor—but they don't have time nowadays.'

George is over 20 years older than Fred and what follows is taken
from notes taken of an interview I conducted with George. Unlike

79

Fred he has not been to prison but he has experienced 'discovery' of his sexual interests and activities. He had been working as a schoolmaster and when his sexual conduct became public within the school administration he was sacked, but through another staff member he was introduced to a psychiatrist with whom he lived as a lodger for seven years. Her attitude had been

'That my sexual interests she understood and was sympathetic about but she was also society-orientated and so she wanted to help me adjust to the rules. I did in that I was celibate for all of this time. . . . At a period when one has been found out, you are grateful for any help that is offered, you are very vulnerable.'

Several years later George became involved with the Gay Liberation Front and a new analysis of his sexual orientation emerged:

'It was either courageous or dangerous, according to your beliefs. My view now is that children have a right to a spontaneous sex life and that one should not oppress them by saying "No". If I could give you a personal example. When I was 12, I was on holiday with my family and a male friend in his 30s took an interest in me and invited me to call on him whenever I wished. I can remember running in my pyjamas to his room in the early hours of the morning. A sexual event occurred but for me this was not separate in my mind from my friendship with him although in the eyes of society it was. Now to what was I consenting? Nothing, it was just part of our loving relationship.

'Although I am supporting the Paedophile Information Exchange, I think that their platform on lowering or abolishing the age of consent is the wrong one. I think we should be campaigning on the issue of children's rights. Anyone who has an "inordinate desire or an obsession" with sex is wrong and this is an antisocial position.'

I asked about what he was hoping for in terms of a change in society's attitudes and the response of those people like social workers who had certain duties in that society: 'I think we are talking about a change over many years and until society's attitudes change and we are not seen as Frankensteins then we are just fortunate if the social worker turns a blind eye to our involvements.'

Probation Officer 6

'A man in his 40s I had on probation who interfered with small boys, fondled them and generally sought them out and

befriended them with sweets, that sort of thing. His relationship
with his wife was pretty abominable. . . . He was terribly
anxious, as in another case which has just come to mind, again
of a man who interfered with small girls. They were desperate
to convey to me their respectability in spite of what had
happened and were most unwilling to talk about the feelings
which had led to the actual need to do that—both of them. . . .
The wife in the first case verbalized her disgust and fears by
being terribly kind and saying, "Can't you do something to him
or for him—change him", and it would seem that with most of
these cases the client was holding the cards in a sense, one
might introduce the idea of treatment for it but they were
always terribly eager to say it wasn't going to happen any more
so there wasn't a need for treatment, "But I'll talk about how
depressed I am in my lousy relationship with my wife if you
like" sort of attitude. But never would they say, "Here is either
a behavioural problem that I have which I will take you
through step by step or something which leads me to have
rather weird needs in relation to the rest of society which I'm
very worried about", they were never openly direct about,
"please help me with this sexual problem". It had to be in the
end looked at in other ways.'
*'What about the conflicts here about what society, the
magistrates, the offenders' family, the offender and the
probation officer wanted?'*
'It's the same with any social work problem you can interpret
what the problem might be, with or without the help of the
client, hopefully nowadays far more with, you can say to him,
"Look these sexual situations got you in trouble with the law
which brings policemen, courts and the threat of imprisonment"
and they will say, "Yes, that's quite right". This is where the
divergence of role happens. You say, "I would like to help you
stop that happening and we can talk about it at great length
and see what leads to it, I can get you in touch with
psychiatrists who will help you look at this". Now if the client is
prepared to play ball, then you can fulfil your role as far as
society is concerned. If he withdraws you then have to
rationalize, to accept he won't let me do it so I can't do a lot
more about that, but part of the whole interpretation of why he
got into that mess in the first place is probably to do with other
things which are less painful to him and you push these. The
conflict in me is dispersed. . . . I could always turn round and
say, I tried this, this and this but he really wasn't keen to talk
about it. There is no way I could impose any sanction to make
him. I probably need someone to say, "But have you tried every

technique there is to make absolutely certain that you as a person have done as much as you can to get him to talk about these things." That's fair comment but in the absence of that you've only got yourself and your client's responses to go on. So for me there wasn't a conflict; I didn't worry about it. Whereas in probation you may not stop somebody stealing, it seems to me the same sort of conflict.'

Probation Officer 2

'A man aged 42, married with two children, placed on probation for an indecent assault of a 4-year-old girl. The offence was non-violent. I wrote in the final paragraph of the social inquiry report: "I have the impression that this couple could have been hoping for some sort of miraculous cure although they may be coming to terms with the fact that this is unrealistic. If he were to be placed on probation, I think it unlikely he would be able to discuss the offence or his feelings about sexual matters. There are, however, other areas in which help may be needed—the effects of the offence on the marriage, for example, and the problems that might arise with neighbours. At the moment it is not easy to assess how far this sort of help will have any influence on the likelihood of him committing similar offences in future. . . ." It was the marriage as the cause of the offence as well as the effects of the offence on the marriage. The other objective was to deal with the very vehement public reaction to the offence. He appeared two or three times with adjournments for psychiatric reports. During each of the court appearances the parents of the child were in court and during the last appearance when he was placed on probation, they tried to attack him in court and they made threats about his personal safety. I was really concerned that he at the very least wouldn't get beaten up after the offence, and attacks might be made on his family, his children. . . . By the time the probation order was made the couple didn't think I was going to be able to literally stop him having feelings of attraction to children or acting these out. . . . On the basis of previous experience of working with sex offenders and preparing reports on them, I think that courts are more prepared to put sex offenders on probation than anybody else and I think that's because they think we can effect cures of some sort. . . .

'I got him rehoused, he was given priority by the housing department. . . . There was a bit of work with the marriage but after the court appearance, neither he nor his wife wanted to talk about the marriage. I finished up working with him by himself in a fairly routine supervisory sort of way with nothing meaty or meaningful in it. He is of pretty low intelligence and finds it difficult to verbalize and almost impossible to talk at all about his sexuality. . . . I suppose there is an element of social control in what I am doing. I am interested in especially how he is spending holiday periods, his wife is at work and the offence happened at a time when he was by himself and I'm slightly anxious about what he does in his spare time. So we might just talk about the ways in which he can fill his holiday time. . . .

'I tried to explore a bit during the enquiry stage whether he had ever felt attracted to his children sexually and I suppose its something which is at the back of my mind that I've never explicitly come back to. The children are older than the one he assaulted. I suppose that lessens the anxiety, I would have been more concerned if there had been younger children.

'The victim's parents complained to their MP who took it up with the Home Office who through an Inspector got in touch with my Assistant Chief who took my records one day when I was out, photostated them and sent them to the Home Office. The comment of my ACPO was liking the conclusion of the report because I had covered myself.

'The psychiatrist had suggested that behind the offence was a marriage problem and suggested they went to the Marriage Guidance Council which annoyed me. I think I virtually told them that anything the marriage guidance could do, I could do. . . . I suppose to put it at its most extreme that if he reoffended against the same girl and the parents went to the same MP who went to the same Home Office Inspector, etc., etc. and they looked at my records and I've not really been talking about sex with this bloke, what then? I suppose inevitably there is an element of anxiety about expectations on me, whether I'm expected to talk about it. For myself I don't feel too concerned about it. . . . I can think of another case where I had three separate probation orders which were based on three separate sexual offences of indecent assault on boys, each time I thought we had a contract when we started to talk about sexual problems; each time it evaporated after the order was made and the anxiety and pressure was off after the court appearance and it happened to me three times and each time a sort of pressure built up to actually talk about it when a new offence was committed and once that was off, it was very difficult, so it's on the basis of that experience that I think we need another offence if we were to talk about it again [in the first case example]. . . . The sexual problems in the marriage are that he doesn't seem to be interested in sex. If he is interested in it then his technique leaves a lot to be desired as far as his wife is concerned which in turn makes her fairly dysfunctional so to talk about that was to talk about an area which tended to show him up as inadequate in a very sensitive, important area of life . . . whether there is anything similar around in respect of attraction to girls I am not sure.

'I suppose with sex offenders we only want to talk about sex to them when their sexuality has been defined as problematic. We are not asking them about their successes. . . . There can be a pride in burglary or taking and driving away, there can be an ambivalence in attitudes towards these offences but it's very rarely there in sex offences. It all seems negative, like with some stealing within a family. . . . I suppose another way of looking at it is to ask the question whether it is people who find sexuality difficult in the first place who commit this sort of offence. Maybe there is something in that, maybe particularly with flashers, the nearest thing for them to a sexual relationship. . . . I wouldn't have expected my client to commit this offence had he not been having sexual difficulties with his wife . . . my feeling of hopelessness in ever discussing beyond the social inquiry stage sex with sex offenders. . . .'

Probation Officer 1

For details of his work involving a paedophiliac client, who was being faced with a chemical approach to change his behaviour, see p. 11.

Probation Officer 8

'There was one instance of a juvenile, aged 16, who I was doing a report on. He was having intercourse with a 14-year-old girl. The teacher went to tell the parents of the girl and I think I would take the same position.'

He discussed how he had to 'accept' homosexuality but

'where I would be a bit more authoritative would be where I felt he wasn't acting responsibly, in the same way this would apply to heterosexuals. With juveniles I wouldn't just allow him, if he said he was performing sexual acts with juveniles then I would feel I ought to step in.'
'Would you like to define "a juvenile" for me?'
'Under 16, although with homosexuals the law stands at 21.'

I pointed out an apparent discrepancy between his definition of a
juvenile and the legal attitude for consent for males and females.

'No, I'm sorry I mean 21 for males.'
*'Would you think that if the age of consent was reduced to 18
you would then think that appropriate?'*
'Well, I have to obey the law whether or not I agree with it. I
expect to have to say to clients, this is the law first of all. I
believe there is a higher law which would be labelled spiritual
or moral. Now if you are asking me personally, do I think the
consenting age for homosexuality should be reduced to 16, I
would say no because I believe homosexuality to be out of the
norm and, therefore, it involves a more serious consideration. I
feel personally I would have a higher age of consent—21.'
*'Would you go so far as to bring in the law if you found out
people were having an under-age sexual relationship?'*
'I almost certainly would have to say yes. I would feel I had to
protect somebody who I considered to be a juvenile.'

Probation Officer 9

'Juveniles view me as some sort of sounding board or use my
expertise in knowing where to go for contraception when they
have begun their sexual life. I might say I have no hesitation in
referring girls who are under 16 to contraception and I've no
intention of reporting any under-age sex that I know of,
qualified by that I would use my judgment on that. If I felt it
was a stable relationship, a boy and girl, then I would not do
anything. If it was someone of 11, then that's a different kettle
of fish, but I'm talking about people of 14½-15, that sort of
age group.'

Probation Officer 4

This officer describes the case of a 15-year-old boy who was on a
supervision order for unlawful sexual intercourse with his girlfriend:

'He got into an awful mess with it because he kept getting
taken to court for it and the magistrates were very good. They
gave him a supervision order the first time and conditionally
discharged him every time afterwards until we got too
embarrassed for words and by then the girl was sixteen so we
all packed up and went home. But in the meantime, he used to
have to talk about what it was like to have your sex life as a
matter of public debate. He wrote to me after supervision and
he said "talking about those things made it all seem

85

normal . . .". It was always at the back of my mind that we had to talk about things—at home for one thing, his father was dead, so part of what I was doing I suppose was standing in for Dad. I suppose if he had an uncle or an elder brother, he could have perhaps talked to—it was the need to talk about him being fifteen, sexually mature and able to do it, doing it and enjoying it and to have to balance against the fact that every so often the police would come—he was sort of raided—and we would have this performance of being summonsed and she would get sick of being carted off to be medically examined.'
'There was certainly a tension there?'
'Oh yes, it was one I was quite explicit about when I wrote to the court. I used to say "You may be expecting that I'm going to tell him to stop it—but I'm not because I don't see what's wrong." I can remember, not having an argument, but a discussion once in a case committee when I was saying that my point of view about him was that there are some people of 30 who shouldn't have sex with anybody because of the emotional, exploitive damage they did to people and here was somebody who was not always sticking to one girl but basically there was one girlfriend on hand, they were all within his age range (they were all taller than him, he was quite a little lad for 15, I don't know if that was what used to get people going, I wondered about the police sometimes). I guess what I'm really getting at is that it did seem normal and talking about something which a kid is anxious about, you can do this when you are talking . . . words were there but it was more than words with him, presence mattered as well. Presence and saying nothing mattered quite a lot and acceptance mediated just through being around. . . .'

Probation Officer 10

Here this officer is considering the question of actually discussing sexual matters with clients:

'With male homosexuality you do have the element of illegality around. I mean if I have a client of 19, for example, and he wants to tell me he's gay, what does he think my response is, given that he is admitting at least the possibility of committing an offence, and what pressure does that put on the probation officer regarding confidentiality? It's a lot easier if the client is over 21 but there is still the element of strong stigma around.
'I am supervising a worker in a case at the moment of a 17-year-old with an IQ of 62 on a probation order from the

Crown Court for two indecent assaults on girls aged 8 and 9. In
fact those girls are his equals in terms of intelligence but not in
terms of age. He is finding it hard to relate to people of his
own age. Given his age he has a sexual drive which requires
expression and he is then turning to people who in many ways
he sees as his equals and cannot see this is a serious matter and
he is now being threatened with the possibility of inpatient
treatment or chemical drugs to reduce the sex drive which is
posing a lot of moral and ethical dilemmas for the worker; to
what extent should he be part of this process and what power
has he got *vis-à-vis* the consultant psychiatrist, for example. . . .
'Dealing with prisons who have psychiatric units with sex
offenders may find the probation officer in dilemmas when
their idea of treatment is different from the prison medical
staff. And the prisoner of course is faced with the dilemma of
"What will get me out of prison quickly and is it worth the
risk?" I think this is a vast area which is very much uncharted.
'That doesn't make me think that there is a common
probation or social work approach to sexuality. Some people
say [sexual behaviour is] "good" and some say "bad" and in a
sense the client can lose out because of the luck of the draw
which social worker or probation officer he gets. . . . If you
have a client with a sexual problem he/she desperately wants to
share, they may get a social worker who is worse than
discouraging; frankly saying "This is a mortal sin". . . . If it's
a voluntary relationship he can deal with it by withdrawing. If
he is under some form of statutory supervision it is not easy to
change your supervising officer and I don't think we often
advise clients of this possibility. . . .
'I would have thought that more often than not, we are
dealing with the people who are embarrassed and full of shame
about their offence. Because I think the other type are perhaps
less likely to come our way. If they display an aggressive front
in court and it's a minor sexual offence, I suspect the court
would deal with them (although I've no evidence to prove that)
but if there is a client who is obviously very confused and
bewildered about what he/she has just done then I think they
are more likely to be referred to the probation service.'

He referred to the refusal of a probation service to circulate details of
the self-help group Paedophile Information Exchange although for
some clients he would see such an organization as helpful:

'I think it's very interesting that that's where many gay people
draw the line. . . . What worries me is that we are not dealing
with two consenting parties. I am very unhappy at the thought

of a young child freely consenting to a sexual relationship. I'm
unclear in my own mind where we distinguish a loving
relationship from a sexual relationship. I think that many
young people desperately need a loving relationship. It's the
sexual element that worries me because I do not think the
young child is able to understand the significance. . . . I think
PIE glosses over the problem, I would not like to say at what
age a person becomes fully aware of his sexuality and needs
sexual expression but I would have thought that some of the
younger age ranges that certain of the paedophiles are attracted
to are unable to comprehend the magnitude of what has
happened. But I fear I may be as bad as the prejudiced
majority which looks at homosexuality in the same light or
under-21 homosexuality. But one of the paedophiles at a
meeting said, "I'm interested in boys and girls up until they
have pubic hair", which was a concept I just couldn't cope with
at all. I think if I was supervising on probation somebody like
that I would be able to supervise them appropriately and
express care and concern but it would take me some time to
understand the nature of the attraction.'
'Would you want to be stopping them?'
'. . . I have no way of stopping anyone committing an act, be it
shoplifting, assault or indecently assaulting little girls. I have
little way of preventing that . . . the danger is that my feelings
are going to intrude into the situation so that if I cannot fully
comprehend the nature of sexual attraction to young people,
that is going to come across and hidden messages are going to
flow between worker and client. I don't quite see how we can
get over that one unless one says something along the lines of
"This is an aspect of behaviour I am by and large ignorant of,
will you educate me" and use the client as a resource.'

For gay social workers, as we have already noted in Chapter 3, the
margin of public acceptability may be felt by them to be very narrow
when dealing with minors, perhaps because of an identification in
the public mind of homosexual people with sexual practices and
sexual corruption. Social Worker B describes how he 'came out'
about his homosexuality to a college medic during a medical
examination:

'The whole situation changed, he took me over and he sat me
down and he sat at the opposite side of the desk and said,
"Well you understand I've got a responsibility for your existence
as a professional person as well as your medical well being and
you understand as a social worker you will probably be dealing

with young children." I said "Yes" and he said, "Well how do you feel about young children?" Well I gave all the pat answers and went off my head and stormed out of the room.'

Social Worker A

'Circumstances forced me to come out in the office on the first day of my first placement. My supervisor was very interested because he had never encountered a gay person consciously, as he thought. One of the first cases he gave me was of a 19-year-old boy who had had sex with a 10-year-old, you know very pretty, blond hair, the whole bit, and this supervisor gave me the case of the boy of 10, as he put it, to see how I got on with it, given I was a gay person.

'It was an extra dimension of difficulty working in my last placement in a children's home with prepubertal boys, whether to come out to my colleagues. What we do is a lot of physical contact, mothering kind of physical contact as well of a fairly intimate sort of nature. I know there is an awareness by the staff of the possibility of some sort of relationship developing . . . now I'm very much into physical contact with the kids. . . .

'I think there is a very great danger of homosexuals becoming very very oppressive towards paedophiles in trying to deny it yourself that you are interested, the way you cop out of it is by putting down paedophiles.'

Social Worker A

'The question doesn't arise so much for homosexuals who are bank clerks and canteen assistants as for those who are teachers and social workers. . . . Although this sounds romantic, in a lot of ways, I really feel I've got a lot in common with the sexual outlaw, no matter what their sex offence has been, apart probably from rape, but even then under certain circumstances it would be the same.'

For an example of Social Worker A, acting to control a teenage girl 'in moral danger' see p. 54.

Social Worker A

'One area where I am concerned with the law is in dealing with young people. If you have a kid on supervision who was 17½ then the chances are that nothing much would happen if you put him in touch with a gay organization, but I'm very aware that if I've a kid of 14 or 15 who came along and was gay, I felt I wanted to refer him to self-help—I would do it, but I'm aware of the difficulties that would arise. Even then the self-help groups may not cater appropriately for the teenager.'

Social Worker B

'When I'm discussing with my kids masturbation—when I've got over that yes it's all right—this brings up this discussion where do we do it and I've got to say things like—well you don't do it in the streets and you don't do it in front of other people and I think "my god, why shouldn't they if that's what's actually satisfying for the kid to do that", and they have got to make that choice and they have also got to take the consequences that a certain sexist society would lump on them. They have got the freedom to make that choice and there is me sitting there saying "no, you mustn't do it" and they are saying "why" and I'm stuck with the same stupid answers—it's not right and people might not like it and I think "What a hypocrite you are!" People would have a far stronger objection to your actual sexual practice than to some kid masturbating.

'I did a social enquiry report on a 16-year-old who had admitted having sexual intercourse twice with a girl aged 14. In writing the report I wondered if I should put in the report what I thought of this ridiculous law but the magistrate would be put in a bad mood and take it out on the kid. I had to create a fine balance for myself by not throwing out my principles into the dustbin and I went through the thing weighing it in the kid's favour and in the end recommended a conditional discharge.'

Probation Officer 11

This officer described a case of under-age sexuality where he was in conflict with his organization, clients, the police and the magistrates:

'My Senior walked into my office and put down one of these "Children in trouble" forms about a 14-year-old boy appearing in Juvenile Court for an indecent assault on a similar-aged boy . . . there had been no coercion, violence or serious after-effects . . . why has this come as far as court?'

The worker described how he made enquiries of the police, one of whom suggested he needed child guidance help 'which I thought was a very severe attitude. My attitude all along was that this sort of thing was rather normal and if all the boys who did this ended up in

court or child guidance where on earth would we be?' He learnt
there had been a senior police directive that this case was to go
straight to prosecution. After investigation he recommended a
supervision order, not because of the offence, which had been
'elementary sex play', but because of elements of violence in the
family. Also the father had been convicted before his marriage of,
among other things, male prostitution. The father made strenuous
efforts to avoid meeting the probation officer. In the social inquiry
report the officer queried the advisability of the case ever coming to
court. His seniors reprimanded him both for his recommendation
and the criticism of the police's conduct:

'I had this feeling that they had given me the case to test out
my own views on the subject because I think they knew by that
time I was gay. They gave me the case to see how I would
tackle it, when they saw how I was they rather wanted to take
the case off me. This I resisted strongly.'

On his work with the boy, he said:

'I did discuss sex and adolescence and various other things with
him in depth and I must admit I didn't record them in their
full extent. . . . It really didn't concern me whether the boy
grew up gay or straight. I thought that wasn't really part of it. I
was concerned though that he wasn't damaged one way or the
other through the court case. I thought he might get this idea
of himself as a criminal homosexual; that he might get this idea
that homosexuality and criminality were mixed so that he might
become avidly anti-gay to almost prove himself the other way.
. . . I think a lot of adolescent boys or girls could do with a
confidante as they are growing up and this is what I tried to
be. . . .'
    'My employing authority took the line that you couldn't be
[publicly] gay and a probation officer. I didn't know at the time
if they were trying to get rid of me or what. They were taking
what they called "a special interest" in this particular case.
Which meant they kept looking at the record and trying to take
the case off me. It was put to me that they were thinking of me.
That I was vulnerable running a case like this. But I knew I
had to carry on because of the casework relationship with the
boy—it would have been confusing if after having lost me,
another officer had taken a different line. But also I was
refusing to hand the case over because I thought it would create
a precedent and it would mean that I wasn't capable of dealing
with a case in which there were sexual connotations . . . with a
weekly inspection of this case I found I did censor my own

records. . . . Strangely enough I didn't feel an over-identification in this case. I felt a certain amount of empathy with the boy but then I do with a lot of clients who I haven't anything in common with sometimes. I felt I was not working out my own needs on the client. My own needs did get jumbled—but more in my seniors' minds than my own. I felt I had to discuss it with somebody I could trust—not just morally but someone who was a social worker or probation officer.'

The worker made the point that usually his supervisor was a good one but that pressures from the hierarchy incapacitated him, also he had seemed on other occasions to find discussion of sexuality a problem. In these circumstances the worker turned to and received help from his training institution.

Social Worker F

This worker talks of how he encounters problems of under-age sexual behaviour, as he puts it, 'at one remove':

'A social worker in another group came to see me with a problem with a 16-year-old lad on his caseload who had talked about a relationship with an older chap to a community worker and this had got back to the social worker who wasn't quite sure how to play it, and there was obviously the question of illegal sexual relations. So although I wasn't directly involved, I was asked to advise on that. I played on the fact that the lad had discussed this with the community worker rather than directly with the social worker and that perhaps it would be better for the social worker not to be directly told there were sexual relationships, maybe if he could collude in knowing there was a significant relationship in the 16-year-old's life and discuss things generally. . . . I also gave information about groups for gay teenagers because I thought it important he should know there were other teenagers who were gay and the possibility of mixing.

'My own view is that gay teenagers don't have access to other gay teenagers as straights have with their peers. I think this is an important and sad situation. From my personal experience that certainly for me was something I lacked. I don't think relationships with a large age gap are necessarily to be advised against—it's very much an individual choice.'

Social Worker E

'I do have objections to under-age sex, not absolutely but on occasion because I do think that physical and psychological damage can arise, as far as I can see, things like cervical cancer, and sex being used in a light-hearted way of enjoyment, but there again, I wouldn't know where to draw the line and where to say it's serious and important and fruitful and helpful and where to say it's devaluing the whole thing. As a social worker alarm bells would ring and I would have to protect myself even if I was terribly keen on incest and terribly interested in paedophilia, I would still have to put a stop to it because of the fact that there is a child at risk and children at risk are a particular section of the population to whom social workers have to be very sensitive. . . .

'I suppose what I am saying is that a 14-15-year-old girl is not at risk in the way a 2-year-old is and at the same time I suppose a 14-year-old girl is not at risk from a 14-year-old boy in the way she is from a 20-year-old man or her 50-year-old grandfather.'

'Do you feel that homosexuals are censorious of paedophiliac sexual interest in order to maintain their own respectability?'

'Yes, gay people in general bend over backwards to point out that they are not paedophiles. One particularly good historical reason for this is that it has always been assumed that they are. I think sometimes the paedophile lobby doesn't realize this— that any identification with paedophilia in the public eye more or less undoes all the work one has tried to do to become accepted. Because the trouble with paedophilia is you are into the realms of when is a person sufficiently old enough even to understand precisely what is happening and to give consent. The anti-gay lobby would say you can't give consent until you are 21 and even then it's too young. And so really it's only a difference of degree; nobody has yet scientifically in a laboratory worked out a sliding scale per IQ or mental age or reading ability or chromosome number or whatever to say that when people get to this age on the scale that they have a right to say yes or no. We just have arbitrary legal boundaries. It makes me feel a bit embarrassed because I realize that what we are doing is climbing up a ladder towards respectability and in order to do that we are really being unjust to a minority. Personally I do get rather worried about people interfering with children, as it's called. I don't worship children in a way that a lot of housing departments and social work departments seem to but at the same time I do feel that a child is a *vulnerable* creature. It may be filthy and dirty and it may swear like a trooper and it may smoke but nevertheless it's an unformed creature. I do realize that some of them make the running and perhaps a lot of them are not damaged at all; perhaps none of them are, perhaps they

93

enjoy it and would welcome this sort of thing—indeed, anyone with knowledge of infancy would know that children are extremely sexually adventurous and active at ages where people seem to think that they have no sex at all. But my emotional response, I'm afraid, is that I suppose until it's proved otherwise, I'd rather not back the practice of paedophilia.'

Social Worker G

'I believe that my sexual orientation has given me a much better understanding of other people's difficulties. I've said to a number of people when they had been talking about paedophiles, "Well a young life must be protected but how terrible it must be only to achieve emotional and physical release with something which is forbidden one." I think I would protect anybody from legal processes as much as I could because I don't think the legal processes are helping the individual, they are simply protecting society, for a time.

'A man in his late 50s was referred by the court to a consultant psychiatrist because he had been having sexual relationships with two 17-year-old boys. The man was working as a petrol pump attendant and the boys I think had probably seduced him as much as he had seduced the boys but in the end they demanded money or they would get the police. I think he told them to go to the police which they did. He was referred to me and I said, "Well about all I can say to you is you had better ask to see their birth certificates in future. The law provides that over 21 this kind of behaviour is acceptable, under 21 it is not." It later came out that he was only attracted to people under age. The consultant went through the motions of helping the man in hospital for something like six months and then felt he could say that all that could be done had been done and he had fulfilled the requirements of the court order and the man was free as far as I know after that.'

Social Worker H

'We have one client in common as a group in the office who is very disturbed and also a paedophile. If it was just the fact of paedophilia, I would feel differently about it to the way I do. I have only interviewed him once myself and I did raise the question of law of which he is very well aware, dead scared in fact of the law.'
'Would you report him to the police ever?'
'That's very difficult because it arises in other things as well.

People tell us that they have done something which is against the law. It really is extremely difficult and once or twice I have had occasion to call the police to collect a client and I feel awful about it and I never know what is the right thing to do. What I have done in specific cases (like absconders from borstal) is to call the police and then tell the client I have called the police so in fact they have opportunity to leave.

'I think that there comes a point where you can't set yourself above the law and there is an absolute in the law but not in morality, but if there was an 18-year-old boy having sexual relations with an adult and I was dealing with the adult, then I would have to think about that, and I would probably talk to him about the law. If it was boys of the same age then that would not bother me at all.'

'Would you want to distinguish yourself from paedophiles?'

'Well you don't know that I'm not a paedophile, do you?—but I'm not in fact. I would want to distinguish myself from a paedophile and homosexuality from paedophilia. I do take a sympathetic view of paedophilia. I approach it from wishing there were an ideal society in which sexuality could be expressed between adults and children and concern wouldn't be aroused by it. . . . If it was just straightforward paedophilia of a responsible mature adult, as my position is now I really don't know what I would do, what I would say. I would try and not prejudge the issue by going in with any particular principles and see what came out as we talked.'

In attempting to understand the accommodation of sexual interest and involvement of and with children and young people, we can be assisted in bridging the gap which sometimes emerges between social worker and client by hearing from this unqualified social worker who during the course of the interview discussed his own experiences of 'help' in the area of sexual conduct. I was asking about actually preventing a client from availing themselves of behaviour therapy:

'In certain cases, for instance in paedophilia, I think I would because I have had behaviour therapy myself. . . . I have also had a libido-suppressing drug, it didn't work and even if it did, I wouldn't advise it—chemical castration is no better than physical castration except you can stop it when you want to. . . . I went to a psychologist via a psychiatrist. He certainly didn't express any disapproval except implicitly by giving me the treatment, it was implicit in the treatment. He didn't verbalize it. His approach was (a) you don't want to be gay (I was 17½

at the time and terribly uptight) and (b) I think I can do
something about it.'

I queried if the change in the law had made any difference to him
and he denied this:

'The law didn't mean anything to me then, it may have meant
more to the psychiatrist, and when it was changed in '67 I
hardly noticed.'
Did you feel he disapproved of you?'
'He didn't show it in what he said or how he looked or the way
he behaved apart from the treatment. He didn't "tut tut" at
me, except as far as that was implicit in the treatment and
that's what I feel strongly about. . . . I'd only come across
people, mostly priests and him and the psychiatrist who were
liberal, tolerant. I took it for granted that that was his attitude
too; that he wasn't going to belabour me because I was
homosexual and that he had a fair amount of knowledge about
homosexuality anyway. And I didn't feel uneasy about his
attitude—I do now because I'm so different myself now—then I
didn't expect him to be judgmental about it. In fact neither
then nor now have I met nastiness about my being gay—to me
personally.'
*'Having had that experience, how do you now see your
homosexuality?'*
'I don't know about the origin. I don't prefer it to heterosexuality in myself, I just am, with advantages and
disadvantages, all of which are social rather than sexual. . . . It
would have been so easy presumably, for the psychiatrist to
have said in half an hour, "There is no reason why you
shouldn't be happy as a homosexual" and he could have saved
ten years, I suppose, of agony. No one ever said it—until very
recently but then I had found out—but very, very painfully . . .
even those who were tolerant never said anything positive.'
'What brought you out?'
'I can remember it very clearly. It was a BBC film report about
the demonstrations after the Stonewall Riot.'

The 'Stonewall Riots' occurred after the police had raided a gay bar,
the 'Stonewall' in New York City, in the summer of 1969. Following
these incidents the New York Gay Liberation Front was founded.
   Concern about the age of consent bears some relationship to the
protection of people in unequal power relationships. Perhaps
nowhere is this better illustrated than in children's residential
settings.

Social Worker I

'I was a housefather in a special school for maladjusted boys.
They weren't out experiencing relationships with the opposite
sex very often. I suppose the older ones who were 16 and went
to a youth club were trying to show some interest in girls but
after having lived in this rather sheltered environment were
under-confident . . . there were times when one found them in
bed with each other in the morning. . . . I said, "That is
nothing to worry about or to feel embarrassed on my account,
come and have a chat sometime tonight", and in that context
they denied everything and said, "I just went in there to talk to
him last night and 'cos it was cold or something, we aren't
homosexual." I just said, "Well what if you are or if anyone is
really?" I was laying it on the line that I was preferring them to
sleep in their own beds. If everyone was doing this it would
make life very difficult for two houseparents and seventeen
kids. . . . I then worked with 10-to-13-year-olds and there one
was dealing with ignorance. The other boys were coming up to
puberty and starting to masturbate. We had 12-year-olds—I
don't know how sexual it was—but they had a power complex
. . . one or two wanted to dominate the group and the
houseparents as well . . . one particular one started taking little
boys into the bushes and sucking their cocks. We found that
the little boys didn't understand anything about what was
happening. The older boy I had to talk to, he was very difficult
to handle, trying to dominate me as well as the whole group . . .
again he was denying any sexual interest. I lent out books on
sexuality for very young children and talked to the younger
ones. I wasn't very good at it but they said they understood. . . .
I was having to give other staff reassurances that it was being
dealt with satisfactorily.'

I asked how his training course had prepared him.

'Well, sex was mentioned in passing when one mentioned
Freud. But it was something which never came up. . . . After
the course I felt very confident at this school because they had
confidence in the course I'd done and in me to run this house
my way. The housemother was particularly cold who I worked
with so these kids were very much looking to me for affection.
I can think of a 10-year-old coming back from a weekend away
crying and I just went in and held his hand while he was in
bed. I couldn't have done that two or three years before. . . .
These kids never queried my displays of affection, they never
labelled me although it must have been obvious that my friends

who came to stay were male. I can think of residential workers whose displays of affection to kids have been very much queried by the children in the peer group. They often pick it up wrongly of course being disturbed kids, very often people who are married have been more strongly accused of seeking physical contact with these kids than I have. . . . There had been various very difficult issues about such matters in the past dealt with at Governor level so one was in a vulnerable position and if one hadn't put oneself in a vulnerable position, one wouldn't have done nearly such good work. . . My relationships were known in a covered way by some members of staff and it was pretty obvious I wasn't interested in young kids anyway.'

This attitude was in some contrast to his previous work experience before qualification. He was 21 and in a working boys' hostel. He described how he felt his own inexperience and sexual interests had hindered him in coping with the boys' need for guidance in heterosexual relationships. Also:

'I felt in conflict with the other staff over many of the attitudes to care. . . . There was one boy who had a particular adolescent passion on me. At the time I wasn't experienced enough to handle it at all well. I thought he was leading me on and he wasn't really and there was no one to talk to about it. He used to do things like knocking on my door with only a towel round him. Nothing ever happened but that was by luck rather than anything else. I didn't really know what was going on with him; there was no support to talk it over. I was aware he hadn't had a father since he was 8 but it got more and more overt. Fortunately his mother had him back quite soon so he didn't go on and become impossible.'

Stewart is 18, studying for a degree and aiming to be a social worker:

'I was 17 and she was 15, we got to a stage where we thought she was pregnant and so we went to hospital for a pregnancy test. Whilst we were there we decided to go and see a social worker and see what would happen to us. The nurses asked if we would like to go and see a social worker who said herself that she was meant to report such cases to the police but she personally didn't think they should betray the trust and with her being in a hospital she used that to make sure that everything you said was completely private. It was OK because she wasn't pregnant and a couple of months later she left home and was taken into care because of conflicts at home. Whilst there her mother called her a prostitute. They obtained another social worker's report and a pregnancy test. They started to treat her like a prostitute, i.e. they wouldn't let her out and said she couldn't go and see me. With her being 15 and a bit independent anyway, she didn't like their attitudes and she used to try and come and see me. The social worker said I should abide by the parents' wishes but she was lonely and used to come and see me, just for a few hours and try and sneak back. Every time she got spotted. The woman in charge rang my home once and said, "She isn't just naughty, she is wicked, every fibre of her, through and through", which was untrue. One day she claimed that this boy in the home had tried to get into bed with her. But the social workers said that she must be making it up as the boy was all right. They treated her as if she was either making it up or it was she who did the enticing and was then trying to get him into trouble. The head of the sixth form saw me at school and told me they had reports on her and she was a prostitute and was that type of girl. The headmistress (there were about six headmasters at our school!) said that "She is that type of girl". That's how they explained it to me. She'll have missed you such a lot that she needed the physical comfort of this other boy, she would have enticed him. The school said "We have got these reports from the social work department", and the social work department said, "We have got these reports from the mother", and so they all fed on each other and gave completely the wrong impression about her and she was trapped as a result. Eventually they decided she was uncontrolled at the home and sent her back to her mother. There was the threat of under-age sex hanging over my head and my parents didn't want any trouble so they said she couldn't come round to the house. The only time I could see her was at school. The main thing about it was the frustration of knowing that what you were doing wasn't wrong but every pressure possible was just put on to split us apart. I used to walk around at playtime, it was always raining for some odd reason, I used to have my arm round her . . . the headmaster came out and said, "I don't know what you think you're doing —you are carrying on! They are all talking about you in there", meaning the teachers' common room. I thought they must be rather odd if that's the best thing they can think of to do in their dinner-time.

'If only they had just, instead of looking at reports, seen her as she was, a normal 15-year-old girl who was a bit precocious, it would have made things a hell of a lot easier and she wouldn't have had so much trouble. All she wanted was to be wanted and liked by someone which is why she clung to me so much. She had no stable base and I suppose the children's home tried to impose discipline on her but you can't suddenly impose it on someone like that. They are bound to rebel against it.

'The major thing became that I was breaking the law and I couldn't justify that. Otherwise it was just half an hour in the school playground, otherwise I couldn't see her. She reacted by more attention-seeking behaviour and the more peculiar she acted, the more difficult it was for me. It got so that the mere mention of her name made me cringe. So although I felt I should help her because she is in the right but it was so much easier for me not to, which is not a very nice thing for me to admit. But I'm proud that I stuck it out for nine months.'

The sexual conduct of children cannot be separated from questions about their growth as people and how caregivers and takers will contribute to that process. Social Worker J, working in a residential setting:

'I'm expected to provide a father figure or big-brother figure almost as a Freudian male stereotype, and the women are expected to be passive and motherly, but I don't feel attracted to either. I feel you should try to be a person and define your own identity so that they have a range of different kinds of human possibilities that they can relate to.'

Social Worker A:

'Where I work they are talking about taking on new staff and they are very much talking about the gender of the staff.'

Social Worker B:

'This is the amazing thing about the [intermediate treatment] unit I work in whose whole philosophy is founded on fairly radical standpoints and when I got the job there was, "We have to decide where you can fit in because we have got to have a balance." If you find out what this means, they mean an available man figure and woman figure who is going to physically relate to the kids and give them an identity. Now I argued strongly against that from various points of view mainly because I did not think that in the unit it was one of fundamental importance to the kids. I do think that a positive identity for them is a very important thing but I don't think one supplies this, but a kid builds a positive identity from a lot of relationships with a lot of different people. What I've discovered since then to my surprise and a little bit to my shock as well—is that some of the kids are modelling themselves on the heavy football-playing male type . . . some of the kids would orientate to a woman of whatever type and some of the kids are orientating towards me.'

Social Worker A:

'It has been argued that one way to split up traditional role attitudes is for men to be involved in child care. Looking at a residential situation, what I see is a complete splitting in the men, whereby in a job situation they can relate in a subtly sexist way by shedding some of the more sexist attitudes towards kids and do non-sexist things like washing dishes, baking, etc. But in their relationships with the staff once the day's work is finished they revert back to being heavy straight men. It's more confusing for the kids, coming through in an invidious sort of way.'

Social Worker B:

'Another thing about this providing of parental roles is that I'm not going to become a parent. This parenthood that they keep telling me about is something I haven't a lot of investment in. So I keep thinking why the hell should I provide a parent figure because I don't feel parental and I'm not likely to—in the orthodox way.'

Social Worker J:

'George Weinberg in *Society and the Healthy Homosexual* says that heterosexuals keep pushing this parent and reproduction thing to homosexuals because of their fear of death. They can't cope with the idea that here is somebody and there is nobody coming after them.'

Social Worker B:

'Heterosexual people always ask me "do you never want children?" and heterosexual social workers will develop it into —does the fact that I have got myself resigned to not becoming a parent, does that affect the way I practise social work with kids. Well it does actually, but not the way they think it does, I would hope.'

Concern about role modelling is one that seems likely to be a feature of the considerations of many thoughtful staff in residential settings. This was a matter raised spontaneously by the officer-in-charge already quoted:

'We have one great difficulty and it was the subject of a long and searching enquiry inter-staff. We have a teenage girl, very well developed, very affectionate and very likeable, my [male] deputy and myself suddenly realized we were not in fact producing the father image for this youngster because of inhibitions. Invariably when she comes in she will give my wife a kiss, and invariably try to do the same with me. Now I have cold-shouldered her for so long so she has now started to give this up.'

His wife:

'At her last case review we wrote her case review notes and then invited her to attend her own review and she did attend the whole review—and one of the comments which we had written into her review notes was the fact that she wasn't taking any interest in the opposite sex. Since when she has swung completely the other way in that anything male that enters the house now, she is there.'

Her husband then recalled another girl who was now 'living off her back': 'You can't help now wondering if because of *our* self-protective urges, recognition of the potential dangers, we didn't in fact deprive that girl of something she is now seeking.' His wife: 'Because she certainly was a very affection-seeking child . . .', husband interrupts, 'And a big girl too!' He then went on to say how he had after the case conference been making a very conscious effort to make physical contact with the girl involved in the case review even though he was not someone who spontaneously made physical contact with people.

It could be argued that the examples given so far in this section are out of the ordinary and that social work's concern with the sexual conduct of its clients is more reasonably assessed by taking account of day-by-day attitudes reflecting degrees of respect for persons of whatever age. There is surely no more severe testing ground than to hear from the ex-recipients of residential care.

Gwen is 30, she had been brought up in care from being a baby to when she was 15 and went out to work. After going to a reception centre she was transferred to a children's home for about fifteen children. There was a full-time housemother between the time she was 9 and 13 and her husband worked during the day.

'Did you have an important relationship with any of the staff?'
'No, largely because I felt the home revolved around one difficult girl who I think was wrongly placed. She was a bad influence on everyone there, she used to have these mad outbursts and the houseparents used to be frightened of any confrontation. Actually I resented her more because I was two

years older than her but she got her own way, she had her own
room and this means a lot to a girl because it was something I
should have had. . . . One person who stands out in my mind
that I would say gave an awful lot to me was, tragically, only a
part-timer. She came in for about three hours each day. She
was about 50, she hadn't any children but she was great, really
nice and she taught me that it wasn't the amount of time you
spend with children that's important but the quality of it. She
gave me far more than the full-time staff. She didn't pamper or
cuddle us but she was extremely nice because she used to
explain things to us or if you questioned anything she would say
why she had said it. If you came in from school, all you used to
get was "go into the playroom, I'm busy". It was always "out
of the way". If you brought your school work home—if you'd
done something well or you had "got a star" as it were, you
used to go home beaming, wanting to show auntie. But this
auntie always showed interest. Yet on the other hand if you
were naughty or did something which displeased her, she used
to show it but I never used to think she was against me because
she'd told me off.'
'Did you have periods when you were very unhappy?'
'Very, I would say as a teenager mainly. I came from a large
family—twelve in all who had all at some time been in care.
Some of the children had parents who visited, mine didn't. My
father was in and out of prison. They never explained why they
didn't visit. You would just meet him in the street drunk and
causing a scene which used to be very embarrassing. . . . At the
beginning of the teenage period I missed having parents most,
it was when it really hit me. When I was younger I didn't
realize everyone lived in their normal homes with their parents.
I assumed everyone had the sort of set-up that we did. . . . I
think I was unhappy there because they never explained
anything and if you queried anything they would either say you
were rude or you were rebelling.'
'What kind of sexual knowledge did you obtain?'
'There was no attempt at all in the home. It was as though it
was a dirty thing that shouldn't be mentioned. . . . I'll be
honest with you, I rather thought that having a baby was like
something which just happened to you. I didn't think you have
to have a relationship.'
'How did you explain your periods?'
'I thought I was dying. I was frightened to ask the auntie. My
brother who was older than me went to school and asked the
boys but all he said was it was something that every girl has
and you will be like it every twenty-eight days. For quite a bit I

was buying sanitary towels out of my pocket money. I went for
a routine examination at the doctor's. He asked the auntie if I
had started menstruating. I said that I had and she got quite
shirty because she didn't know! Of course I thought it was
something which shouldn't be talked about. I did find out a bit
more about it because the year before I left school they used to
have sex lessons at school. They gave a bit out about
menstruation and having babies and that.

'I was never allowed boyfriends. I was never allowed out—
only on a Sunday for church!'

'Was there any sexual interest between children in the home?'
'No, not really. I can remember being very interested in one of
the lads in the children's home when I was younger. I used to
think he was lovely but never showed it. Obviously he knew I
was interested. But nothing like a girlfriend-boyfriend situation.
I got the impression for a start it was wrong to be interested in
the opposite sex. . . . I went to a large secondary modern
school. The boys' and girls' schools were next door to each
other but separate. There was the brother of a girlfriend who
was a heart throb at school but I daren't have said anything to
the auntie because if I had I think she would have stopped my
friendship with his sister.

'After I left the home I lived-in where I worked at a home for
mentally handicapped children. I used to have a number of
boyfriends for short periods. I found it very hard to get involved
with anyone. I always thought men were rather like me dad.
Dirty old men; they would let me down. I always thought
people would let me down. I still have this actually. I find it
hard to believe that people who mean the most to me are not
going to let me down. Because my father was one for women.
. . . I often met the other women, his mistresses. . . . When I
went to my parents' flat one day he was lying out, naked with
this other woman in the back garden. I am still wary of people.

'Between leaving and getting married when I was 21, I had a
relationship with a boy who I started going out with seriously.
He paid a lot of attention to me. He was nice and I became
pregnant. He didn't want to know then and I had the baby and
kept it and I've no regrets. I didn't hear or see any more of
him. I went on working for a while, my son was at a nursery
and then I met my husband.'

'Was the pregnancy unwanted?'
'No, I wouldn't say that. I was horrified when I found out
because I had no family and nowhere to live. So in that sense
there was a lot of fear and I thought, "Oh no, I don't want to
be pregnant." But in actual fact I was glad I was, because I've

got something that was mine and I was rather possessive of it.'
'Does your experience affect the way you deal with your kids?'
'Yes, I think I tend to be very demonstrative. I'm always
kissing my kids and I like to have them on my knee. I like
them to be with me and I like to cuddle them which is
something I never had. I don't like to see my kids upset. . . .
My father's relationship with other women has I suppose
basically made me a one-man girl.'
*'Would you say that sex knowledge and attitudes were the most
important aspects which were missing or unhelpful in your
experience?'*
'I would say they were one of the important things. Another is
that I didn't get and would hope children would now is
encouragement, through the later years of schooling and going
to work. I was just packed off to the youth employment officer,
an old woman who was determined I was going to go into the
glass factory. I was *told* what I was going to do and because I
wouldn't do it—I wanted to work with mentally handicapped
children, the welfare officer and houseparents were up in arms
about it. They saw it as rebellion. They even said I would end
up in a girls' remand home.'

Brian is now in his early 30s, a qualified youth and community
worker. He was brought up in care from three months old until he
was about 16. He said that he now had a thing about emphasizing
the importance of relationships because he had missed out on them:

'Earlier on they were single-sex homes. For example when I was
at junior school, there was up to forty boys in one establishment.
The only females were those in charge and those were single
women. They didn't employ married women at all. . . . There
was one big house for the lads on one side of town and a
similar establishment for girls on the other side. My personal
development in terms of relationships with the opposite sex was
arrested somewhat and I took a hell of a time to get over that.
When I got to the age of going out with girls there were very
few. I was courting my wife for ten years before we got married.
It was stormy in the sense that she found it extremely difficult
to accept my expectations of a wife figure because they were so
demanding and so varied. I expected not only a wife and
mother but confidante, a mother figure. A substitute all in one
for all the things I needed. . . . Parents of children in care were
allowed to take their children out for the weekend and that
didn't matter to a great extent when I was in this huge forty-
odd establishment. Because a lot of the kids were in the same
boat as me—they didn't have any. . . . In the home I finished up

in I was the only one left and that *hurt*. When you were mixing
with other kids at school it was very easy for them to make out
the fact you were different. You were in a home and you were
always in a home because you had done something wrong. Your
parents had done something wrong—it was this sort of image
and kids are cruel. . . . We ganged together from the home in
an aggressive way, there was always fights. . . . Towards the
end of my time in care I was in a family group home and they
employed a married couple and not only that, the married
couple had a daughter. . . . This came at the right time—I was
in my early teens . . . if they hadn't been around at that time,
if there had just been a housemother and warden, I think I
would have turned out different. . . . In terms of my
relationship with girls, I found it very difficult. The only
relationship I saw was a sexual one. . . . This whole relationship
thing was so difficult. Because when I started off, I was moved
around from home to home about five or six times within the
same town. They used to make you change schools as well and
that was bad because it meant that early on when you started
to make friends at school—lads your own age—you needed time
and were just beginning to make real friends and I mean as
different to acquaintances, all of a sudden you would be up and
off after three to five years. After a while you never did it
because you began to build this sort of armour, this shell of
self-sufficiency and hiding inside it because relationships hurt
and so you built this shell to stop relationships happening.'

On sexual instruction:

'The Victorian attitude was made obvious by the physical
separation of the homes. At school this was not helped by even
my secondary school being all boys. . . . The reasons for the
staff may have been because they themselves were unmarried,
spinsters, and may have had all sorts of weird and wonderful
ideas about boys and girls and the sexual bit. . . . I never ever
remember having a discussion on that sort of topic . . . yet
there were all sorts of questions I wanted to ask.'
*That was a long time ago, what about your experience now of
kids in care?'*
'Two or three years ago I worked in a youth centre where kids
did come from a mixed children's home. The person in charge
was a spinster and I know the kids who came to my centre were
having similar difficulties in relation to girls in a way that I had
experienced. So in that sense, it hadn't changed hardly at all.
It may have been the situation of the spinster in charge. I know

that these kids like me felt inferior to women for some reason.

'About three years ago the woman who ran the huge children's home, spinster then about 50, left and went to live in Canada and married. Then came back and wanted a reunion with "her boys". . . . Ninety per cent of fellows were married, we spent the whole day together. A number of them had been in serious trouble with the law, had been in prison, remand homes, etc. A number had had to get married. . . . I think they had experienced similar difficulties to me.

'I remember going on holiday—the homes went all at once, we stayed in individual boarding houses. At one point we were set in groups in rows awaiting the Children's Committee and the Mayor in his big black Austin Princess and he would walk down the beach and say, "He's looking well and he's got some colour in his cheeks", and all the people would be sitting round and wondering what the hell was going on. But the image was deliberately created and sustained and maintained . . . the children of the Children's Committee. Councillor Smith always got dressed up as Father Christmas. He came round the children's home on Christmas Day. One guy, the eldest in the house, he was about 16, out at work, Councillor Smith was doing his Father Christmas act, "Well, what have we got here!" sort of thing, called out this guy's name and handed him a parcel and it was expected that one said, "Thank you very much Father Christmas" but he didn't, he said, "Thank you Councillor Smith". All hell was let loose. One Christmas I was heavily committed in this relationship to the girl who is now my wife and I was invited across for Christmas afternoon, but couldn't go because Father Christmas was coming round and everybody had to be together.'

Interim conclusions

This section has contained descriptions of a variety of sexual expression in which the only constant is the behaviour being under the age(s) of consent. From the views of these workers and clients we shall now focus on some points of special interest.

First, a major problem which is also an important finding is the lack of an agreed definition as to what is paedophilia. We have already touched upon this subject in Chapter 3. Legally 16 for a girl and 21 for a boy are the limits below which a man can be said to be having sexual relations with a minor. For a woman to be having illegal sexual relations the boy or girl would be under 16. Some people involved, including PIE, want to evaluate the quality of a relationship between adult and child to determine if it is merely

107

sexual usage—paederasty—or child love—paedophilia. Gay Probation Officer 10 recognizes this possible distinction and doubts its
validity. George implicitly is discussing paedophilia as a total
relationship with children rather than a sexual outlet. Fred could
also be describing a general liking of young boys although he
specifically mentions teenage boys and differentiates himself from
people who are interested in 4- or 5-year-olds. However, his probation
officer stated that Fred had been convicted of offences against boys
aged between 10 and 14.

A common definition of paedophilia which can be observed as
running through the responses of the social workers is that it is
about sexual relationships, with or without love, of pre-pubertal
children. We have noted the limitations of such a 'common sense'
stance (p. 57). We will now deal with the responses in this section
under different headings noting the congruences and incongruences
of attitude between the clients, the gay, and the straight social
workers.

1 Attitudes towards paedophilia

All the heterosexual workers felt that sex with children should be
stopped, controlled or redirected. This comes over as primarily a
personal disapproval of paedophilia but also contains a practical
awareness of workers needing to be seen as agents of social control.

The gay group were less unanimous in their disapproval. Probation
Officer 10 thought 'I don't think I could stop them' and that he
would have to learn from the client about what was the nature of the
attraction. The unqualified social worker described a situation
where a man was so disturbed in his behaviour that he would not in
any way encourage the man to have a relationship with a child
although he wished that society could permit sexuality between
adults and children.

Social Worker E separated his responses into personal, organizational, and gay public image but in the end came down against
paedophilia, referring to the need to *protect* children, even from
themselves.

Disapproval may not, therefore, be unanimous but none of the
gay group stated they would actively approve of or encourage
paedophilia as they defined it. There does emerge a differentiation
of homosexuality from paedophilia as an obvious concern of the gay
workers; this probably affects case decisions although (with the
exception of Social Worker E) the gay group held a political analysis
of adult/child sexuality, which might lead in practice to a more
tolerant or 'eye-turning' response. This is all George asks for from
social workers.

2 Treatment of this type of sexual conduct

The 'straight' group contains people who would encourage or approve of chemical suppressants of behaviour but Probation Officer 4 in Section E (pp. 151) describes his opposition to chemical therapy in another client situation which would no doubt be generalized to case decisions involving paedophilia.

Within the casework relationship, the workers find themselves wanting but unable to discuss the offending behaviour. They turn instead to marital relationships, practical problems, or rely on routine supervision to control the client's behaviour. Dealing with practical problems is approved of by Fred whilst he is still apparently hoping for a 'cure' of sexual interests towards which he can be said to have an ambivalent attitude. Certainly his public response to his problem as defined by the law is that the professionals should 'treat his sickness'. He has no other way of presenting this part of his self to the world. His private response may well be very different.

George at one time coped with societal pressures by seeking treatment and also by living without expression of his sexual interest. Since that time he has undergone a political conversion and now sees his behaviour as worthy of private and public expression.

Probation Officer 2's statement to the court concerning the likelihood that direct work on the paedophile offence or sexual matters would not be undertaken is very important as is the officer's concentration on the public reaction to the offence.

None of the gay group supported aversion or chemical therapy. They varied in their degree of active opposition to such procedures. Perhaps the strongest response came from the unqualified social worker who had been at the receiving end of such attempts to change behaviour. Probation Officer 10 discusses the dilemma of the officer who is in opposition to such treatments which may be used by higher-status professionals.

3 Working with under-age sexual conduct

The responses in the study illustrate how the existence of an age of consent creates a special interest in people's specific sexual acts related to their chronological age, rather than their emotional maturity, their relationships with others, or respect for their privacy. Probation Officer 8 saw this as no problem because of his acceptance of the law's need to protect juveniles. Probation Officer 9 did not take such an absolute view but relied on his judgment about a stable relationship existing between a boy and a girl. The fact that the legal age varies according to the sex of the participants is a problem of which the (male) gay workers are very aware. Probation Officer 4 discusses his and the magistrate's attempts to humanize the application of the law and the effects of making public, behaviour which privately causes no concern to the participants. It is very important to note the way in which he attempts to carry the magistrates along with his way of thinking in this case.

We must also take account of beliefs shared by gay Social Worker E about moral and physical danger in under-age sexual expression. Stewart's account emphasizes the detrimental results for individuals of having a particular age below which sexual behaviour can easily become synonymous with such assumed dangers.

4 How social workers react to their own sexuality in working with children

It is not surprising that the gay social workers referred to their own sexuality in dealing with minors as they felt themselves to be on display, or in the case of Probation Officer 11 on trial, when they were dealing with such cases. It may be that what they were reacting to was not so much their own sexual feelings as other people's view of their sexuality, as when Social Worker A describes his having physical contact with pre-pubertal boys. As Probation Officer 11 puts it, 'My own needs did get jumbled—but more in my seniors' minds than my own.' When there is a confrontation of their own sexuality with a child, as with Social Worker I, then they are under pressure in a similar way to, for example, male social workers in residential homes with teenage girls (see p. 56; pp. 101-2).

Social Worker B finds a dilemma in socializing children into the expression of sexuality in acceptable ways, given that his own gay orientation is seen by other people as unacceptable.

Social Worker I described how his own lack of experience and sexual interests had been a handicap in helping boys in heterosexual relationships.

5 Special problems relating to residential work

(a) *As experienced by the residents*   Gwen and Brian clearly were in need of more information about sexuality. They both describe an atmosphere where such discussions were hardly a possibility. Gwen was unable to experience alternative models of males to the unfortunate one provided by her father. She left care unprepared for close relationships. Brian's anger still comes over at his own deprivation of care—the single-sex institutions, unmarried house-mothers. Both Brian and Gwen *feel* that they are very demanding of their current partners but of course they lacked intimate knowledge during childhood of such partnerships in process. Both went to single-sex schools which failed to dilute the overall impression of a care experience that may have been little different from other children of their generation. However, it is still felt by them to be the determining factor in their current relationships.

(*b*) *As experienced by the workers* Gay Social Worker I recognizes the special problems of the residential setting; a lack of choice about partners, power struggles where sexuality can be used as currency and where the deprivation of certain experiences may result in an over-emphasis on relationships within the home or school. He recognizes clearly that physical acts cannot be separated from their meanings within the residential group, and are situational rather than life choices.

(*c*) *Sex-role differentiation* The officer-in-charge and his wife discuss 'male image' in association with physical contact with children. Their 'great difficulty' is in their attribution of meanings to the teenager's behaviour. They believe that children should be provided with parent-like models. This involves physical expression which is problematic for them because of their view of sexuality between staff and children.

The whole basis of sex-role behaviour is questioned by some gay social workers. At one level what is being challenged is the rigid separation of traditional roles between men and women. However, there is also in Social Worker B's response a deeper criticism: 'a positive identity for them is a very important thing but I don't think one supplies this, but a kid builds a positive identity from a lot of relationships with a lot of different people.' The implications of such a position for traditional mother and father roles is spelt out by Social Worker J and Social Workers A and B. Their view is that rather than attempt to provide one or two parent-figures for children usually without such people, the children should be able to relate to a range of people with whom they are in contact. They may choose to identify with aspects of a variety of women and men.

We can only guess at Brian's response to such care provisions, given his concern about the marital status and sex of the staff. Gwen, having experienced 'houseparents', seems to have felt a great loss of ways in which to define herself. Given that her experiences of parents had serious negative aspects, she may have welcomed knowing more closely a range of people. She clearly understands the importance of the quality of the relationship rather than the length of time involved.

The policy and politics of social work

B Sex in the family

A sexual problem family?

Probation Officer 9

'Two brothers, elder now 23, in prison. Long history of sexual offences beginning with indecent exposure and moving on to rape, buggery, gross indecency. I find it difficult to see what influence I can have on his [the elder brother] sexual behaviour because of his upbringing and his sexual needs and the way he meets them. There seem to be two levels in the family. One is that they don't talk about sex openly and the other is that anal intercourse is used as a contraceptive method. He is saying that when he comes out if he gets a girlfriend OK, but if he is frustrated he just doesn't take much responsibility for his behaviour. . . . I've explained it's not socially acceptable but that doesn't really cut any ice. . . . On the one hand anal intercourse is fairly tolerated in his subculture whereas rape will never be acceptable. . . . I haven't really worked out a social work task with him.

'With his younger brother aged 21, there was a spate of offences around the same time, nothing before or since. He is a gullible, much less intelligent character. He confessed to everything and threw in a bit more . . . this happened with his girlfriend but there were also homosexual offences in his case but I see him being a normal heterosexual. . . . There seemed to be some emotional undercurrent in the rape; he had tremendous resentment against his mother-in-law who he saw as having done some very rejecting things to him. He was very angry about this—had a few drinks and was not used to drink, he raped this barmaid. Again I think he had anal sexual intercourse with her or attempted it. . . . It may be the main method of intercourse now in his married life as a form of contraception on either side. I've discussed this with him, it's a very touchy subject, he is very rigid and inflexible, although I've tried to educate him about birth control. . . . He is conscious of the need to report and be in touch and he uses that as an excuse to be over-dependent and to bring any minor problem along. . . . With his getting married I saw it as decreasing the risk of offending which was doubtful anyway as they were just a spate of offences as compared with his brother.

'What is also frustrating is the inability to get across to the parents either, they are of very low intelligence. The daughter aged 15 goes to an ESN school. We are very concerned with possible so-called promiscuity. The mother keeps saying she

stays out with men, she has no control over her . . . we took
her along with the parents' agreement to have her put on the
pill. . . . I explained everything to the mother and a female
colleague went along the next week and she recalled nothing.
She is one of these women who appears to understand but
doesn't of course . . . the father is much the same really.'

Probation Officer 4

'Martin, early 40s, married fifteen years, five sons, he was
convicted of buggery with three of the boys and with his wife.
He also liked to hold his wife's windpipe during intercourse. I
think she has got a slate loose somehow because it took her the
best part of two years or perhaps longer to complain. He is a
very selfish man and she is a vacillating woman so I think the
things work together very nicely and the children don't seem to
have suffered a great deal. What was done I think was given
and received as something at worst playful and boisterous and
at best actually rather tender. He would go on and on
alarmingly about how much he loves them. His love for them is
a very egocentric thing, their importance is that he loves them,
not the other way around. His wife eventually went to the police
and he holds it against her.'
'Your aims?'
'First, it was prevention. Two things will help, the boys are
getting older and will presumably be in a position to say "no"
and stop him and the other might be some kind of fear. He is
as selfish as ever but I am pushing the reality thing; what he
has actually done, what people will think of him. In some ways
I'm trying to instil a bit of guilt, or a bit of shame.

'The sort of effects I'm worried about is that I'm concerned
about their capacity to grow away and achieve independence if
there is a sort of closeness with parents. I think that is the
concern with incest more than anything else. The judge
muttered on about sort of turning them into little homosexuals
and I thought that's a load of cobblers. I don't take any notice
of that but what he has done to them is to use terror tactics at
the same time. Holding on to his wife's windpipe was one thing
but he played very teasing games with them which was quite
cruel.'

'In prison he is seen as a model prisoner. What happened
was in the home, no great harm done so there is no horror
attendant. There is a bit of this, "this is funny-peculiar,
naughty but it's not nasty really." As I say there is a nasty side
to it which hasn't been shown properly so there is pressure to
release him on parole. My attitude is no, so long as things are

113

not resolved about the final outcome of the divorce his wife is seeking and the custody of the children. But I do want to have him on parole because I would like to have some kind of hold. I don't think he responds too well to relationships as a means of moderating behaviour. He is a user and a manipulator.'

Probation Officer 12

'Jill is in her 30s, her offence was an indecent assault on her 18-month-old son. She was living with a man, the child became involved in their sexual activities. He was encouraged to emulate the sexual acts on his own mother and was stimulated by both of them. There was also some question of the man performing other acts but it wasn't proved. The man was sent to prison and she was put on probation. A friend of Jill's reported to a colleague that this was going on because it was almost a public performance. The probation officer informed the NSPCC and the police were involved, both admitted the offences. Jill denies it absolutely, "Someone else did it." All four of her children were taken into care which is very sad for her because she did love the children. Jill is of very low intelligence and socially backward, she is just like a child, she fantasizes to an enormous amount about relationships with men. One of the aims was to get her to accept the children were away and she was unlikely to gain custody of them. She also has financial problems but as far as the offence is concerned I haven't felt able to bring the reality of the offence to her as I think it might finish her. Recently we have got a bit closer, she has been saying "Well it was my fault really because he was my child. . . ." I don't think that until the police arrived she thought there was anything terribly wrong. He wasn't being hurt, he was enjoying it so the whole thing has been a dreadful shock to her.

'The tension for me in this case is this very pathetic woman who has lost her children and doesn't really know why. . . . I did experience in the beginning a lot of tensions, this was a case which caused quite widespread revulsion in the office. I think probation officers can accept almost anything but they couldn't accept this and I experienced similar feelings. I suppose it's something to do with images of a mother but it's much more understandable when you meet the person.'

I asked about the origin of her different response to this case.

'Perhaps it was above all training or logical thought, I don't know. I can almost understand everyone else's feelings in the

case better than mine . . . although I think the bit about it
being less damaging came from training, the learning as you do
about relationships between parents and children.'

I asked if there were cases where sexuality was important in her
estimation but she didn't deal with the subject.

'A married couple, I had the man on probation for taking
without consent. I was aware from the beginning that this man
had been going to see a psychiatrist because he was very
depressed over money matters but one thing which had cropped
up was his physical relationship with his wife. I never ever
pursued that at all over the two years.'
*'Was that because you thought the psychiatrist was dealing with
that?'*
'I couldn't honestly say that because he didn't see the
psychiatrist for very long. One of the reasons was that they were
both so terribly depressed, I wanted to help them through that.
. . . I suppose I really did have feelings about approaching
them. I suppose I would have found it much easier if they had
broached the subject themselves. Maybe, I also felt I had this
information behind their backs and it would be wrong to bring
it up.'
*'Do you think they would have seen you as being interested in
their sexual relationship?'*
'I think they would have found it very difficult to talk. It was a
difficult case, they tended to put me in a daughter-like role and
tended to want to look after me. If I was giving them something
they wanted to give me something back.'
'Had there been a difficulty in other cases?'
'In a problem family I have currently I have endless discussions
with the parents both separately and together about family
planning. We obviously have talked about physical sexual
matters. I suppose they are about the same age as me, it's more
of an equal thing. We have talked about it endlessly—family
planning is the most important thing as far as they are
concerned—but they have got nowhere. They have peculiar
notions, the man in particular about how it will affect him as a
man if he has a vasectomy. . . . At one point I brought in a
male colleague as well, we did think about getting somebody
who had actually had a vasectomy.'

Probation Officer 13

'Mother is now in her 50s, son is 23. Their sexual relationship
began when he was 14. This went on for nine years before a

prosecution. She is a very disturbed woman, she has been a psychiatric inpatient. She enmeshed him and prevented him from making contact with women of his own age. I thought it would be appropriate to get Bill disentangled from his mother, in view of this I abandoned her from the start, feeling that she was in a sense such a chronic case that any efforts I put into her case wouldn't make things much better and that the time was better spent with Bill. The aim was to get him out of the house. This he managed after eighteen months from the beginning of the order. He was accepted into a hostel. Unfortunately this didn't work out in that his personality was such that he couldn't cope with the demands of the hostel and in a matter of weeks he came back to the nest. So in that respect my efforts were a failure as he stayed at home until the order was terminated.

'She seemed to take a terribly destructive delight in discussing not only the offences but the things that Bill said to her whilst he was present in the house. So although we were able to discuss the sexual angle, it was in a very destructive way. For instance she took great delight in taunting Bill with an admission he had made that he wanted to have sex with young boys. He had been assaulted by a man when he was younger and he wanted to do the same thing to a boy now he was a man. So seeing them together wasn't useful at all. Discussions with Bill in the office were more detached but he was able to become involved in discussions . . . he was concerned that people mocked and despised him, not just because of the offences (the whole neighbourhood knew, not least because his mother had told them) but because of his physical appearance which was small, gnome-like. He tended to withdraw into himself. He never left the house because of his feelings that people were looking at him, he only saw his mother and they could only argue with each other. He only saw me and he just hadn't the practice in talking . . . he had also been in children's homes for ten years and they are not the sort of places you can confide in people.'

'What about other people's expectations in such a case?'
'The incestuous relationship drew me in as well, I tended to forget about everyone except him and her. In terms of the organization, my superiors, I am left with a lot of discretion to make my own decisions. I got very little interference, the only restraint is supervision sessions and it's in those I have to justify my ideas and if I can't then I'm open to altering my ideas. The courts? They are so remote I tend not to take them into account. The neighbours? I didn't even think about them.

'My own views about sex are "whatever turns you on" unless it's hurting other people. I could no more get excited about these two having sex than I could about man and wife. Because they weren't hurting anyone but themselves. I mean that a father having sex with a child I would deplore because there is an element of harm to a minor.'

Probation Officer 9 dismissed other aspects of sex and the family:

'The reasons vary with every case, the reasons why I have felt close or confident enough to raise it. With the married couple where I didn't do so, the man is very powerful physically, he is a very aggressive, very likeable man and perhaps there was an element of I was afraid of what might happen with him and what might happen between them. Would he be violent to her, she was in a different sense being violent to him emotionally. I didn't want to provoke, to stir. This couple's sexual life had waned. He had a serious accident at work which had made for physical difficulties. Sex was very awkward for the man.

'One discusses with women the attitudes of their husbands towards sex—the fairly common attitude of the husband going out for a drink, coming back, having sex with his wife. In no sense having it together, just going to sleep and perhaps going to work next morning and that epitomizes their marriage. Also once or twice I've talked to women who have been living with men and their relationships have been very happy until they get married when the whole thing seems to change. The man stops wanting his wife so much and this has raised serious problems as regards the relationship, "Does he want me, he's got me now, does he still want me?".'

The question of marital counselling is one where the values and attitudes and experience of the social worker will obviously be important. It is also an area in social work where traditionally more than one client or worker has been involved (Bannister and Pincus, 1965). How relevant are the worker's personal characteristics in this area?

Social Worker F

'Marital work is the sort of work I enjoy. Where I wouldn't be comfortable was where one wasn't free to if appropriate talk about one's own sexuality. To a certain extent in the marital counselling situation the couple want to know whether the people concerned are married/boyfriend/girlfriend. Have they got a sex life? One's uncomfortable to the extent of not feeling it's possible to bring it up, that it would throw the people completely and make it impossible to continue just because you are a member of a minority group. . . . This came up with a consultation session I attended. It was advised that the counsellors themselves should feel very much at ease with one another's sexual experience and relationships. The crunch problem was the attitude of the couple we were trying to help, should they know I was homosexual. The fact that my co-therapist knew I was gay helped ease the tension quite a bit.'

I asked about his attitude to family life.

'I wouldn't put a great deal of store by fidelity or exclusiveness in relationships. Counselling a married couple I would see the outcome of them being strong enough to split as right as the outcome being that they have sorted things out sufficiently to be able to stay together.'
Do you think your moral value judgments should be made more explicit to the client?'
'On the one hand I very much support straightforward contracted sort of work, on the other hand I think it's important to look at what's appropriate to the client and to his/her situation. To give the person your curriculum vitae at the outset can be totally inappropriate in lots of situations.'

This worker described an incest case where he had discussed the actual sexual involvement with the girl and her father and he had also tried to ensure that the girl did not share her parents' bedroom:

'I think what had happened, he had just come home pissed one night and touched up his daughter whilst his wife was in the bathroom. The girl wasn't very happy about it and complained. But I don't know if one can say across the board that one is happy or unhappy or worried about incest. I would not want it to be a criminal matter but there may be a role for social work in individual cases.'

Social worker K described how her attitude to roles within the family has changed, particularly over the last five or six years:

'My whole attitude to the traditional roles of husband and wife has altered a great deal. At one time I would have thought that a woman who wasn't happy looking after young children and was depressed about it had somehow failed to come to terms with her maternal role and this might have been due to a failure in her own relationship with her mother; failure in acceptance of her own womanhood and femininity. I would

118

have seen it in those kind of developmental terms. Whereas now I'm likely to see it as a woman's role in society, expectations placed on women to be in the home and look after children, often in the case of clients without the wherewithal to do it—without the housing, money, the possibility of self-help playgroups. So that my whole way of looking at that situation in marriage would certainly be to relate the woman's feelings to the wider society and social expectations rather than to her own maternal development. . . . I would almost certainly look for a much greater flexibility and not let the man sit at home waiting to be waited on. So that would be an enormous shift.'

She also spoke of the narrowing division between previous liberal judgments of clients' behaviour and her own fiercer judgments about herself and her friends.

'The clients have had a liberating influence?'
'Yes, but what's made the shift in my personal life is the whole gay liberation movement. Because [of my Christian background] I'm still trying to work out and it's still important to me, I'm very affected by the gay Christian liberation bit . . . this has had a much bigger affect on my shift and particularly a personal relationship I've had over the past four years with the woman I live with.'

I asked her to place her views within an organizational and legal context:

'I think it's very important to know what the law is and to distinguish between that and practice. I've always got very annoyed with social services departments when sometimes the two things have got confused. . . . I've always thought it important to know what the law is so that I and clients and social workers know where they are. . . . Having said that, the law has never been where I derived my moral code from. I think this is because I've a Catholic background and part of that was to see something beyond the law so that my religious background rather than the law was my super-ego . . . so if people have behaved outside the law, although I know that may be dangerous for them and may also be immoral, it isn't necessarily. . . . So when clients have behaved outside it, I haven't felt as a social worker I have any responsibility to inform the people who impose the law that the law has been broken and that may be because I think the law in a particular instance doesn't make good sense. I certainly don't think I would be justified in reporting anyone's breaches of the law unless it had dangerous implications for society. . . .

119

'Though I'm prepared to accept . . . that some people find
happiness and satisfaction in a whole variety of sexual
relationships, for myself there has always been a very strong
link between my emotional feelings and my sexual relationships.
. . . I'm not quite sure how one would manage to accomplish
more than one sexual relationship at a time because I think
that if I was having other sexual relationships then my
emotional feelings would be diffused. It's very difficult to know
whether my feelings that all the intensity goes in one direction
is just a kind of very strong expectation because of marriage.'

I asked about 'value contracts':

'You have to make some judgment about whether your being
explicit would inhibit them more than it helps. For example, I
wouldn't want to be saying, "I just think you ought to have one
sex relationship with the person you are very fond of", because
that may make a nonsense in terms of where the other person is
at. . . . And if you do try and work from where the person's at,
then they do find a working out for themselves if you really
genuinely believe in the importance of their doing that.'

Social Worker L pointed out to me that the majority of his work did
not involve any overt discussion or consideration of sexuality, a
theme echoed by a number of other workers:

'In marital cases, it tends to be primarily separations, whether
the wife has been battered or not, the wife is coming in wanting
to separate or has just left the husband. She is wanting initially
to be rehoused . . . that's an obvious case where we could
discuss the sexual relationship but I do find that we tend to
concentrate on relationship and practical problems.
'. . . to what extent it's a result of my being gay, to what
extent it's me as a person, I don't know but I think it makes it
much easier for me, let's say in a marital situation, to get a
feeling for both sides. . . . Because I don't feel bound up in any
set sex-role, I feel I've probably had a much wider range of
experience in a range of sex-roles than people around me may
have done and so I may have had the experience of being with
someone who is very masculine and I may have had the
opposite experience and this most straight people may not have
had. . . . I think that the client can tell, especially someone you
are getting involved with, whether you do have some sort of feel
for that experience. I've worked with a lot of the wives but I've
also taken on battering husbands as clients and feel I've been
able to identify to some extent with both.

'I am gay all the time but I only work with a gay client once
in a very long while . . . so it's much more important for me to
be aware of how being gay influences my work with all the
other kinds of cases and in a gigantic chunk of things it
doesn't have any influence at all . . . if I'm sorting out anything
with DHSS my being gay is not something of which I'm
conscious.'

In dealing with responsibilities within families for dependant
members, this worker traced his strong emotional feelings about
obligations to his early life in a country which took extended family
responsibilities very seriously. He felt that he had not yet analysed
the way his sexual orientation might affect his dealings with
families. 'Also, in our team every one of us is single and in the same
age range.'

In relation to the law, 'I lived in a country [Latin America] where
homosexuality was illegal and having lived with that for so long it
does undermine one's identification with the law, I wouldn't ever
apply for a job in probation because of this.' He described the case
of a West Indian family in which he and a female worker were
involved. There had been an incestuous relationship going on
between the father and the girl aged 14 for about a year when the
workers had discovered it:

'I felt I had a very good rapport with the mother. The other
social worker and I didn't feel it was our responsibility to report
the incest. The mother didn't want it taken further. The dad
and her talked about it and decided that he should move out
. . . my assumption is that it's up to the mother and daughter
to decide.'

Social Worker D

'I don't think in the conventional terms of family life. I don't
think that I'm there to keep families together because they are
the best thing invented. In terms of working with people I do
think that meaningful units, families or whatever you want to
label them, are important and the people involved in them . . .
the idea of an ideal family life isn't something I relate to,
mainly because I don't see that even in the families that don't
come to this agency and I do see it as a television ideal and not
a reality for the people I know who are my friends, as well as
for my clients.
'I'm sure that social workers pick their cases. It would take
me a lot of working through to work with this kind of thing
[incest]. If you want Freudian terminology, that stage I

121

haven't really worked through at all. I would respond with distaste—that would be my *feeling* even though my head told me to look at the situation as it's at. My feeling would be if tomorrow this case came up in allocation, if somebody else would take it, I'd let them. . . .

'I do make value judgments but I think they are different from moral which suggests right and wrong. Value suggests to me that something is better than something else. I definitely do make those decisions but the value judgment is based more on lots of factors that make something better or worse from my point of view and my experience. . . .

'I try to explain a little in a very general way about not necessarily who I am but about where I stand as a social worker in relation to a particular situation. It would be very different if it were a welfare rights case as opposed to if somebody came to me for casework help. But I would try before I started getting involved to work out with them what I was here to do and what we were going to work on and not just plunge in without any kind of statement of where I stood, or try to find out where they stood.'

Social Worker E

'Being the way I am I'm not terribly struck on families. . . . I am aware that there are for example, schizophrenic families. It is, however, a social work tradition, or has been in the past, to keep families together. I haven't really managed to form a water-tight, sound, copper-bottomed attitude to this, one adopts a hand to mouth response. Somebody else would dignify it by saying it was a flexible response to changing situations but I think it would only be honest for me to say—one's first response is to keep a family together. One's second response is to hang on and see if this is desirable and then one may have to change one's view and say, "No, this family will have to split up." Now it all depends on for instance if you are dealing with a young child rather than an adolescent. Adolescents ought to be helped to grow away from their families. With a child it's much more difficult. I can't make up my mind, for example, of the importance of a two-parent background for a child's welfare. I have a suspicion despite all my feelings against families . . . that children are better off if they have a mum and a dad but that's only an emotional reaction I think. But clearly there are many situations where children are better off with one parent. The other being just a visitor to the house or

perhaps barred from seeing the children . . . but the whole
question of adoption and fostering raises very problematic
questions over what's called inclusive or exclusive fostering. If
you have parents who are inadequate or perhaps doing their
children harm. How do you reconcile yourself with taking the
children into care, preventing the mother who may be an
alcoholic or a neurotic person from having them? The trouble is
I have a political or ideological feeling somewhere that says this
is wrong.'

Social Worker G

'Recently I've been involved in two cases where mongol children
have been born. In one the caseworker and I [as supervisor]
worked with them for over six months and now the family have
come to accept the baby and can't think how ever they said
they would have killed it had it been sent to them. In the other
we have worked to a situation where we have decided that the
child cannot go back to the family—for its own sake, not for
the parents' sake. These two parents are so ill-adjusted that
they can't bear a fault. . . . I think so much depends on the
marital relationship here.'

The complexity of some marital situations is nicely caught in this
description by Probation Officer 10:

'A woman in her late 40s, put on probation for shoplifting. For
many years she worked as a prostitute specializing in sado-
masochism. From my point of view the difficulty is in focusing
at all on her past. The main reason I think it is relevant is that
she is married to an effeminate homosexual with a number of
convictions for soliciting and drug abuse and several suicidal
gestures, numerous prison sentences and hospital treatment. He
is the father of one of her children. At the moment the marital
relationship is a very dicey one indeed. He tends to have nights
out. There is a lot of indirect communication between the pair
but none directly. I make a number of offers to work with the
two of them. These are accepted in the first instance but when
it comes to the actual visit, everything happens to prevent this.
It's a peculiar relationship with this woman's background of
prostitution with a presumed lesbian element plus her husband
who is clearly involving himself still in the gay world. I'm not
concerned for her about the likelihood of reoffending but I am
concerned about her happiness and lack of it, especially as
there is a 9-year-old daughter living with them who experiences

123

father's absence and the tension between mother and father. This case highlights that no matter how caring you think you are about what you feel you are getting across to the clients, the client will still resist talking about sexuality and I don't quite know how one bridges the gap because clearly if we are going to get anywhere with the areas of difficulty in sexuality, then you have got to encourage the client to talk and if they refuse to talk we are stuck. . . .

'The court had very little information on this woman when she was placed on probation. The police antecedents had got mislaid. So nothing was known about her previous convictions which included keeping brothels. She was also in breach of a suspended sentence for a more criminal matter. There was no social inquiry report so in fact the court had very little to go on except her *appearance* in court.

'But at the moment I don't think I am adjusting them—I think they are adjusting me to their equilibrium. . . . I would have thought a better relationship would ensue if they would just talk to each other. I certainly wouldn't aim at a better sexual relationship between the two of them. They know one another well enough to know what is possible and what is not possible. It isn't the question of latent homosexuality coming to the surface shocking the other partner. Their sexual life is known to both of them. I would think that in the sado-masochistic bit she played the active role which is a very good way to have a sexual relationship without having sex. She does nothing except crack a whip—her body is not used in any way. I would (morally) tolerate anything if I felt the passive partner was a willing partner, how one finds that out of course is another matter. If I was dealing on probation, for example, with the active partner, then I've only got his or her word for it. . . .

'But what is sado-masochism? . . . We think, in terms of extremes when we talk of sexuality, that's the trouble, so that scratching with fingernails could be deemed to be sado-masochistic but we don't think of that when we talk—we think of whips, racks and the like and very rarely is that sort of information presented to a social worker.'

Probation Officer 11

'I have a man on suspended sentence supervision order for incest with his daughter. The court more or less told him never to see the girl again, whereas he has and it's fairly important for them both. They have a lot to work through and I think for them to meet occasionally with other people there is quite a healthy thing. . . .

'Really the incest has been discussed in relation to the marriage, rather than in relation to him. I can see the danger of the incestuous relation but the thing is that he has been so punitive towards himself since it happened, so terribly judgmental and censorious that I haven't needed to express society's views to him. He has more or less said since the social enquiry stage, "I ought to be put away for life." I said, "No, No." I did think he needed a certain element of punishment. That's why I thought him being given a term of imprisonment but suspended and he had got the support he needed over a period of time. I didn't think he could get over what he had done unless he felt he had been punished for it.'

A certain view of aspects of the family and social work may emerge from these excerpts. It should not be forgotten, however, that some workers are involved in social work in which the family has operationally no function, except as an image of the unattainable. In such a situation is Social Worker H:

'I work with mainly single homeless, with some sort of social or personality problem. A lot of them are alcoholics, a good number are drug addicts—or both—and I suppose in some sense of the word or another, inadequacy covers them all. Some of them are just plain mad and some are more or less mad. The age range is from teenage to a few old-age pensioners, but they are better looked after by the state after they are 60 or 65.'

Interim conclusions

Views of family life

It is worthwhile considering the overall impression created by these cases. The bizarre nature of the sexual conduct is apparent which is in some contrast to the sort of intra-psychic problems which are described by the Family Discussion Bureau (Bannister and Pincus, 1965). It could be that the workers here are separate specialists in dealing with people who do not recognize they have problems of relationships. Indeed the workers often appear to be unsuccessful in helping such individuals acknowledge that they have a relationship problem to be worked on. These workers seem to get caught up in the client's definition of the problem—their behaviour is against the law and so the law should be avoided, or certain events have occurred like the removal of children or a family member and it is

125

this situation which needs to be changed. This entering into the client's viewpoint should not be seen merely as unhelpful colluding. It undoubtedly does require a special sympathy to listen to the viewpoint of people whose behaviour causes revulsion in many people. See especially the case described by Probation Officer 3 (pp. 46-7). Gay Social Worker D admits to avoiding a case like incest which would threaten her too much at a feeling level. Apart from dealing with the sequela of their sexual conduct becoming public, the workers in such extreme cases were often not able to offer any help to the clients.

In this environment it is understandable that a distorted view of family life emerges. The family is a place for intimate relationships and behaviour which are therefore not the concern of legal and social agency. If the sexual aspects of the family life do become public, then they are likely to be of a dramatic kind. It also seems reasonable to assume that those involved will want to quickly remove their behaviour from public scrutiny.

The encounters of the social worker with such private and public problems of living together would allow few illusions about the ability of such a unit to contain all the individual needs of clients.

For those social workers who themselves do not live in such units, the alienation from advertising images of 'ideal family life' might be even more pronounced. However, there was no general condemnation of exclusiveness in relationships by the gay workers—both lesbians mentioned their own commitment to one person (see also p. 161).

One gay worker spoke of how his early background was still very important in his views about dependant relatives and extended family commitments. Another expressed himself divided on the importance for children of two-parent family life and the interference by social agencies in the way parents bring up their children.

Within the gay group there was criticism of attempts to keep families together as an ultimate value. However, when discussing family life problems there was no evidence of any general, radical alternatives in operation. Exceptions might be the unqualified worker who worked only with those for whom the concept of the family was of no practical use. Social Worker D referred to 'meaningful units' as well as the family. However, when we are dealing with traditional roles and behaviour within marriage, then the influence of a radical political analysis can be observed. This is best articulated by Social Worker K who nicely follows her own conversion from psychological theories of personal inadequacy to a political view of the position of woman in society. She discusses the operational consequences of such a shift in relating to clients' roles within marriage and the family. A similar concern about roles and behaviour is shown by straight Probation Officer 9.

Marital work

A variety of reasons were given for a neglect of sexual aspects in marital work; the age of the worker, marital status, fear of the consequences for the worker or other family members. Where separation is the priority, or where the worker felt personally inhibited from themselves raising what was seen as private sorrows. In the case of Probation Officer 9, sex could have been important to discuss in view of the husband's physical handicap. Social Worker G refers to the importance of the strength of the marital relationship in a successful outcome of accepting a mongol child. A marital focus was used in incest cases.

The gay group showed no inhibitions about being involved in marital counselling—Social Worker F: 'Marital work is the sort of work I enjoy.' Social Worker L felt that his being gay enabled him to identify more easily with both partners in a relationship, 'Because I don't feel bound up in any set sex role.' Social Worker F mentions the necessity of being free to talk about one's own sexuality if appropriate.

To what extent do the workers feel responsible to people outside the family?

We have already mentioned the workers being adjusted to the client's view but other forces impinge on their work. Probation Officer 4 describes his first aim as prevention and sees his achievement of this partly by opposing parole. In the same case he dismisses the Judge's view about homosexuality being caused by his client's incestuous behaviour.

Probation Officer 13 feels he is only accountable in supervision sessions. In the incest case he refers to, he equates the sexual conduct as being of the same concern to him as sex between a man and wife but this is an individual evaluation and he would not extend this to all incest cases. In incest cases the social workers imply they would prefer to deal with such problems without recourse to the law.

The gay group vary in their views about the relationship to the law by social workers. Social Worker E feels that he would need to protect himself (see pp. 92, 93). Social Worker L describes how having himself been a sexual outlaw 'does undermine one's identification with the law', and the operational consequences of this. Probation Officer 11 disagreed with the court's wish to permanently separate a man and his daughter who had been involved incestuously, whilst feeling that a suspended sentence penalty was helpful for the father who needed to feel he had been punished for the offence.

Social Worker K nicely distinguishes between the often confused organizational and legal rules. Because of her religious background she does not see the law as the final arbiter of behaviour and she feels under no obligation to report breaches of the law 'unless it had dangerous implications for society'.

The flavour of some of these responses is captured by Social Worker D. In her separation of moral and value judgments she prefers not to think in terms of absolutes of right and wrong, rather to consider individual value judgments which are personal to the experience of the individual. As Social Worker K puts it: 'And if you do try and work from where the person's at, then they do find a working out for themselves if you really genuinely believe in the importance of their doing that.'

C   Prostitution

Smart (1977, p. 77) makes the point that 'The legal definition of prostitution invariably refers to a woman selling her sexuality rather than a person of either sex selling their sexuality.' It is worth, therefore, turning again to Social Worker H:

'He is a male prostitute who wanted to get over that . . . he stayed in the hostel where I am a warden for two or three months . . . although he was getting lots of money he couldn't hang on to it, in a sense being a prostitute wasn't his problem, it was not being able to cope anyway and prostitution almost by accident was his source of income. . . . He was gay and made no pretence about doing it for the money when he was really heterosexual at all. He had problems with relationships. I guess this was one reason why he was a prostitute . . . he did it as much for the sex as for the money, he was fairly selective who he went with, depending how hard-up he tended to be. He probably would have been very promiscuous anyway.'
'Did he know you were gay?'
'Yes, I told him fairly quickly when he moved into the hostel. I didn't tell him before. Any tensions were small and only momentary in either of us. Because the fact of being gay was no great hang-up to him so it was no problem to me. He told me that he went once to a social security office and the little chap behind the counter asked him what his last job was and he told him "male prostitute".'

Probation Officer 12

'She is now 31, has been soliciting since she was 16 or maybe much younger. She has four half-caste illegitimate children plus one who was killed. The youngest of a large family, her sister was also a prostitute. She currently has a fairly stable relationship with the father of her youngest child. I've known her four years and I really now hardly think of her in terms of being a sex offender at all. She is the one client of mine I know better than any other. I do feel that with prostitutes you have to establish a relationship over a long period of time. I have never talked about her giving up soliciting in terms of the offence. I've only talked to her in terms of the effect it has on her life and the children's lives. This is becoming very apparent to her because her eldest is 12 and has discovered her mother is a prostitute when her mother last went to prison. I think of prostitutes as a client group with very special needs and problems.

'I think the experience of the probation service is that to discourage prostitutes from their way of life doesn't have any effect. There is a personal dilemma for me which I think is shared by my colleagues as to whether we would regard soliciting as an offence anyway in moral terms. . . .

'I think she is a very insecure person, she feels that no one will respect her because of her way of life. She doesn't rate herself very highly so I think the aims are to build up some self-respect in her and to build this sort of relationship where she can feel there is someone outside the circle of prostitutes that she can have a relationship with. . . .

'I think there is a tension not so much with my employers but with society who would take one view of prostitution and I would probably take another and I think that's a difficult dilemma. I would always try to make that fairly clear in court when I'm making a report that what I'm doing is not necessarily related to stopping her soliciting. . . .

'I think at the beginning I did have a view of prostitutes as being overtly sexual in the way that they dressed or their conversation. It does happen sometimes but very rarely and it certainly doesn't apply to this client who relates fairly normally in the way she keeps her house and looks after her children. . . . I probably expected at first some indulging in salacious conversation but that rarely happens. . . .'

'Do you discuss specific sexual matters with her?'

'Very rarely indeed. . . . I feel she rarely wants to talk about sexual matters specifically. When we get onto those areas she does feel embarrassed to talk to me about them. . . . But this is specific to this client, with other prostitutes I have discussed sexual matters particularly in relation to how they started off and what their feelings were about it rather than what actually happened. I don't think they do talk much about what actually happens, what they actually do. . . .'

129

'What about health matters—VD and birth control?'
'Yes, I do find with the girls that area is discussed much more.
I think they tend to be fairly careful in relation to VD, most of
them. They're aware of what they can do, where they can
go. . . .'

Probation Officer 9

This officer was discussing the importance of the words one uses to
discuss sexual conduct:

'With this prostitute I was able to use more vulgar words. . . .
I would use "masturbate" and she would look blank and I'd
say "wank" and she would know what I was talking about and
only slightly be embarrassed. . . . I would switch from one to
the other according to what she was understanding.'
'What were your aims with her?'
'I was just reacting to crisis. Her marriage was always looking
as if it might finish. There was always tremendous friction. Her
husband encouraged her to solicit, if anything, or at least
colluded with it. . . . I don't think she was that bothered about
the money, she wanted to get out of the house, the kids were
getting on top of her and it was a bit of social life and a bit
adventurous in a way and she also had a deeper need to have a
stable relation with a man. . . . I'm pretty sure on that fact
from discussion with her, some of the clients became close
friends, not just in a sexual way, just a way of meeting really.
. . . [The husband had] some kind of expectation I would
disapprove of soliciting and be wanting to stop it. . . . I would
see that as an ultimate aim but not anything I'd expect to
achieve necessarily. . . . I suppose I've got my own personal
feelings about legislation on prostitution. I suppose I'd have it
decriminalized for a start. . . . I wouldn't disapprove of
soliciting in the same way as I disapprove of, say, robbery. . . .
I see prostitutes as being victimized. . . . If a prostitute is
placed on probation I see it as so unrealistic for somebody to
stop them ever soliciting and change their life-style overnight.
. . . I suppose society out there, the man in the street, might
hope for that but I'd hope that magistrates and people more
closely connected with the courts would see that these people
have got social problems and you help with that and hopefully
they may not solicit so much. . . . I can see the nuisance value
to the neighbourhood but not much more than that . . . but
there are other laws to deal with that. Similarly if there are
pimps and violence involved there are other laws to deal with
that. . . .'

The image that the client presents to the social worker in a particular situation is perhaps too often taken to be 'the truth' rather than a situational response to a number of interacting pressures which result in the client playing out a role for the worker. I was able to meet a total of six prostitutes in an informal setting which they used as a drop-in community centre. Most of their discussion together appeared to be about the particular stresses of the occupation. There was a lot of 'obscene' language used and emotions were easily triggered off into laughter and angry scenes. Children played around their mothers and there was a feeling of belonging about the centre. I discussed the general aims of the centre with a number of the probation officers involved (who do not figure in other aspects of this study). There was agreement that social problems, health of the women and kids, housing, money, relationships with pimps, boyfriends, were areas with which social work was concerned. Any aims about the women ceasing prostituting were seen either as long-term or not desirable—no agreement emerged from the workers about this. There was awareness of 'prostitute trade union' activity but the general belief was that this was a self-help movement to be managed by the women themselves. The probation officers also were aware of the need to decriminalize soliciting but were not taking any active steps to achieve this aim. I had the opportunity of interviews (not tape-recorded) with two of the women without the presence of the probation officers.

Mary was 27 and looked ten years older. She had very firm views, as did others, about the need to decriminalize her way of obtaining employment. She thought that there were other groups 'like those men who interfere with children' who should be locked up in prison. She saw the role of the probation service as limited in that her problems were financial. In terms of individuals Mary was quite sure which of the four probation officers she had been involved with were useful and mentioned them by name. I asked how officers make their impressions on her: 'Oh, Ms X. was a waste of time, she just didn't care, with others it's been that they showed they are available to help.' I asked if she had experienced a probation officer trying to change her way of life: 'Oh yes, they disapprove of what you do but they don't think there is anything wrong in it.' Mary said that she could never discuss sex with probation officers and was amused at the apparent contradiction as she went on to describe how she was a puritan and embarrassed with sex. Mary gave as an example that with the man she lived with she was shy of undressing in the light, although shortly before she may have been doing just that for a client without any difficulty: 'It's business only with us, we are only selling what is ours—do you ever get tired of money?' Her attitude to her own daughter was 'If I thought she was going on the streets I'd break her neck.' She recalled that shortly before she and some other women had reported some young girls from a local children's home to the social services. Apparently these children had been offering themselves to men 'at 30 bob a time'. Mary was quite open about the economic aspects of her decision to report the girls. Generally Mary was pleased with the informal setting of the centre. She thought that the probation officers got to know the women better than in office interviews and they weren't 'nosy' in the way she had experienced supervising officers to be in the past. Her test of a good probation officer was 'could you invite them to a party?'

Angie is now 35 and was in care by the time she was 15 and says she has been on probation 'most of my life'. She spoke of how she had expected to dislike Sue, her last probation officer, but one day they had a discussion in which Angie felt able to ask Sue about her sex life. 'Was she on the pill? "Yes." Did she live with someone? "yes, another probation officer". After that I felt better about her and I told her about my own sex problems.' She contrasted this experience with other probation officers 'who know all about us before we know owt about them'. She lives a distance away from the pick-up area. 'It's two different worlds with me. Prostitution is just a job but sometimes with the punters I feel like giving them their money back—almost—I feel sorry for them, old and lonely, it makes you realize you are not the loneliest person in the world.'

Angie was also pleased to meet probation officers in a more informal atmosphere as she did not like reporting and preferred the 'normal atmosphere' at the centre. Angie's experience of social work now extends to her 15-year-old son being in care and having his own social worker. 'I know he has had sex but I couldn't discuss it with him.' Her daughter is in borstal having also been a prostitute. 'I tried to stop her but she was brought up by my parents although she did discuss sexual problems with me.'

Angie says that her soliciting is now only occasional and her problems are not connected with the occupation but are rather money difficulties or concerns about her son. She also saw the probation officers as disapproving of prostitution, 'but they don't go on at us, and anyway, that's a waste of time'. She saw very clearly that the officers were 'half on our side and half on the courts but the Vice [police] hates this centre'.

Angie also had an important idea about ways of working for probation officers involved with the women: 'I think that all the probation officers should get all of us together to see us not just on our own but to see what are the major problems we all have.'

These discussions with the women could only have taken place in an informal atmosphere. They were impossible to prearrange and were in the middle of their working hours. These factors constrained the type of tape-recorded interview used in other parts of the study. I was able to complete one such interview with a prostitute (Diane). She was the client of Probation Officer 14 (Anne) from whom we hear first:

'C' 'I've known her since she was 15, she is now 23. Her very first appearance in the juvenile court was for theft, ever since it's been prostitution and she has been on probation numerous times. She has five children between 8 and 3. The main thing was to try and keep her together, try and stop her going to prison, and try to find something on which to build for herself and the children. . . . I don't think stopping her prostituting has ever been the main focus but of course it must have been somewhere because if she continued she would go to prison. . . . She is now under a suspended sentence, she has got a house, she almost lost it once when she floated and went to prison . . . she is pretty good with the children but when they were very small there was a concern that she was neglecting them . . . they are smashing kids. . . . She is at the stage now where she only goes out when she has a bill to pay. She has one or two regulars who go to the house, you know we have never really dwelt on this at all a lot, it's much more been the relationship she had with the bloke she has been living with and I've known a few. The last one lasted quite a long time and she has just been through a very difficult period on the breakdown of that relationship and I think she has come through that and is quite enjoying her own freedom. . . . She is quite open that she doesn't know whether she will get through the suspended sentence or not . . . she will say "Perhaps I should go to a bar and pick up a bloke there, and not be likely to get caught so much."'
'Would you encourage that?'
'I suppose I do, I suppose one is making one's own judgments on this sort of thing, it doesn't seem very wrong to do. If it means she is not going to get picked up I would be all for it. I would hope really that she would mature sufficiently so she would be able to get through the whole thing. But if that's going to be her way of doing it then fair enough. . . . When she was 16-17-18 and was really being exploited by a lot of people I found that very sad but the fact that she has gone out to earn a living that way doesn't bother me. It's the effects—the ponces —and her need to be subservient and not see herself as a woman in some ways. . . . She was very unrealistic and out of this world and gradually she has I hope begun to see herself as

a person with rights and needs of her own. . . . She is a person
who couldn't express any feeling, she would keep it all bottled
up inside to the stage where she would almost *steam*. I could
feel the heat coming from her body. I think that she has
changed a little . . . it was difficult to make any contact with
her and I was just another authority figure chasing round trying
to say "No, No", and it took a long time to change that. . . .'
'How do you see the future for her?'
'I suppose it worries me that there is a risk of prison. . . . I
think that if she can weather the next year or so—she is quite
hard-working in fact and if it was possible for her to get a job
that would earn enough money. The problem is that women are
not very well paid. If she continues to work out her
relationships, I would hope she would be able to cope. I am not
saying she would be stopped soliciting but do it in a more
sophisticated way.'
*'Do you think there would still be a social work task for you if
soliciting were no longer a criminal offence?'*
'Yes, one of the children is nicking at the moment. Yes I think
there would still be a task at the scene she is at now. . . . She
has worked though a lot of feelings over the years and I think
she feels better about it and is not the compliant little child any
longer. That's in the context of our relationship and it feels
better.'

'C' *Diane*

'I think I was trying to screw in a telephone box when I first
got to know Anne. I was 15 and pregnant. I was quite crackers,
a crazy lady. . . . I didn't like her, I'm a funny person. At that
time I didn't talk to people easily, I kept everything bottled up.
I think it took a year before I had any faith in Anne at all.'
'What happened to change that?'
'I think it's that she is so easy to get on with. She doesn't push
me to talk, she leaves it to me to do the talking. . . . If I
thought I wasn't going to get Anne on probation I probably
wouldn't want it. She doesn't push you into anything, she
leaves it to you whereas a lot of probation officers, they ask you
and expect you to answer. Er, what's the word, they tend to
bully you around. Anne's got the patience of Job, with me
that's what she needed. . . . I didn't know I was pregnant until
I was six months. I was as green as an apple. . . . I was put
into a mother-and-baby home. That I disliked because I hate
being penned up. . . .'

*'When you first were into prostitution, how did you think Anne
would react to that?'*
'In the kind of crowd I was in I didn't really care because I
never turned up for appointments anyway. This is what I mean
about Anne, she was so good, she used to turn out and find
me . . . she used to go to cafés where black men go all over
looking for me, she could have taken me back loads of times
for breach of probation but it never happened, a lot would have
done. She's wrong basically but then again, if she had've done
it wouldn't have worked out. I needed a push for everything,
even for appointments at the hospital when I was pregnant she
used to come and pick me up and bring me back . . . and so
it's built up.'
'Are you quite dependent on her now?'
'No, not now, probably when I was younger, every problem I
took to Anne. I'd rather talk to her than me own Mum. . . . I
think since I became more settled, before that I moved around
Midlands towns and more often than not I took the kids with
me. But I always kept coming back to see Anne. I'm far more
independent now and Anne helped me to be that way—a lot of
time and patience.
'I think Anne honestly thinks that I could do better for
myself than soliciting but it's such an easy thing to fall back
into when you are short, easy money. . . . I wouldn't say she
disapproves . . . now it's once in a blue moon since I got
settled. Obviously I couldn't go on the way I was with five
kids. I would have lost them moving from town to town. . . . I
thought the suspended sentence was harsh, for two years but
obviously the magistrates are trying to wean me off as well. . . .
I don't think they have got a clue—magistrates. . . . Basically
for me it's just money, you do get some punters who get
attached to you and you get to like them, I've got a few who
come. . . . I've got a very lively sex life but as far as I'm
concerned, when it's business it's business . . . there were one
. . . I did get attached to him, he had a bit of money. When
you are in this you've got this little dream and when it did
actually come I haven't got it in me to be hard enough to live
with him or marry him and take his money.'
'If the law were changed, would you be problem-free?'
'Yes, if it were legalized brothels. But who the hell wants to
look at 25-year-old women—the girls would all be so young we
wouldn't stand an earthly. . . . Most of my problems have
arisen from prostitution.'
'Unionization?'
'It's a waste of time until they legalize it. . . . It seems stupid

135

to me, the tax they would get back in return. . . . If the coppers decide to have a purge on you they do, I remember one year I got six or seven convictions. Older girls said report it, they are harassing you, but what can you say. . . .

'I've got four lads, all good-looking, under 20 who come here and I say you must be mad, coming here paying money. But it's like they say, if we aren't paying cash to you, how much is it going to cost us to take a bird out, drinks, and then at the end of the night you aren't sure you are going to pull her anyway?

'I know some girls who are bisexual and on the game. If a punter said to me I'd give you £20 to £30, we get a lot of this, he will want to see a lesbian show. But then with me it's just for money although a lot of chicks get quite a kick out of it. If they asked me I'd automatically go for one of the girls in town who is a bit that way anyway. It makes a better show for him.'

'I think Anne was on the right wavelength from the beginning. It was me. I'd no faith even in my own parents . . . social workers I find don't know what prostitution is all about, they don't know the problems. More so if you have got a pimp. I think they just tend to listen to a pack of lies . . . they would take it in, I don't think a lot of them have got a clue, Anne is good, I'd recommend her to anybody, you couldn't easily con Anne. But a lot don't know what makes you carry on. It is something you fall back into so easily. . . . We look at it this way—if we have got probation we have got off, that's how we see it. . . . If I had nowhere else to go, Anne would have no hesitation, she would let me and my kids come to her. Her husband's been down and done repairs. They are involved, when I was having stress with this bloke, I was phoning up at all peculiar hours—if it were her husband "Is that you Diane", straight away they *knew*. She will turn out at any time. I've met her children, we got on quite well, 'cos even her daughter has been down at Christmas, 'cos she has played guitar for the kids. I know her husband, I know where she were brought up. I know her father was an alcoholic. Really and truly a lot of her circumstances were the same as mine. She was brought up in a little village with her father—she tells you, it's not as if you are sitting there with the attitude "She thinks she's better than me"—she tells you.

'As soon as my kids are old enough they will go on the pill. I wouldn't want them to get lumbered like me. I don't hide anything from them—I don't think they know what I do. They have seen one or two blokes come but if I've got somebody coming I'd get them out of the way. This is why I try and make it that they come during school hours or after eight at night. I can't even remember me mum telling me to change me knickers. Then again I think I baffled her. She hadn't got a chance to handle me, 'cos I were a proper rebel. If one of the kids wanted to be a prostitute, well fair enough. I'd advise them not to be. But if this is what they wanted I wouldn't stop them either.

'It's easier to tell em straight at the VD clinic that you are a prostitute. If you go down for a check every four or five weeks . . . it causes problems if you have got a dose because then they expect you to remember every punter you have been with. . . . I think it would solve a lot of problems with VD if it were legalized so you could book in and not feel embarrassed about it. There were a social worker down there who put my back up alarming. I went and got my treatment but you should go back for your check. I were going with the lad I'd lived with for three years and with me being a prostitute, she automatically expected it to be me who gave him the dose. As it happened it were him who had screwed out and come back and give it to me. She wanted to see me and I went and saw her, an oldish woman, she turned round and said, "How do you think your husband (she didn't know one way or the other) is going to feel if you continue to go around with different men and keep coming back and giving it to him?" Well I've got a temper at the best of times, up went all the papers on the table, I stormed out and that in itself put me off 'cos it's not her place . . . she kept writing and she apologized and all this crap but it just put me off her. They have got a young one who I did see and she is OK. Business is business, fair enough but when they get nosy. It's like with social security—it puts me off going up there. When they want to know *how* a child is conceived and in *whose* bed it was which is what they do. To me it's irrelevant if you are claiming for kids. Everything about sex is weird really. It's like with social security how they expect you to just not have a guy. I think you can have one staying either one or two nights. But common sense should tell them it's just not going to work. If they find out now that this bloke is staying four or five nights. He doesn't give me any money, he signs on. . . .

'I don't want to be soliciting in ten years' time. If there was something which interested me I could work. . . . Anne keeps on pushing me to go to nightschool to study design but I don't think I'm ready for that yet.

'Some guys will come here for us to dress them up like women, which they have never told their wives. You approach a car and get in and he's sat there in suspenders and stockings

which is something he wouldn't do at home. It's like when they
want oral sex; they turn to us for something different. I think
marriage would be such a bore if there weren't something
outside somewhere. I think there would be more busted
marriages if there weren't something somewhere on the side,
whether you pay for it or not. Your punters vary, I've got one
who has never screwed a woman in his life and he's nearly 30.
He's a nice bloke, he comes here and if his mum knew what he
was into she would drop dead, heart attack on the spot. 'Cos
he's all goody-goody as far as his mum is concerned . . . he
says I look like a female wrestler and this is what turns him
on. . . . I prefer to do 'em here, if you get a funny customer
you can control things better than in a car.'

Probation Officer 3

This officer and her prostitute client have already been referred to
(p. 20).

'When she's going to court she lets me know and I feel I am
now working through a system whereby she comes out of prison
and we are working back through the fines, probation,
suspended sentences and imprisonment routine. . . . We put it
to the courts and said, "Look you can't expect a probation
order on a prostitute to be worked out in the normal way. We
wouldn't want you to think that when we take them on a
probation order that we are doing it with a view to stopping
them committing offences, we are doing it to stop them from
going to prison" and they said "OK". That's the name of the
game. I think that the only sort of constructive social work, if
you like, the type I am doing is working with her mother and
her father to a certain extent because her mother has worked
through from being appalled at being unable to control her
daughter and then shocked and ashamed and then extremely
worried through the stage where she felt she had to decide in
herself whether she was going to continue the relationship or
she could say she can't take any more and, "I don't want to
know you." She wanted to maintain the relationship and in
order to do that she has had to adapt her ideas and feelings
about prostitution and she uses me as a sounding board for
doing that. . . . My own feeling is that prostitution should not
be imprisonable. I'm a bit ambivalent about whether or not it
ought to be legalized. I certainly don't think they should be
"going down" for it and I feel I'm into a protective game in
collusion with the courts almost. The magistrates will deny
that, because they are subject to a series of sanctions.'

We have heard from some prostitutes and social workers about each other. Both see themselves working with or for clients. Sometimes their boundaries may become diffused. I met Liz, who had just returned from court where she had been fined £175 for soliciting. She was very upset and angry and unsure of her immediate plans. A young woman probation officer asked somewhat coolly, 'Where are you going to stay tonight Liz?'—'For £10 I'll come back with you'.

Interim conclusions

The emotive charge in the word 'prostitution' is diffused by considering the women quoted in this section. The impression is of working women, usually with children and sharing all the financial, environmental and emotional handicaps of such people in our society. In addition they face the constant threat of prosecution and imprisonment. We have also noted that it is traditionally women, or rather 'girls', who are seen, inaccurately, as the perpetrators of this crime.

As working women their jobs are sometimes involving and sometimes not, for it's clear that the clients and women do at times achieve something other than just a business transaction.

The prostitutes' views of their probation officers seem to be most favourable when a very close relationship is achieved—Mary: 'Could you invite them to a party?' Angie had heard about her probation officer's own sex life and Diane knew about her officer's background and saw her husband and children as also involved in helping her. Trust is seen as taking a long time to build up by both parties.

The relationship between Diane and Anne is long-term, hard-won and on a very personal level. Both appear to understand the rules within which they operate and both appreciate that these are bent on occasions for some such purpose as keeping Diane and her children together. They don't appear to agree on the scope for social work intervention beyond the criminal aspects of prostitution. What is agreed upon is the strength and purposefulness and dynamic of the relationship that has been built up between them. The openness with which Diane discussed many aspects of her life with me can be seen as part of a testament to the trust in that relationship.

Angie articulated the dilemma for probation officers as being 'half on our side and half on the courts'. The officers seem to have achieved an understanding with the courts that the purpose of a probation order was not the prevention of soliciting but rather to concentrate on the social problems of the women involved in the work. For most of these probation officers, social change by the decriminalization of prostitution was viewed as desirable but none made any active attempts to unionize the women in order that pressure would be brought to change the law.

It is difficult not to leave this section without feeling that the probation officers are involved in a 'protective game in collusion with the courts almost', as Probation Officer 3 puts it. It is an area of work in which the maintenance of role distance is under obvious pressure and it is necessary for the women and the officers to move beyond stereotypes of each other's role if anything useful is to be achieved.

Angie's suggestion that the officers should bring the women together to discuss major common problems may point to one future direction for social work in this area. Other probation officers in England are among a group of people helping to organize prostitutes into union activities with decriminalizing soliciting as a priority aim. The National Association of Probation Officers has also adopted this aim.

D   Other manifestations of sexual conduct: exhibitionism, fetishism, transvestism, transsexualism

Probation Officer 3

'A case of indecent exposure which was transferred to me from another officer. The person concerned was married and on his second probation order for indecent exposure.'
'Presumably it was the usual few feet away and there was never any threat?'
'Yes. He is in his early 20s. I looked at the case when it came to me and I saw the officer who had had it before had chosen positive non-intervention and seen relatively little of him. He told the guy that he was going to do this and said that his confidence had been knocked enough and that he didn't want to be on his back all the time which would have reinforced this by analysing him all the time. He'd had a bit of contact with the wife and sort of checked that situation out and then had not seen him for several months. His wife was about to have another baby. I thought, "I've picked this case up and I ought at least to make contact." I phoned them up and made an appointment which they cancelled and so I made another. They were rather surprised and not wanting to know. They were very happy the way they had been going before. The wife phoned me back and said that she was going into hospital this week to have this baby and it'll be difficult for me to come down. I said OK and explained that I just wanted her to know who I was. It was a new order, it was only six months then. The order is still

running. I told her that I was her new probation officer, "I want to meet you and don't want to change things." She said OK and I've not been in contact since. I can rationalize to a certain extent about not getting in contact. I couldn't to my employers. . . . I think what it's about really is "indecent exposure". I just don't have a first notion of what I would do with him. I think I cross my fingers and say there's a child in there now, he's proved his potency with his wife. Stand back and see what happens and if he does it again, I'll worry! . . . This is my first case of indecent exposure.'

Probation Officer 6

'A man in his early 20s, single, living with parents, tended to indecently expose himself now and again without knowing why. Everything else about him was satisfactory. I tried very hard to talk about this area because it was the only one which caused him any concern and got him into trouble and was potentially the area which would cause breakdowns in relationships . . . he didn't want to talk about it, called it "that mucky thing" he did . . . towards the end of the probation order he got a girlfriend and he talked about his [sexual] relationship with her . . . as far as looking at sexual problems there was little overtly said but we made a relationship and discussed things and he was very co-operative. . . . I was trained as a psychodynamically equipped and organized caseworker and so this sort of problem was a great one for me to look at at these levels . . . the tension was that he wouldn't let me play my game but I was happy to play his after a while.

'His parents were in their late 60s and they saw him as being punished for this thing and so his regular contact with me was part of the attitude that so long as that was happening everything would probably be all right. They didn't want to talk about it at all. He hasn't reoffended again as far as I know.

'A more difficult one was a 14-year-old. He used to stand in his maisonette window when his parents were out and expose himself to people going by. He used to make an effort, standing on chairs and tables so that people had a full view of him. He has done this twice, once for which he was placed under supervision and once during it. Again he hasn't reoffended. I see him as a very confused adolescent, quiet, fairly withdrawn with very caring parents but there wasn't a lot of communication but things never got violent at a verbal or physical level. I really did want to talk about the way he thought about things sexually, he was at a good age to look at these things. But he just clamped up, he became upset, looked away. I remember discussing it at great length with my senior—what else could I do to help him look at this—but it was quite clear I was trying every method of *personal* help—laying off for a few weeks, then trying to introduce it gradually, being a bit ruthless at times . . . but he would never discuss this with me. His parents were very co-operative and wanted to look at it in terms of their relationship with him and talked about sex; what they felt he was getting from school and the media and so on but in particular their relationship with him . . . so it was a good casework case. . . .

'Almost certainly in view of the nature of the subject matter I probably thought that if they were going to discuss it it would be with one person who they could trust and that was in the casework sense going to be me, so I condoned a perception of privacy which would be required if they were going to talk. I think if I'd had half a dozen on my caseload at the time, the possibility of a group might have hit me.

'There was a bloke in his early 30s. A lot of identification here because he was my age throughout the lengthy period I knew him. He stole women's underwear and then masturbated into them. As far as I know, he never wore them but they used to really turn him on. This was worrying because his marriage had broken down as a result of these offences. It happened in a pattern—he was convicted for this offence every three years for nine years. . . . As a relatively new probation officer when I got him, the whole thought of this sort of offence interested me, purely as a voyeur if nothing else . . . there were questions about if he should have access to his children. He was very much more open about what he did, what came over him when he got depressed. But again, we had to look at his depression generally, usually breakdowns in relationships, rows with women when he felt the need to do this. . . . He had to steal worn knickers—he was done for burglary, breaking into a flat for this purpose.'
'You don't remember suggesting he could get hold of such things without stealing them?'
'No, I don't remember suggesting that. . . . He was made the subject of a probation order plus medical treatment . . . he was assessed as possibly suitable for treatment involving being given electric shocks whilst being shown pictures. He was discharged from hospital after six weeks . . . he apparently then led a reasonable life, then right at the end of his probation order, he did it again. . . . Whilst the aversion therapy was on I supported him as he didn't like it. I said "well it might do you

some good", sort of thing. . . . He was far happier to talk
about how depressed he felt about the way his marriage had
broken down and what led up to it, his relationship with
women, all good-quality stuff to look at without ever directly
looking at his involvement with the actual offence.'

Probation Officer 7

'A 31-year-old man, about to be paroled, in prison for burglary,
marriage broken up although ex-wife still in contact, they have
one child. Long record of offences, previous probation orders.
His ex-wife was having an affair with a student teacher and was
writing to tell him this whilst he was in prison. In prison he
told the welfare officer that he had been a transvestite and this
was really the reason why his wife was divorcing him. . . . He
presented the problem to me in prison of being a transvestite.
I must confess it floored me a little bit, I just wasn't sure what
to say to him. Because I wasn't sure if it was a problem for him
because he was in prison and it had emerged or if he genuinely
saw it as something he wanted to clear up. If it could have been
accommodated within his marriage then it might not have been
all that much of a problem, whereas in prison it would have
been—he would have been bashed up for it. . . . He seemed to
view himself as some kind of complete outsider because of it.
His wife had said some particularly nasty and cutting things to
him. I spoke to the welfare officer and wondered if it might be
helpful for him to go to a psychiatrist about it. He was quite
interested in some form of therapy. I felt I was underskilled
when he came out with this—you know, where do I take the
conversation from here? I don't think it was an inability to cope
with that kind of information. He gave it to me in a fairly open
manner, didn't seem all that embarrassed and I felt myself
reassuring the man, and offering him some sort of comfort, like
him being ill or something. Strange really, I just felt that I
could have handled that situation better. I was conscious that
the interview was a one-off, probably for a couple of months.
. . . I referred the matter on. Whether I thought it was to
someone more specialized or whether I just didn't want to talk
about it. Certainly I didn't feel quite sure what to do with the
information he was giving me.
'I don't see that I have to stop him . . . but if he is grossly
unhappy and cannot reconcile himself to it then I think we are
going to consider if he can stop, simply so he doesn't have all
the guilt to cope with, that seems to be the real problem—the
after-effects. . . . I wonder if he had some sexually fulfilling

143

relationship if there would be the need to indulge in that—I just don't know. . . .

'One thought which does occur to me is that we do seem to be the agency who has contact with people who commit sexual offences and it might be helpful to have some sort of self-help group set up . . . we are very busy setting up self-help groups for addicts and alcoholics.'

'C'   Roy was 14 when he was placed in residential care for breaking and entering with intent to steal. The staff had a hunch that there was more than appeared on the surface concerning his offences. The officer-in-charge and his wife (their details are given on p. 74) described how they felt 'he had a feminine side to his nature'.

Officer-in-charge: 'There was something very wrong. We researched back into the family history and found that his father had been convicted of attempted rape. We had to reassess why he was in care and our aims were then to see if we could help him come to terms with the problems his environment had produced. . . . It took 12 months before he was able to talk to me. . . . [The problem was that Roy liked to dress in female underwear and had been using his sister's at home, breaking into houses for this purpose, and also occasionally dressing in staff or girls' underwear in the residential home.] We felt we couldn't help Roy on our own and this is why we called in a clinical psychologist, fortunately he was someone we could easily talk with. I don't think we could say that we hoped to cure him but we wanted this youngster to come as near to normality as possible. The single most important factor was that he wanted to overcome it himself. . . . He had used the delinquency to shadow it because of the sexual problem which had been at home when sex was never discussed in any way and because he didn't want to appear in any way to be abnormal in the eyes of his family. He considered what his father had done wrong and what he was doing was wrong . . . he had no normal sexual upbringing at all.'

His wife: 'There had obviously never been any show of affection at home, no demonstration from his mother. This first went to me and then to the other female members of staff. He behaved as you would expect a 5- or 6-year-old to be in wanting cuddles, to be held.'

Her husband: 'When he did appear in court we had arranged the treatment. Roy had agreed to it and we put it to the magistrates, we wanted him to stay at our home during this.

... We got full co-operation from the police and the
magistrates. . . . People in the wider society do not have the
slightest idea of the type of problems with which we are
dealing. So many of them still see us as having little children
who are orphans, nowhere to go.

'At the end of the treatment, the psychologist wasn't
prepared to guarantee a cure. All he would say was that there
was sufficient of a relationship that if Roy found these very
powerful urges returning he felt that he would return to him. He
talked of channelling these into socially acceptable avenues
rather than unacceptable. . . .

'He did in fact take himself back to the psychologist when he
broke up with his girlfriend. . . . He had told the girlfriend
about his problem, and I think she was more understanding
than her parents were. . . . On one occasion when the children
were all using the same bedroom and the dirty laundry was all
in one basket, one evening fairly late Roy had come down and
attired himself in a girl's dirty linen. Unfortunately one of the
more disturbed boys caught him and made quite a thing of it. I
think we certainly searched ourselves as to instead of keeping it
to ourselves we should have discussed it a little more with the
children. We shouldn't have allowed this situation to happen.
It's difficult for these kind of problems not to become common
knowledge in a home like this . . . we find that contrary to
popular belief, children in care are very understanding of
others' problems. . . . Informally there has been quite a lot of
group therapy in this type of problem in the house.'

'C' When I met him Roy was 18. The interview took place in the
children's home, although in private. Roy was living with his
parents, there was some suggestion that he was unemployed at that
time. He still visited the home frequently and there was no doubt as
to the mutual affection between him and the staff. It should be
noted that Roy apparently found it difficult to verbalize his thoughts
and feelings although he had volunteered to discuss this no doubt
still sensitive area of his life. My interviewing style on this occasion
did little to help Roy.

'When I was in court, they gave me a care order, I thought I
was allowed to go, I didn't realize I had to go in care myself. It
didn't click until my social worker grabbed me and said "you're
coming with me". . . . I was told by the houseparents that I'd
be in care until I was 18. It seemed a long time then but it
went quicker than I thought. On the first day I came here, I
ran away and was brought back. After that I was all right.'

'Could you have been helped not to come into care?'
'I could have helped myself to stop myself but I was too
embarrassed to tell them at the time. . . . They could have got
me a psychiatrist early on to help me.'
'Was your problem just breaking and entering?'
'Yes, but getting in and what went on inside the house was
entirely different. . . . I would go breaking and entering, do
what I had to do and get out quick as I could. . . . Funny
enough sometimes I felt terrible about doing it, other times I
was fairly happy to do it. . . . Mostly it was the fact that was I
going to get caught or not. . . . Me father knew about the
problem 'cos I used to do it to my sister but he didn't say
anything. . . . I found it a bit harder to talk to a lady social
worker than a male. I would find a male social worker would
be more on my side so I could talk to him better because they
are the same as me.'
*'Really, outside social workers haven't been very important in
your life—who has been?'*
'Barbara and Tony [officer-in-charge and his wife], I have been
able to talk to them since I came here about most things, they
have given me a lot of courage. . . . They go deep into it before
they see you, whatever you have done, they talk to people first
to find out about it, then they talk to you, see what you have to
say.'
'How far back did your problem go before 14?'
'About a year and half. Looking back now to 14 I must have
been mad, I had a lot going for me at home and I chucked it
all in really. . . . I've got a good job now, I'm all right, I've got
something to take my mind off everything now.'
*'If you hadn't had the help you had, do you think you would
have grown out of it?'*
'No, definitely not. I've had all the help I need. If I'd stayed as
I was who knows, I'd have probably been inside. . . . There
would have been no one there to help me—me father wouldn't
have—it would just have been a belting, that was it—forgotten
—and I would have just carried on and on. . . . Talking to
Barbara and Tony was the main thing, I couldn't talk to people
at first. . . .'
'So what was it additionally which the psychiatrist did for you?'
'*Treatment*, I needed treatment and nobody else could give it to
me apart from the psychiatrist. He was the nearest one to me,
he could get hold of the equipment that was needed fairly
quickly. So we thought we'd try him. Tony had been to see him
and he seemed a good bloke so we went from there. He talked
to me, near enough from birth, well at the age of 11-12, right

through, family life, everything. It was taking bits off my mind, I was worrying quite a lot, I'd then forget about them—they were being dealt with, seen to. We were getting through to me what was wrong, what was right, what to do and what not to do. He gave me a lot of advice, so did Tony and Barbara. . . .

'None of the kids in care talked about our problems. It's one thing we've never really done. The odd one or two may be proud of it but the rest keep quiet about it.'

'Would you plan on telling people you got close to in the future the problem you had?'

'No, I wouldn't tell them. I told my ex-girlfriend. It took me one and a half years to tell her. We were going through a bit of a rocky moment, she wanted to know why I was in care so I told her and that was it. We split up. She had heard so many stories; that I'd raped someone, that I've broken into the Post Office. . . .'

'What things [about relationships] still puzzle you?'

'Girls, I don't know [why] they always have, it's one of the things I never looked into. . . .'

Probation Officer 10

'One of my students a couple of years ago had a client who was a male transvestite, married with children, whose wife had deserted him and he was coping with bringing up the children and with his transvestism. I did discuss with my student the possibility of referring him to one of the self-help organizations but the client didn't feel that was necessary. I felt he was a very isolated transvestite, as far as one could gather and his offence was stealing ladies' clothing from clothes lines. He had other commitments bringing up his children, etc. which took up a hell of a lot of his time. He was doing very well at it and this was with the approval of social services. He was also seeing a psychiatrist and the client didn't feel at that point any need for contact elsewhere. I think probation officers and social workers are reluctant to share this sort of client. There is a sort of feeling of this is really an interesting type of case and I'll keep this one to myself. I think we are all at times voyeurs and want to learn something about the client's private life. The other problem is that social workers would have fantasies about the nature of the organization' (he goes on to discuss PIE, see p. 87).

Probation Officer 11

'My personal value system says to me things like, a transvestite or a transsexual, I would feel OK, fair enough, that's their right, they can do what they want and isn't it terrible that people put them down and I try to be as sympathetic as possible and yet I sort of think, well it's a bit of a peculiar society we live in, in that when we are trying to get rid of gender-roles, they want to change from one set to the other. Maybe that's just something they have to go through in order to find themselves.'

Interim conclusions

Indecent exposure 'as a problem' does not appear to evoke a particular response so much as the criminal record or age or social circumstances of the perpetrator. The probation officers consider possibilities ranging from radical non-intervention (or benign neglect) to aversion therapy, casework, group work. There are again descriptions of the difficulty in clients *talking* about the actual problem behaviour. In the case of Probation Officer 7 the inhibition was the officer's in dealing with transvestism. Lack of knowledge would appear to be his difficulty. He says he would consider some kind of therapy. Aversion therapy was seen as the treatment method of choice in Roy's case. His problem could be assessed as breaking and entering, fetishism, transvestism, fetishistic transvestism, transvestic fetishism or the effects of his family background. How much any of these labels should properly be attached to a 14-year-old boy is probably the most important question illustrated by this case, alongside a consideration of the implications of the particular treatment method. However, it was not just aversion treatment but relationships which clearly mattered to Roy. Like Fred (p. 78-9), he seems to view his behaviour as a 'sickness'.

Roy's 'problem' could also be viewed as the reaction of 'helping people' to an example of different sexual behaviour. Probation Officers 6 and 10 both refer to voyeur responses by social workers. There is belief in some responses in this section that the problem sexual behaviour would disappear if some 'normal' aspect of sexuality was found satisfying.

In respect of transvestism, Probation Officers 7 and 10 consider the use of self-help groups. Probation Officer 11 has a radical perspective on transvestites and transsexuals which comes from his views on adhesion to gender-roles.

Because of some general confusion appearing in the responses in a number of areas reported in the study, it is necessary here to distinguish between homosexuals and transvestites. The latter cross-dress in order to obtain sexual gratification but they may be heterosexually or homosexually orientated. The transvestite is usually seen as male in our society and it may be that female transvestites are either not so visible because of fashion or that social attitudes to dress in particular and women in general make female transvestism a less meaningful activity for women.

Both homosexuals and transvestites should be distinguished from transsexuals who feel trapped in a body which is for them of the wrong sex, and help may be sought through surgery. The transsexual should also be distinguished from the hermaphrodite who at birth has physical manifestations of being of both sexes (see Green and Money, 1969; Money and Ehrhardt, 1972).

E   Where sexual conduct is apparently a secondary issue

Probation Officer 12

'Especially with younger males there is always a sexual element. It isn't very deep but it's there and can be quite useful. I've found that 19-to-20-year-olds do relate more easily to a woman . . . you can sort of adopt this flirty attitude and it helps the relationship.'

Probation Officer 6

'It's very clear that women will use male probation officers to work out all sorts of things. One terrific case was when a woman went through the whole relationship with a man before dropping me. She was up for a first offence, burglary. Had a shocking relationship with her husband. Being flirty for the first few months—as that went on she said, "When you're coming up again, why don't you come after 9 o'clock when it's dark?" I told her, "No and you know why." After about six months it turned into a sort of nagging relationship . . . a recognizable relationship with one's wife. And then gradually she went off me and I felt we had achieved what it was like to be 45 and married to the same person. And then she dropped me, got another bloke, came in and said can you get my probation finished. . . . I don't consciously think or state any values attached to sexual behaviour. No doubt they do colour my perceptions. I can't remember a time when I felt revolted or pleased. I suppose that if a lad comes in and said he's made it with his first girl then I express a pleasure at that, taking it back to my first experience. . . .

'It's been an experiential thing of saying I'm a probation officer, I know I sympathize with minority groups and in the end I do it, but I don't know how you would teach that. . . . Sexual offences and those against young children make it socially acceptable for even social workers to be revolted.'

Probation Officer 15

'A man in his early 30s is on probation for arson. . . .
Throughout the supervision he gradually formed an attachment
to me and started writing me love letters. It was very difficult
for him to talk about it face to face. . . . When faced with the
idea that his expectations of this are unrealistic he breaks down
very quickly and says the letters were just written in a mood of
depression and he doesn't mean anything but I think that all
his life the only women have been his mother and sister and
now suddenly because of his involvement with a court, being
put on probation—he has been given a woman probation
officer. . . . I think he could be hurt very easily. . . .
I think people are very loathe to talk about their private
intimate relationships, and why not! There is very little that is
protected from the prying probation officer.'

Probation Officer 1

'I should have lots of moral views . . . but I'm so non-
judgmental now I sometimes surprise myself. I have a code
which is *mine*. . . . Having been a confirmed bachelor it was
like discovering a new world . . . experiences of being married
and having children. If I hadn't had them I'd be a lot less of a
person than I am. I used to imagine as a celibate that I could
think myself into these experiences and empathize. I now
realize that's virtually impossible. The real thing is so different
from the imagined or reasoned thing.'

Probation Officer 3

'If a woman is dealing with a male offender then you get into
the male-female dialogue and tensions between worker and
client. The client usually wants to sound you out and know who
you are as a woman. The articulate client can do that verbally
and probably quite subtly. The inarticulate client is going to do
it non-verbally and probably not so subtly. How do I respond to
that? . . . "Do you understand what I really mean or do you
think I'm giving you the 'come on'?" and it's common to all
cases, not just sex offenders.'

We have already mentioned (pp. 52) a case of Probation Officer 5,
who attempted to discuss possible homosexual feelings with a
teenage client.

Probation Officer 9

'I think I steer clear of sexual areas now more than I used to when I finished training. I approached some middle-aged couples and got negative feedback and possibly also because of my age [29] and that people know I'm single.'

Probation Officer 4

'There is a general assumption among the people I talk to, both men and women, that I'm married, that I have two if not three children. Probably that I love my wife even and that on the whole I'm a figure of moral rectitude and correctness but sort of openminded about it. . . . A lot of my clients like me to be like that. For one thing it means that I'm happy. Another that it means I'm fairly conventional and boring. For some it sums up certain aspirations. Also it confirms a morality, which is common across many of our clients, which is pretty strict. When people talk about their own sexual conduct in marriage there are things which are assumed to be wrong even down to husbands fancying birds outside. It is assumed that I believe that it is wrong . . . people assume I'm sitting on very safe ground . . . however open-minded I am they assume that's where I stand. It may say something about me, it may also say something about probation officers and divorce court welfare officers.

'I work by getting generally close to my clients . . . with the lads I like to see them growing up and getting on and getting off with lasses. . . . I don't see clients as prospective sexual partners any more than I see colleagues (with certain notable exceptions who know about it!). . . . I'm certainly not what you'd call a promiscuous sort of person so in that sense people's perception of me is pretty right. I'm sure that at different times, different clients (I'm not talking about sex offenders now, just people) obviously go through what in one set of values you'd call "transference". In my sense people get quite affectionate, feel quite warm about me, that's OK. I use that and I like to use any warmth I feel towards them. . . . For a large number of people if you are not leaping on top of people that's not sex. What these incest things bring to light is in some ways how fine boundaries are between one way of loving someone, one way of feeling drawn to someone and another. A lot of it is about setting boundaries. This could be important in the long term with incest cases. . . . There seems still to be an attitude in society that you can *do* something to people who are

151

sexually aberrant. Like give 'em the tablets—like the old lady
who came into the office aged 80-plus and her husband was
making excessive demands and she was wanting to know if they
had any of them tablets that they used to have in the war—God
bless her . . . it's a misconception of what sex is. That it's in a
box, "the sex department of the human being". It also tends to
have its own rules which are quite separate from normal
healthy bodily rules.'

Probation Officer 8

'I am an Evangelical Christian. People would expect you to be
puritanical and in one sense I am as a standard. I would
imagine my morality standard to be higher than the average
man in the street. At the same time, I feel I've quite a
sympathetic understanding, especially of homosexuals. It's very
difficult. You try to understand without condoning or
condemning. I personally don't think God intended us to be
homosexual but I do accept there is a feeling or condition
whatever you call it defined homosexual. I don't think they
differ from the heterosexual in morality in that they should not
be perverted.

'I personally would want to discourage any physical sexual
acts outside marriage and the family. One of the problems of
this job is very rarely do you see a *Christian* family. . . . I
certainly find it very difficult in that what I want for this person
and what he is may be poles apart. At the same time I have to
accept I have no right to change him, although I want him
changed. [See also pp. 84-5 regarding this officer's views on
juveniles.]

'I did counsel a girl in prison who had had one abortion and
was considering another. I tried to put over all the alternatives
and she asked me what I thought and I said I was against
abortion and explained why on ethical and Christian grounds.'
*'What about clients knowing in advance about social workers'
views? Was it like the middle class generally finding their
professional advisers by personal recommendation?'*
'Clients we deal with either like or dislike their probation
officer, GP, or social worker. There is a certain amount of
understanding [about their personal qualities], it's not on an
intellectual level or on the same level of perception; they like or
dislike more on the way he presents himself rather than what
he believes, more on personality rather than evidence.' [See this
comment in relation to Andrew below.]
'How much is your sexual experience and interests important?'

'To be single and Christian I find very difficult, particularly in
this sexual area. The sexual side of life is greatly emphasized in
our society. . . .
'C' 'Andrew is 29. I'm currently preparing a report on him in
respect of two charges of stealing. He is a confessed homosexual
and in 1974 served two years for gross indecency and buggery
with a man in a mentally handicapped hostel. He attributes his
current offences to his unemployment which he says is partly
caused by discrimination against his homosexuality. He also
says he is lonely as a homosexual and in this depressed state he
committed the offence.
    'I go along with his evaluation to some extent. . . . I see him
as very manipulative. He wants to be put on Community Service
and probation because he feels I can help him with his
problems. He was on probation in 1969. Last time the officer
said he wasn't very co-operative and he didn't think supervision
had great value for him. From the records he didn't seem to see
any forward change. The word selfish appeared. In a sense he
was using the probation service. . . . I feel he is quite an
intelligent, articulate fellow who has been able to express his
problems to me in some depth. I'm not sure I can help him
that much to understand himself. He has got quite a good
understanding of himself. One of the problems is that he has
admitted to being scared stiff of going to prison again which is
understandable, given the homosexual side of his nature—they
have quite a rough ride in prison.'
'C' Andrew: 'I was first put on probation for stealing. I didn't
react to it very well at first. I didn't understand what I was
supposed to do and I wasn't then very good at talking to
people. Now, seven years later, I've learnt a lot about people
and I'm more sure how they could help me. . . . I felt that the
probation officer would accept me but whether they would like
dealing with me was another thing. One of them had to speak
about homosexuality but I thought he was only speaking out of
politeness to me rather than in actual fact he was interested in
it and thought it may have had some effect on my life. . . . I'm
sure he wanted to change me but obviously that's impossible.
You have only got aversion therapy and that's not a hundred
per cent. I'm sure that someone's view that you are homosexual
and ought to be heterosexual is just ridiculous. Whatever he
said could not have altered me. Before I went into prison I
went to have aversion therapy but really to swing it my way to
avoid going to prison. Also I was confused and I thought
maybe I could avoid going to prison and come out straight. But
if I dig deeply I suppose I didn't really want to change. . . . I'd

had a relationship with someone at the hospital where I was working which was completely wrong. . . . One of the patients noted I had been buying this certain person gifts and he reported it. The person involved was interviewed and he said he had had sex with me. . . . In prison the welfare didn't discuss homosexuality—(a) they didn't want to know or else (b) they weren't experienced enough to deal with such things. Although I did see a psychiatrist in prison and went through various things with him. . . . One of the social workers did ask me how I felt about mixing with other prisoners who had done so many other crimes. . . . I didn't have much faith in social workers in prison anyway, they seem to be ordered about by those in charge of the prison. . . . I saw a probation officer after I left prison who was helpful, apart from just talking about it he said the obvious thing that he didn't want it to happen again. Obviously I didn't. He gently brought it into the conversation, then got on to another subject and then would no doubt come back to that later on. As for remembering what he said, I can't but it was helpful whatever he said. . . . Obviously he mentioned things like you don't go with blokes under 21 . . . but I think he asked me if I did have a relationship . . . I did have, earlier for eighteen months but that ended. Of course I spoilt all that by being somewhat promiscuous myself. If I found someone who was attractive I wanted them as well although I did want to stay with this one person because I loved him. Now I don't think I've any love left in me for anyone in particular, I'm sure I haven't.

'I got into trouble last year over a possible fraud situation and I rang up and arranged to see the same probation officer again of my own accord. . . . The current probation officer—I think he just accepts me for what I am, as a homosexual. Whether he approves or not, only having had two interviews I wouldn't like to say. He doesn't seem against people who are gay and he would obviously help people as much as he could. I think he is a little inexperienced, in relation to gay people. It's just an *impression* I got. He has probably not met many people who are gay. I think he is a good probation officer. I spoke about this with somebody else anyway beforehand. I like him because he is young which I think is helpful as he is more likely to have an understanding or accept it more. An older person might have Victorian ideas. . . .

'It would be very very interesting to know what a probation officer would think if paedophilia was legalized as gay people are. . . . He might think, "I've got children of 9 and 10 and I wouldn't want anyone interfering with my children, boys and

girls." I am totally against paedophilia. I think it's disgusting
really. . . .

'I know there are gay social workers and probation officers,
although they don't go shouting it around in social services . . .
it may help if they are gay in understanding a personal situation
but I wouldn't say it's something vital that needs to be there.

'From what little I've seen of this probation officer I think he
is a person of principles and standards. It's just the way he
speaks about things in general and how you should conduct
your life. . . . From first meeting social workers/probation
officers you don't really know them, they don't really know you
apart from hearsay or what they have read on sheets of paper
in front of them. By the second time I should have been able to
form an opinion probably as to whether you could trust and as
to whether that person's advice would be good advice and how
far to believe in what they tell you. . . . I think it's the way they
conduct the interview and certain things they ask you. Things
probably which you don't expect, they bring up something
which isn't totally relevant to what you are speaking about.
This would show that they are really interested in you as a
person. You are more than just a name and a number; they
want to help you.'

Probation Officer 4

'C' 'Kevin is happy, well he isn't, he's as miserable as sin but
loves every minute of it. . . . He's got personality problems.
When he was talking about a sex change, Dr X said, "You
have a maladjusted self-styled homosexual and after that you
will have a castrated maladjusted self-styled homosexual
pretending to be a woman." There's no problem about asking
him what he has done—one doesn't ask—it's private. His
sexual behaviour isn't a problem in itself. . . . I assume he
picks up 18-to-19-year-old lads . . . which is offending in one
sense but who's looking? . . . So many of my cases I'm dealing
with, sex is quite a distorted thing. . . . I'm quite interested in
Kevin's supposed homosexuality because some of the time I
don't quite believe it. . . . I just don't believe there is a section
of the human race that's homosexual and a section that isn't.

'I warm very much to Kevin, I like him very much and know
he is a pig and a fool and various other things but I like him
very much, we like one another and it's a good working
relationship. It's probably a bit different from the model of the
professional relationship that I was given when I was training
but it's a relationship which works, probably because I'm old

and big enough to set boundaries. Sometimes they are just lines that are unseen.'

'C' Kevin is 30, unemployed and he wants to work in an old people's home. He lives in an attic room where the interview took place. He has had a number of convictions connected with his homosexual and transvestite pursuits. He is currently on probation for stealing. He described how in the past he had taken four overdoses, been in prison 'for prostitution' and 'taken to the bottle'. He had also found his psychiatrist helpful in talking to—

'I asked him once if I could alter [his sexual orientation]. He said, "I wouldn't advise it, we could give you male hormones but it would be drastic, probably kill you if we did." At one time I wanted a family. . . . My brother is homosexual, he lives at home and me mother has more or less accepted it with him. But with me getting into trouble with the police, it's been bad for her.

'I've known this probation officer for five years . . . he comes here pretty regular. To me he is not like a probation officer, more like a natural human being. I had one probation officer who did me for breach 'cos I didn't go and see him one week. . . .

'When I was 22 I had an appointment to go and have a sex change done in London, Dr X gave me this, two of me mates had had it done. I really wanted to be a woman. Even two years ago he gave me a second appointment and again I didn't go. Soon as I left the psychiatric hospital I was bang on the bottle again. . . . Now I think at 30 it's too late. I should have been a lot better off with a sex change. . . . I should have wanted to settle down with someone, I should like an affair now but I can't get involved with people. . . .

'I was dressed as a woman, made a packet as a prostitute for twelve months, kept this bloke all the while. . . . I have a bloke comes now, he's nearly 60, it's just company, he brings a Chinese meal and asks me how's me food cupboard and puts me £20 on the table. . . . When I was in drag, a lot of blokes are that stupid it's a shame, before you get them back to the house, it were all over and done with in the car. . . .

'I still get depressed, the psychiatrists have only taken me in and dried me out. In a psychiatric hospital there is nobody you can talk to; married women and middle-aged housewives suffering with depression. In fact when I first went in I couldn't even talk to the doctor. He used to come on his ward rounds and you used to have to go and sit in this room and there were all staff—nurses, social workers, the bloody lot all sat round in this room and you have to sit in front of this desk and tell him your problems. It's virtually impossible. . . . Second time I went in there were two more homosexuals, one had slashed his wrists, only 21. The other couldn't accept his homosexuality. He worked for the government or something. I said, "You are stupid, you can't alter what you are, if they find out and you lose your job you have to get another" and I really helped this lad, he accepted what he was.

'I first realized it when I was 12 or 13. My first experience was when I was 13 with a school teacher. I used to go to his home for three or four years. When I was 15 or 16 I met this very rich chap. It was an easy life, I never used to have to work when I was young.'

'What is it about your probation officer makes you want to go on having him as a probation officer?'

'Well I think he's nice, I like him as a person, I think he's great. He is so easy-going. I've been up to his office once or twice and he has said, "Come on, we'll go for a beer and a sandwich". There's not many probation officers do that and not many who will come and visit you. . . .

'One old bag of a social worker I met in hospital, described me as the scum of the earth, mind you I was being aggravating what with the boozing.

'Whenever I've gone to court, my current probation officer has given me a good report. If it hadn't been for him and the psychiatrist's report this last time, I would have gone down.'

Brian is 50. He is a manual worker. Two years ago he had been on probation for a homosexual offence to Probation Officer 5:

'It was an offence for loitering. Previously I had been on probation for buggery. The other probation officer said that probation had been good for me so they made another order. I was wary of this second probation officer as he was younger and made it clear he didn't know much about sexual offenders. I was afraid he might think it was an illness which it is not. . . . Gradually he had a way of talking, getting it all out of me. There were times when he had to speak to me very seriously to pull me round, to give me confidence. I was afraid of losing my job, at my age, but although they found out my boss said that my private life was my own, provided I did my work. . . . Gradually the friendship actually happened. I wasn't just a number to him. . . . Obviously he wouldn't do anything like it himself but obviously he was an understanding person to realize

157

a homosexual has feelings and the actual sexual side I think he understood to a certain point.

'I'd been to my doctor to ask if there was any treatment to change me, he said no and as soon as I came to accept I was a homosexual the better it would be for me. . . .

'I thought probation was going to be a question of reporting, saying you were in work and where you lived. I didn't think there would be the welfare part at all. . . . After a while the authority didn't seem to be as severe as I'd anticipated.

'He suggested that CHE was going on in the country which I didn't know about. I told him I'd joined and he said that was a good thing. It was to keep me from going on the public conveniences. . . .

'I'm not saying he eventually does stop you. Let me make it quite clear that there are times now when I still go although I've been on probation. [For further discussion between Brian and myself see Appendix.]

'Just as my probation order was ending my relationship with a man broke up. I automatically went to see the PO. He could see I was heartbroken. He made it quite clear that I could see him any time. He would be the one person I would fly to. I look on him as a friend and I know he would be able to help.'

'C' *Probation Officer 2*

It is important also to read this officer's remarks concerning Charlie and the stereotyping of homosexuals (p. 17).

'One of the closest relationships I've had on probation is with Charlie, a homosexual, who isn't on probation for homosexuality —something like driving without insurance—but we have talked at length about the problems as he sees them of being homosexual. Mainly about the reaction of society and his feelings that it would be nice to be heterosexual then he wouldn't have to face what he feels to be people talking behind his back. I think we have had a very warm, close relationship in which I've been able to empathize a great deal with him. OK, I'm not interested sexually in men to the same extent as he is but nevertheless if he is talking about sexual attraction, I think I know what he is talking about. . . . I can feel fairly safe about him being attracted to me. . . . I think there is a little bit of paranoia in him anyway which gets focused on his homosexuality. . . . He was always in work, never out of a job for more than a day or two but he was always changing jobs. The reason was that being away from work he thought gave

them time to talk about him behind his back. . . . Gradually
letting people know he is homosexual and finding that a fair
number of those anyway are not disgusted by it but remain his
friends has been very important and far more therapeutic than
I have been to him.'

'C' Charlie is in his early 30s, a manual labourer. He recalls how
he was first placed on probation in 1962—at that time he had not
told many people about what he described as his 'bisexuality'.

'I had no intention of telling my probation officer but after a
couple of interviews he perhaps saw it in me and started
mentioning a couple of gay pubs or coffee bars in London but I
pretended not to know. But through little things that he said I
could tell he was gay. Then I went inside and during the time
I was there I suddenly had a visit from someone I didn't know
of who introduced himself as my new probation officer. With
tongue in cheek I asked him what had happened to my old
probation officer. He replied, "Oh well, he wasn't tempera-
mentally suited to the job and he left." Then over the next few
years I used to see the original one in town and various places
and we both admitted to each other that we were gay. As soon
as he wasn't my probation officer, it's funny but I could tell
him. Ages later when I was in prison again I met him. He had
ended up getting three years for things like indecent assault.
Anyway on appeal this was reversed to three years' probation. I
didn't keep it from him because it was against the law—in fact
I always trust probation officers. I imagine the same way that
people trust a priest, I feel I can almost tell them anything, on
the moral side and I don't think they would get on to the phone
and report me, even when it is illegal when people are under
21. . . . I don't tell the neighbours, relations or my mother with
whom I live, whereas I do tell my social friends about being
gay. My fear was that if I did tell a probation officer he might
put it in a report to help me and that might get in the papers
or the police might get to hear and they could put something
on me.
'Two or three years ago I got into trouble for some motoring
offences. Well I was living with this boy then. I more or less
thought I wasn't going to get into serious trouble again and
feeling that my relationship was going to last for ever, I thought
it was so obvious that I might as well mention it. And then I
was told that when I was going to be placed on probation it
would be with my current probation officer who of course I'd
known for about eight years off and on. Of course then there's

no point in hiding it or not speaking about it anyway with him.
Plus the fact that socially things have changed in the last few
years. He said to me that his impression of me had been so
mixed up with pills and crime and that sort of thing that sex
had been pushed into the background. It was a flippant thing! I
suppose I'd also exaggerate my contact with girlfriends to give
the impression that everything was all right in that respect. I
often felt that I'd bring the conversation around to the subject
but it got to the stage where I thought he'd feel I was a right
idiot for not mentioning it before. I'd got plenty of other
problems, I think he would have gone grey if he'd found out I
was gay as well. In respect of his attitude, I know that he's
trained almost not to be shocked but beyond that as a person
he seems such a placid calm sort of person; whatever his job
was I don't think he would have bothered anyway. . . . I think
he might have read between the lines beforehand but he
thought he wouldn't push it because it might put me off.
Actually if he had brought it up and asked if I had had any gay
experiences then I might have told him but I would have
added "Yes but this is just between me and you." . . . I'm not
quite sure whether having had gay experiences would help a
probation officer with gay clients. The first probation officer
obviously had had loads of experience but it didn't seem to help
him!

'I didn't like the first probation officer. He was a bit Uriah
Heep-like. I think liking is very important. Feeling you don't
want to let them down.'

Social Worker F

'A woman being treated in a psychiatric hospital. It had been
mentioned in her past medical notes about her identifying with
men and her masculine behaviour. She and I never talked
about sexual matters at all. Mainly because I felt that all her
problems had been gone over in great detail for so long that I
wasn't going to do the "new social worker bit" and start all
over again. I did also wish it hadn't been dealt with by social
workers in the past as that her femininity should be reinforced
all the time; that she should be praised for such manifestations.

'I think that [using sexual attraction] is often bolstering the
worker's security . . . more than doing something for the client.

'In the hospital where I worked there was still left-overs of
Freudian analytical attitudes. But I didn't generally meet it
head-on because of not feeling strong enough in a social work
organization to challenge the medical view. . . .

'There have been hassles about my orientation but it's easier now in my present job as the cards are on the table.

'I think that the worker's first- and second-hand sexual experience is very important in the way they handle cases. . . . I was involved in counselling a lesbian couple—just the fact that it took place—I was quite pleased that the psychiatrist was able to refer this. There were relationship problems, one was into drugs and the other into booze.'

Social Worker L

'I feel the need to be very controlling of [sexual responsiveness] with male clients. I feel the need for them not to pick up on that feeling from me and, therefore, because I do it with males, I do it across the board, although with females it's not usually there to be picked up on.'

Social Worker D

'It depends what you mean by sexual. I haven't felt any pangs of arousal for a client, but then I've only felt that in relation to the two primary relationships that I've had in my life anyway. But I do feel attracted to clients in a way that one could develop into a meaningful or sexual relationship and I'm quite happy about that. It may make me a bit tense because it may develop in a way in which I would choose it not to.

'If clients ask me who I live with I tell them. If they ask if I'm married I say, "No, I'm in a permanent relationship", and they usually say something like "Does he beat you up?" and I say that I live with a woman. The last time I said that to a client she said, "Oh Sue, you aren't a lesbian are you?" I said, "Oh yes I am." She said, "How terrible, you are so nice!" I said that we all have our different life-styles and that I didn't see hers as invalid, and that if I had any choice about the matter, I would rather she accepted mine. Next time I saw her she was perfectly OK with me. A few days later she saw me and my girlfriend and she came later to say, "Oh I saw your girlfriend, she looked quite nice you know." . . . But usually I don't come out to clients because of *time*. I really don't want to go through the hassle every time and it is a hassle every time.'

Social Worker E

'On my training course the students adopted so-called radical or liberal stances and so didn't consider the fact that I was

161

"bent" to be a handicap. One member of the group I know was called by her tutor a "bloody lesbian" at one point but I think he meant it as an insult and he was notorious for being an unpleasant individual in any case.'

Social Worker I

'I suppose I don't have very great respect for the law myself . . . the whole law pertaining to gay people is so unsatisfactory that it colours one's attitude to the law in general.'
Do you expect your course [CQSW; he was already qualified in residential work] *is going to equip you better to deal with matters of sexual conduct?'*
'I very much doubt if it will, I suppose experience will do that. I suppose I know very little about heterosexuality. I understand it but I don't experience it. . . . I suppose more to the point I understand very little about women's sexuality.'

Probation Officer 10

'I think one has to create a climate in the first instance and part of that is how the PO is seen before sexuality is talked about. If I am a cold, aloof military-type figure and say, "You use the words [to describe sex] you want to" I'm giving out two messages. . . .

'One of my students dealt with a social enquiry report on an unmarried man in his 30s charged with stealing a tube of lubricating jelly which to me straight away suggested he might be gay, he lived on his own in a bedsitter in the city centre. I might have been totally wrong but it's right for me to suggest to that student that the evidence suggested that the client might be gay. Equally one has to know the student. . . . I think one would advise the student to look at this if the client wanted and perhaps to think in terms of a period of supervision to help the client understand himself. I think it is wrong to assume the client may be homosexual, therefore the client is homosexual, therefore the client needs help, then offer probation. The danger is that one follows that linkage. But I think one of my first tasks is to help students question and assess situations, collect facts and this case is a good example, where the student needs to be aware of possibilities and maybe discard just as I need too. Otherwise I'm going to end up with students seeing homosexuality everywhere. . . . In fact the lubricating jelly according to the client was for the treatment of piles. . . . He also stated he was bisexual and that it wasn't a problem for him. The student thought that was so and it wasn't included in the report and the person was treated as a first offender and given a conditional discharge.'

Social Worker B

'If I walked into a house and a man said, "My wife and I have a sex relationship and tell me what you think, I lie on the floor and kiss her feet and she hits me over the back with a table leg." My response to that would be quite different from if I went into a house and a woman said, "My man comes home every Friday night and beats me stupid." That's to do with my morality . . . it's what I would call healthier and unhealthier relationships. I don't think in this society there can be totally healthy relationships because I don't think we live in a healthy society.

'There is such a lot one feels as a social worker and a homosexual. About the type of things you come up against from a wide spectrum of the population; from the general public, from your clients, colleagues, employers, agencies you deal with, and from yourself, the way you deal with your own self-oppression. It's trying to have all that integrated into a professional practice. . . . I would like my employers and social work as an institution to recognize that and make available as much resource as possible to enable as many homosexual people as possible to fulfil themselves.'

Interim conclusions

This section shows the workers to be generally aware of the presence of sexual elements in the casework encounter even if the primary aim was to deal with other matters. This is acknowledged by using sexual attractiveness as an aid in making a helping relationship (Probation Officer 12). This is not approved of by Social Worker F. There can be a somewhat stereotyped male-female role-play (Probation Officer 6). More problematic situations exist when the workers feel that the client is in love with them (Probation Officer 15) or will misinterpret the worker's interest as being a specifically sexual one (Probation Officer 3).

The ways of handling such meetings are seen to depend on a number of variables including the ease with which the workers handle their own sexuality (Probation Officers 4 and 2), the way the worker is perceived by the client (Probation Officer 4), the worker's previous experience of dealing with such matters (which may be a

163

negative one, Probation Officer 9), the worker's moral beliefs (Probation Officer 8). Sexual orientation seems to be important for the gay workers. Social Worker I mentioned lack of knowledge. Social Worker L felt he needed to be very controlling of his sexual responsiveness with all clients. However, as we have already noted, other gay workers saw their orientation as helpful in their work.

Andrew makes reference to his straight worker's possible lack of experience but knowledge and experience of being gay doesn't appear to be of crucial importance to the gay clients. Indeed it may be seen as a handicap (Charlie).

The client's views of a successful worker comprise: liking, being a friend, taking a thoughtful interest, being treated as more than just a number (mentioned by both Andrew and Brian), being a person within, yet additional to the officer of the court role.

Probation Officer 10 reminds us that creating an accepting environment prior to specific discussions of sexuality is important. Sexual orientation may be of little use in assessing a client's situation, either from the worker's or the client's viewpoint. Knowledge of sexual activity is not always considered to be appropriate by Probation Officers 4 and 15 because of respect for the client's privacy. A similar implication might be read into Probation Officer 2's remarks concerning the focus always being on sex offenders' problematic sex as opposed to their successful experience (p. 84). This has to be balanced against probation Officer 2's concern at not knowing about Charlie's sexual orientation during a relationship lasting several years. Charlie considered that he didn't want to bother the officer with problems and that knowledge about his orientation was best kept within a certain social group. There was also some indication that he wanted to ensure the information was kept away from the police. Changes in the law and social attitudes are important to consider alongside Charlie's personal changes. He believed wrongly that his Probation Officer had guessed about his sexual orientation. Probation Officer 2 clearly feels he should have been more perceptive but what would this have achieved specifically in Charlie's case?

Social Worker F reminds us of the negative effects of labelling clients with having certain problems of sexual identity.

If specifically sexual aspects of worker-client encounters impress as being of less importance than more general personal qualities, we have also to account for Social Worker B's belief that individual sexual orientation has political as well as personal status and as such should be integrated into professional practice.

The importance of 'coming out' is mentioned in relation to the organization by Social Worker F and with clients by Social Worker D. She also counts the personal costs of such ventures. It is worth noting the report of Social Worker E on the social work tutor's term of abuse for his student.

Probation Officer 8 has an ideal of morality which is daily in conflict with his work experience. His solution 'understand without condoning or condemning' is a familiar Christian one which does seem to work for Andrew at the social inquiry stage. The officer appears to underestimate Andrew's ability to assess him. Andrew's behaviour could be seen as rational rather than manipulative as the worker suggested. Andrew's articulate and conscious awareness of himself appears to be interpreted as a negative indicator for the usefulness of a probation order.

Probation Officer 8 is by implication without experience of sexual relationships. Probation Officer 1 has gone through a similar state, left it, and now sees himself as radically changed by personal experience, and able to compartmentalize his personal moral code from a general non-judgmental attitude.

Kevin has important things to say about his perception of hospital treatment and 'ward rounds', and of the short duration of the prostitute's career. He also illustrates the problems of labelling— prostitute, homosexual, transvestite, transsexual. Kevin and his probation officer agree on the special nature of their relationship and that for them it works.

On probation Andrew and Kevin would experience different attitudes to them having a sexual relationship with an 18- or 19-year-old male. Charlie considers that probation officers would not report such a situation. Brian was informed about a self-help group as a preventive measure in relation to law-breaking. Social Worker L mentioned (see p. 121) being personally at risk in respect of law-breaking as affecting a total attitude to the law. In this section Social Worker I makes similar comment about the effects of the law relating to gay people.

All the clients seem able to separate the court aspect of the officers' role from the person. It is also observable that the clients still experience interpersonal problems.

F The workers' training

I had intended this section to be concerned with how well the social workers and probation officers considered that professional training had equipped them in dealing with matters of sexual conduct. In fact none of the workers mentioned finding their basic training as being of any relevance specifically in the area of sexuality. On the other hand there were workers who, having completed a professional course, felt more confidence or a changed attitude and therefore more able to cope with clients' problems—including sexual ones. For example, although Probation Officer 12 considered her response to a client as 'perhaps it was above all training or logical thought' (p. 114), she considered that training taught her about relationships between parents and children and she was able to transfer that to a sexual conduct problem.

Many of the group could not remember sexuality being mentioned during training. Another noted a passing reference in relation to Freud. The workers had experienced qualification training from as long ago as twenty years to having left the course in the year of the interview. When sexuality had been on the curriculum, its relevance to practice had not been proven. For example, one probation officer referred to specific behavioural treatment techniques as having been taught in the area of sexual problems but the worker had not found such treatment to be appropriate for clients on the probation caseload.

Post-qualification training was mentioned frequently. This consisted of self-help groups, lecturing on specific problems of sexual minorities, personal life experience, marriage guidance training and, as we have noted, being taught by the clients.

Interim conclusions

These workers valued experience rather than specific qualification training in aspects of sexuality. We have therefore to understand the uses of knowledge before we decide on the content of education and training in social work and sexual conduct.

Part three

Conclusions and implications

Chapter 6

Conclusions and discussion of the study

Let us take the section on prostitution as a way of ordering, and inevitably reducing what may appear as rich in interest but unrelated accounts of the meetings of social workers and their customers.

Certain people become the clients of social workers because their sexual behaviour is seen both as different from, and a threat to, what is regarded as right conduct. It is believed that they still have some ability to choose although social or biological determinism is seen as explaining much of their behaviour. It is further believed that the effect of these pressures can be alleviated and the person may respond to such changing circumstances through the agency of a social worker. The result will be a prevention of further wrong conduct. To achieve this the social worker will have to find a way of influencing the offender. This has traditionally been through a relationship with that individual which goes further than considering the offending behaviour in isolation. As we have seen, the workers find that behind the label 'prostitute' are young, working women with little job security and only occasional job satisfaction. Sometimes they suffer organized and sometimes individual exploitation by men. Because of the nature of the work and the hours it entails, there are dangers to health and it is short-lived. Housing is a further problem for these women who are often single parents. The study shows that all these stressful circumstances are quickly appreciated by the workers who set about helping the women, often through years of difficulties. The relationships achieved are impressive but what are the results? There was general agreement that the offending behaviour—soliciting—was in no way changed by the social worker's efforts. Indeed there was an impression that such behaviour went on independently of the social work task except in the way the social workers attempted to protect their clients from the rigours of legal penalty.

The workers and the women saw quite clearly that, in addition to the personal problems involved, the social pressure on a prostitute came from the law and its interpretation by police and magistrates. None of the workers in the study saw it as their task to achieve the alleviation of this major social pressure on the women, with the important exception of informing magistrates that they would be unable to prevent soliciting.

Is this the appropriate stance for social work?

How far can we extend this analysis of a certain aspect of social work and sexual conduct to others?

In respect of sexual conduct such as exhibitionism, fetishism, transvestism (and transsexualism) we are not dealing usually with a way of earning one's living. These are more properly leisure pursuits in which the perpetrators do not usually come into contact with a recognizable 'victim'. (Rooth (1973) studied a group of thirty persistent exhibitionists and concluded that sexual violence was exceptional among them. He added that other sexual activities—paedophilia, hebephilia—were a feature of a comparatively high proportion of them. There were three cases of incest. He considered that we should not regard exhibitionists as a homogeneous group and that persistent may differ from occasional exhibitionists. Also in relation to exhibitionism we should not ignore the feelings of the women or children involved.) They are, however, disapproved of in the same way as prostitution. Instead of or in addition to the scale of punishments involved in the tariff system of justice, we have to consider the psychological, chemical or surgical treatments of such behaviour. Social workers are not unanimous in their attitude to psychological, or legally imposed treatment. The reason for their attitude to the psychological would seem to be that those people who have such sexual interests may wish to change or be rid of them. Workers who may themselves have been on the receiving end might wish to discourage certain treatment endeavours, both from the viewpoint of morality and efficacy. Outside such personal responses, social work has no guidelines to offer on treatment technology. The result is that some practitioners can take an active part in the giving of aversion therapy to a 14-year-old boy because he enjoyed masturbating in women's underwear. The facts that he wanted to change his behaviour and that he had other social problems are quite separate from the question of social workers' attitudes to manifestations of sexual secrets which are not dangerous to other people.

Another area where the behaviour is legally and morally ambiguous is under-age sexuality. As with prostitution, the major social problem for the 'customer' was the law and the administration of the law. The workers adopted a range of responses to such behaviour, attempting to argue against a chronological age of consent with magistrates, ignoring the illegality of the behaviour, considering reporting their clients' under-age sexual activities. The public uncertainty about a fixed, sexual moral code, separate legal evaluations of homosexual and heterosexual conduct, and differing organizational responses to precocious sexuality among boys and girls, gave scope for social workers to exercise moral and political judgments here, as did the previous aspects of sexual conduct discussed.

Within the context of a professional relationship, would one know as a client what these judgments and actions were likely to be? In respect of prostitution the answer from the study is probably yes—the worker would understand that soliciting was your major problem and would attempt to teach the magistrates about your plight (and his/hers in trying to change your behaviour). The worker would then try to negotiate a 'contract' with you to deal with your personal problems in respect of your total life-style and chances. The worker would not suggest you joined a union to decriminalize prostitution and would not do anything active to bring about that aim. But s/he also would be unlikely to report your soliciting to the police or the social security.

If you were discovered indecently exposing yourself, stealing underwear or dressing in order to assume another sex role, a range of judgments would be made dependent on the way each individual social worker assessed you as a person—your marital and family status, age, previous criminal history. It is not clear if the workers would regard the law as creating a problem larger than any personal difficulty which might be assessed as being relevant in your case. The worker might attempt to form a relationship with you which located your behaviour as being due to psychological causes. As we have seen, they might also consider a specific psychological treatment which attempted to change your behaviour. S/he might also consider you joining or even the formation of a self-help group.

If your 'problem' was under-age sexual activity, any of the foregoing stances might be adopted. Behavioural treatment or chemical treatment would only be likely to be recommended if the age gap between you and your partner was a large one. In this area the worker's moral and political views would be very important in deciding how s/he dealt with your behaviour. Imagine, for example, being a client of Probation Officers 8 and 9 (pp. 84-5) and having the same 'problem'—under-age sex. The treatment you received would differ considerably with each officer. You would have no way of knowing what judgments would be made before entering into the professional relationship. Would the gender of the worker give you some clue? It is possible that women with a radical, feminist analysis might attempt a process of conscientization to your low status and exploitation as a woman. Would the worker's sexual orientation be important? The gay male workers did show some alienation from legal rules which might have operational consequences. Perhaps this aspect of the worker's personality would be likely to have a visible effect in working with under-age sexuality. However, the study points to a range of responses in which sexual orientation was not a determining factor.

If we turn to paedophilia, we are dealing now with sexual conduct in which the idea of a victim in need of protection is a very strong one. Sexual orientation is an important fact to be taken into account. Straight social workers appear as morally disapproving the behaviour and presumably supporting its legal prohibition. On the other hand some gay workers had a psychological or political analysis which was sympathetic to relationships between children and adults and disapproving of legal prosecution. However, because of their status as recently and ambivalently rehabilitated sexual outlaws the gays were wary of being seen as 'child molesters' and therefore were likely to take a conservative stance in relation to advocating the goodness of such relationships. There is just an implication that the gay worker would be more likely than a straight colleague to turn a blind eye to paedophilia.

This book contains examples of behaviour where, as one worker puts it, it is 'socially acceptable for even social workers to be revolted'. Here the moral and legal attitude is unambiguous. What may we learn about the social work role from such cases? First, that the concern with the *individual* client suggested as being so important in all the social work literature and seen as a central tenet by the initial group of probation officers referred to on p. 70 does not always have an overriding status in the way these workers deal with matters of sexual conduct. Prostitution is the only area where the individual always seems to come first before organizational, legal or the workers' moral considerations. Other 'victimless' conduct has some variation in where the workers place themselves in the CLIENT-SOCIETAL-ORGANIZATIONAL-LEGAL configuration. The decision is not inevitably client centred. For example, in relation to Roy, 'we wanted this youngster to come as near to normality as possible'. The fact that Roy wanted 'treatment' after his problem had been 'discovered' by care-givers is a similar problem to the one we face with Fred, who is still seeking a cure for what other people have defined for him as his sexually deviant behaviour. In Fred's case 'victims' have been identified. The worker's response to Fred is a mixture of wanting to get alongside him, organizational and legal pressures, concern for the possible victims, plus his own views about sexual conduct. Hence his approach to Fred was not client-centred.

This is a major if unrecognized problem for the worker. It is possible to see such unclear encounters as partly explanatory of another finding of the study—the inability of many sex offenders to discuss their conduct with their workers.

The social worker is motivated by a mixture of political and personal reasons to be concerned with the individual. S/he is socialized on training courses to be suspicious of her/his motivations from both political and psychological perspectives, but nowhere is it suggested that the person is not the main focus of interest. Even if the client's welfare is to be achieved by structural social change, the evaluation of the goodness of that change would be for social work in terms of the gains and losses for individuals. Within such a socialization process, the bureaucratic structures in which the majority of workers will be employed are seen negatively—a work setting to be survived rather than enjoyed. Consideration of obligations to such social institutions as legal and welfare agencies are not given equal weight in the selection and training process of social workers. These are, however, the main providers of their practical work and later employment and are integral to every qualifying course in social work. Even if they are not recognized as having such a status in teaching about social work decision-making, the statutory and moral ideal functions of social agencies do pose a direct threat to the primacy of the individual.

To return to the people who were unable to discuss their sexual conduct with the workers. Given the above it is possible to see such muteness as entirely appropriate behaviour, a meeting of an internalization of social hostility, with a social worker who doesn't know his/her own mind let alone the client's. The social worker may believe s/he is client-centred and in some instances, as in prostitution this is obviously true. In other aspects of sexual conduct the client's needs are superseded by the worker's concern with personal views/ beliefs or organizational or legal constraints. In 'serious crimes' this may be a quite conscious decision—the worker is deliberately setting out to act as an agent of direct social control. In less ambiguous threats to the safety of others—as in under-age sexual conduct—the worker's evaluation is not so open, and respect for persons may be negated by a desire to protect people from themselves or maintain absolute standards of public morality. More personal views may also compete for recognition. What the study points to is that these evaluations are unknown by both parties prior to entering the client-worker relationship.

How do we account for the differing analysis of paedophilia between gay and straight social workers, but the lack of any clear-cut operational differences between the two groups towards a range of sexual conduct, including sex roles within and without such

173

institutions as marriage and the family? Simply that if the study has any validity then it shows that a concentration on sexual activities or preferences is of lesser importance than understanding the roles that all social workers and clients play in our society. In other words, the question is not, 'Do we want to allow homosexual/lesbian social workers to have the care of children or other vulnerable people?' It is rather, 'Can we allow people who do not have a clear political and personal knowledge of their role as professional social workers in areas of moral ambiguity to enter into asymmetric relationships with their customers?' The fact that the gay clients felt that the personal qualities of the social workers were of more importance than their sexual orientation emphasizes the point. In its emphasis on personal qualities social work both hits and misses the political dilemmas in its relationships with society and those designated as clients. The one area of consistency among the responses of gay social workers was in their opposition to aversion or chemical therapy for sexual conduct 'disorders'. Here personal experience achieved a unified, articulated public response to the possibilities of the control of behaviour. Individuals in the study achieved such a conscious approach in certain situations. For example, one of the gay workers described his identification with the sexual outlaw and his response to the rapist in our society (p. 89). However, such articulation is not a function of having certain sexual interests but rather an achieved awareness of the ways in which one's own and other people's sexual conduct is influenced by personal and structural pressures in society. This may lead to supporting or controlling the client's particular manifestation of sexual conduct according to the worker's view, of the effect of such conduct on society and of professional social work's role with that particular person. Sexual orientation may assist the worker in such awareness by virtue of being a member of a minority group. It does not of itself lead to such a state.

If the implication of the above is that the concentration on social workers' *sexual* orientations is at best a diversion from clarifying the social work role(s) in relation to sexual conduct, can this different emphasis be extended to the clients' behaviour? In a very general way the answer is certainly *yes*, in respect of prostitution. Rape is best seen as violence. Incest is a matter of family problems of communication. Under-age sexuality is about the prevention of uncontrollable social change by the next generation. Marital problems are personal power politics whilst other sexual expression is best seen as testing our tolerance of diversity and public display. Of course this is crude simplification and does not take into account people's misery at being found out as different let alone criminal. As an alternative to a 'sickness' definition, it is vital for a client to have access in any dialogue with a worker to both a political and a personal definition of their conduct (see Roy and Fred).

It is no wonder training in matters of sexuality was not found by the workers to have been of use in the field. Teaching about sexuality in isolation from considering the policy and politics of social work is like learning to dance blindfolded.

The responses of the small number of social workers/probation officers in the study can in no way claim to be representative of the possible range of views held in social work. This is especially true of an occupational group at least half of whom have not been professionally socialized by a qualifying course. We need, before proceeding on to the implications of what has *so far* been found, to suggest some hypotheses for further testing.

1 There is a range of moral evaluations in respect of sexual conduct made by social workers.
2 The evaluations are not associated with the law or organizational pressures or work setting.
3 The evaluations are not necessarily associated with the workers' sexual gender or orientation.
4 The evaluations are not necessarily related only to the needs of the clients.
5 The evaluations are associated with the moral and political views of the social workers.
6 The evaluations in relation to sexual conduct will also be linked with evaluations made in respect of other social work concerns.
7 Moral evaluations and political views may be held which are separate from operational conduct.
8 The evaluations in certain cases are held independently of the 'danger to others' involved in the clients' conduct.

In the meantime social workers and their customers are daily faced with decisions about matters of sexual conduct over an even wider area than that discussed in this book. To finish suggesting 'further research' is not a good enough response to them. If we are correct in our assessments here, then the meetings between helper and helped, may involve the morally lame being led by the morally blind, to a destination about which there is no prior agreement.

Chapter 7

Towards a normative view of social work and sexual conduct

Even within the scope of the issues presented in this book we can see that social work as an emerging profession has a direct concern with sexual conduct. In so far as all encounters between clients and workers, social service managers and employers, social work teachers and students have sexual components, this is an obvious if neglected assertion. It has been suggested that the ways in which these meetings are handled depends on a range of factors which are in a sense personal to the worker and client. However, in each's relationship with legal, organizational and societal pressures they are also public issues. An emerging theme has been the apparently arbitrary nature of the workers' responses from the viewpoint of the potential consumer of social work service. Before going on to discuss the implications, at this stage we should acknowledge that (a) throughout the book the reports are illustrative rather than representative of the range of all possible social work responses to all manifestations of sexuality; (b) the reports reflect the diverse and dynamic nature of more general public attitudes to sexuality; (c) in specifying sexual conduct the study may be masking findings which are related to social work in general.

Any hope of consensus in discussions of right/good sexual behaviour is not likely to be found in society generally. Amongst specific groups such as social workers there are often conflicting opinions held and diverse sexual practices contained. It is when these become public concerns that social workers are expected to respond as administrators of social policy at a personal level. When private behaviour becomes visible, social work is both part of the problem and of the solution. Given the many eloquent examples here of the everyday problems of workers and clients, I now want to offer my own direction indicators, from the problem towards a solution. It is my view that such 'solutions' take place in a society which is not unitary but rather composed of many different groups with unequal opportunities to express their sexual needs and rights.

Of central importance is to ask again, 'What does social work stand for?' A past answer has been something along the lines of 'Respect for the individual', or as Perlman (1971, p. 182) defending casework serving 'one purpose that cannot be brushed aside as trivial', writes: 'its existence stubbornly asserts the importance of individual man and of the individual, small, frail clusters of persons called families.' It is my contention that in operational terms for British social work this is not the all-embracing value. As Plant (1970, p. 1) warned, 'caseworkers because they are involved in this dual concern, need to be very clear about the relationship between the individual and society.' The findings imply that no such clarity exists, and this may be directly related to the prevailing myth of an individualized mandate and operation which has obscured the policy and politics of social work in a conflict situation.

To observe the results and suggest alternatives to such a situation in a number of crucial areas of sexual conduct, we will divide these areas into: (1) sexual conduct without a victim; (2) sexual conduct involving a victim; (3) sexual conduct where the status of victim is questionable. (None of these categories are watertight but will for our purposes suffice if the reader thinks of exceptions to these rules.)

These divisions will enable us to observe more clearly the role of the law in relation to public threats and private morality and the relationship social work has with legal, organizational, public or private behaviours. Acting as moral agent does not necessarily involve the enforcing of legal or organizational rules.

1 In this category we will place prostitution, homosexuality, transvestism, fetishism, exhibitionism. These acts are freely entered into, they usually come to the attention of social workers because of laws which are aimed to reduce their public display or to limit the location or ages of participation. The role of the social worker has varied from advocate of the sexual non-conformist, to intermediary of psychologist or psychiatrist or magistrate who is intending to change such behaviour. Laws relating to the prohibition of such different expressions of sexual conduct are a false reassurance to those who choose not to express their sexuality in such ways. Traditionally social work skills have been aimed at individual adjustment. Such a role may still exist for those who are ill at ease with their sexual conduct. However, in its contribution to social welfare, the profession will need to use the developing influence it has in central and local government to advocate the removal of expressions of sexual diversity from the criminal law. There is also a task within communities to rehabilitate the concept of sexual difference. Advocated here is a concern for the individual client but not at the expense of 'public social health' duties which will need to become a more up-front task for social workers. This might mean

arranging for groups of prostitutes to meet with residents in areas to see what are their common problems and conflicting interests. It could also involve alliance with magistrates and others to campaign for the decriminalization of prostitution (those under 18 still being subject to children's welfare legislation). It could mean meeting with homosexuals in an area to discuss the general contribution they can make to community life. Social work may aid such groups in helping to prevent the prosecution of their sexual activities or in acting to minimize the sequelae of such prosecutions. For example, *Gay News*, No. 137, issue of 15 December-11 January 1978:

SUICIDE OF METHODIST MINISTER
Huddersfield: A Methodist minister killed himself the day after being charged with 'gross indecency'. On the dashboard was a suicide note and a prayer book lay beside him open at the service for the burial of the dead.

A PC of Wakefield Police told a Skipton inquest that the minister had seemed to be 'deep in thought' after being arrested and charged. Police warned him against taking 'drastic action' before allowing him to leave the station. The Coroner heard that he had taken a high dose of pain-killing tablets— but death was caused by carbon monoxide poisoning from the car exhaust.

There would seem to be here a unique opportunity in such situations for social work, with its statutory and personal mandate, to find ways of acting on a primary or secondary preventative level.

A similar case could be made out for the discouragement of the prosecution of under-age consensual sexual activities between peers. At a national level it might be appropriate for the profession to find ways to press for equalizing or even abolishing an age of consent, relying on other existing laws to protect the vulnerable. The study shows how such arbitrary age limits are a hindrance to helpers and of doubtful moral protection to individuals or society. (For an evaluation of the physical dangers of youthful and/or promiscuous sexual activity, see Schofield (1976, pp. 111-12). In surveying the studies concerning the association of such activity and cancer of the cervix he concludes,

It seems that promiscuity, early marriage, remarriage and multiple pregnancies are no more than secondary factors. Early coitus, high frequencies of intercourse and sexually transmitted infections appear to be the major factors in the development of cancer of the cervix. Consequently the earlier onset of puberty and the more permissive attitudes towards premarital sex are likely to result in a marked increase in the incidence of this disease in the coming decades.)

It has been implied there is no room for social work in the redefinition of public issues into personal problems—what of the prospective client who wants to change his/her sexual conduct? The prostitute may wish to change his/her occupation. The homosexual may wish to become less sensitized to males or females in order to form a heterosexual relationship. On the other hand the heterosexual person may wish to become less sensitized to people of the opposite sex in order to maintain a homosexual relationship. Here is the importance of the worker presenting the prospective client with details of his/her own social values and, where appropriate, knowledge about psychotherapeutic, relationship orientated, behavioural or chemical treatment for the person to evaluate. It would be hard to envisage justification for the worker independently recommending or encouraging any of these treatment procedures. A question to be faced is the 'encouragement' of homosexual behaviour. Will its toleration/legitimization lead to more homosexual and less heterosexual conduct? If we are discussing exclusive sexual preference and behaviour and if one takes the view that there is a process of sensitization to heterosexual or homosexual preferences, then an increase in homosexual behaviour is likely. This should, of course, be seen alongside the possibility that heterosexual activities will also be increasing in our society.

Here is outlined a role for social workers which is both client- and community-centred and politically committed. The prevailing commitment here is to a view of social relationships where those who are sexually different form part of a wide spectrum of sexual expression within which any absolutes such as sexual normalcy are meaningless and as moral absolutes harmful to everyone. The aim for social work intervention in such cases is the rehabilitation of such outcasts into the society of which they are part. In this operation social work has something to learn as well as to give in the range of alternative helping services now provided by such groups as the women's movement and gay self-help. It is to their relationship with such 'voluntary' or more properly consumer groups that social work must give urgent consideration for I suspect we have little idea how to deal with situations where you cannot 'Start from where the client is'—because s/he isn't! Equally we have to respect the person who does not want to join a self-help group.

2   Do similar strategies apply to the serious crimes involved in sexual conduct involving a victim? Of course social work may be working towards an ideal society where such violent crimes as rape do not exist. Many people, particularly in the women's movement, would see rape as the logical ultimate expression of a sexist society. Certainly social workers involved in the care of children can provide non-sexist models of relating to each other and, as we have noted in

previous chapters, this problem is urgently in need of consideration in residential care. Such a difficult structural problem in society is likely to remain at the status of 'work in progress'. This will involve a range of educational activities, ensuring clients can learn self-defence or the teaching of ways into relationships in which sexual behaviour is mutually desired and expressed. If the individual client is a rapist or someone who sexually abuses children and this appears as an isolated act, he may be offered long-term moral education to change the way he regards sexuality alongside social skills training. If there is continual danger, then the person will have to be isolated from the community at risk. Social workers may or may not wish to be decision-makers or providers of control/care in such cases.

As in sexual conduct without victims, social workers are acting as moral agents. They are advocating societal and individual change to protect the community against violent acts. The workers cannot be said to be client-centred or non-directive as they are usually assumed to be in casework. The worker is community health orientated and the prospective client needs to know this so that s/he may decide not to undergo parole, probation, supervision or other forms of social work but instead be treated according to a Justice model. The additional technical and moral problem here is that the rapist or child abuser may be offered an alternative to penal punishment in the form of psycho-, behavioural or chemical therapy. Social work as a profession should be actively opposed to any procedures which were undertaken with the threat or sanction of the criminal law. If the person wanted such treatment the worker would present his/her own values, political analysis of their behaviour and the opportunities for moral reform. Together they would evaluate the consequences intended and unintended of such treatments and the likely results of the person's further criminal behaviour. If treatment was still desired, there is likely to be personal variation among workers between closing the case, pointing to or opening the door to such facilities.

3 The above evaluations of sexual conduct are reasonably clearly based upon an assessment of physical danger and the rights of the individual to sexual expression. If we move on to sexual conduct where the victim's status is questionable, the issues are more complex. We have to consider paedophilia and incest. The physical aspects are relatively easy to consider. The law would appear only to have a place when people force sexual relations on children, to ensure they are isolated from such opportunities. Incestuous matings should be counselled about birth control, involving abortion as necessary because of the high risks of infant mortality and congenital malformation (Seemanová, 1971). In other aspects of such conduct we are essentially dealing with more controversial moral evaluations.

We judge, for example, that those involved in incestuous unions are likely to upset family relationship balances and later prevent young people from developing unions based on a wider choice. Also in paedophilia it is assumed that the behaviour is likely to affect the children in adverse ways. Balanced against such concerns is the lack of any certainty that individual incestuous or paedophiliac relationships are more liable than other types of relationships with adults to make the particular child less able to live and love in our adult society. It may be that cases which come to public notice should be referred to social workers to try and ensure that the individuals are choosing the relationship and it is not unduly exploitive, on either side. These evaluations would be, for social workers, on a level with their concern with teenage marriages where the judgments made are that unwanted children should not be the outcome of (or reason for) a union. Also that the marriage does not represent a premature closing of relationship options. In case 3, as in previous examples, the workers would need to make their values very clear as their concerns would not necessarily be centred on the client but rather on evaluating and *possibly* helping to equalize the power relationship between the child and adult. In this the risk would be that the adult would have his/her needs denied rather than met by his/her social worker. Here also is a role for social work influencing the legal status of such consensual behaviour.

If we now extend this analysis to residential care, we have all three categories to consider—victimless deviance, under-age sexuality, sexuality in semi-public places and the concept of victims—the abuse of vulnerable people with little choice. In addition there are occasions when the sexual conduct involves a questionable victim—loving relationships between under-age residents or between staff and residents. Obviously such semi-discrete categories require a differential response according to the physical danger involved. A general point in relation to institutions, however, is that both young and old people are disadvantaged through a lack of choice of partners which may also affect staff members. Rights have become privileges. We should strive at an organizational level to decrease the need for people to be separated from the community, either through the avoidance of institutional care or through attempts to break down the isolation of people who have to live in such circumstances. Relationships will develop among residents and these should be evaluated in respect of their mutuality and power-sharing within the context of a person's life which is to be lived before and after the period in care. Will the sexual conduct help, hinder or have little effect on any relationships which will flourish during his or her life? If the answer is to hinder and the sexual relationship is about a seeking after power, then as in the example on p. 87, the worker's job would be to curtail such expressions of sexuality. Otherwise the worker would ensure the client's privacy and where necessary offer encouragement.

When we are dealing with children, the elderly and the handicapped, we are faced with a problem upon which perhaps an earlier focus should have been made. So far the worker has been seen as an outside agent. What happens if s/he becomes sexually involved with a client? Given the above framework, the demands on the social worker are heavy when evaluating the goodness of any sexual relationship which comes to be their concern. S/he would have to judge the absence of physical abuse, the degree of mutuality, the power structure, the meaning of the relationship with the person's possible life outside the institution and the meaning of the relationship for other residents. In residential social work, even though it may be partially isolated from the wider community, the individual's needs are not necessarily of prime consideration.

This is a formidable list and not one which can be gone through with any degree of clarity by a social worker involved sexually with a resident. A more public discussion is necessary—hence the need for a more specific social work code of practice which in itself should lead to such sexual issues being the legitimate concern of supervisory discussion. Such a code should relate to both the sexual rights and the responsibilities of clients and workers. A code should not be confined to residential social work, for if our suggestions towards normative social work and sexual conduct are adopted, then the profession will have to face going beyond client-centred or non-directive principles and recognizing in such a code the organizational, legal and personal elements in the worker/client encounter. If these constraints and opportunities are made known to the client it may well be that the worker's evaluation is not to the client's liking. Any code of practice needs to recognize this and in a somewhat similar way to Catholic gynaecologists in abortion decisions, provide the opportunity for an alternative worker. The provision of another worker is important to help take away the feeling of failure on either side of a professional relationship which does not work. This does imply an opening up of the mystique of the professional relationship with, hopefully, evaluations of behaviour more known about on each side. This will enable clients to have a more equal power relationship. This is especially important in statutory relationships. Clients will be able to choose their worker in a similar way that those of higher status in our society, shop around for their solicitors, general practitioners, schools. In addition to concern about individual conduct, the author's stance undoubtedly implies for social work policy a shift towards prevention rather than intervention.

Into the 1980s: from the reproductive through the relational to the recreational—the challenge for social work and sexual conduct

It has been my intention in this book to address social work's present problems. We also should, even if briefly, suggest some of the likely future concerns of social work and sexuality.

We are moving into an era where the elderly will form a larger client group for social work. Undoubtedly, sexual satisfaction will be among their expectations of a worthwhile existence.

The delightful prospect of a multi-racial society should not blind social work to the stance it will have to take to the already emerging problems of the liberation of immigrant women and children.

The future of marriage and the family is outside the scope of this book. We can only note that other types of units providing for the care of children and other dependents will become the worker's concern. Also social work will need a worked-out response in such areas as the custody of children of lesbian or homosexual parents and towards the conception, care and fostering of children by sexual minority groups. Such a response will also be necessary in dealing with instances of men bringing up children, after broken marriages for example. The decision of women to become unmarried mothers will also have to be accommodated.

Within marriage there will be total demand for sexual satisfaction and an expectation that professionals will provide the technical means of achieving such satisfaction, for example the treatment of sexual dysfunctioning (already television programmes are providing general knowledge of ways of acquiring skills in behavioural treatments of minor sexual dysfunctioning).

Both within and outside marriage, the treatment of sexual dysfunctioning will require social work to consider the implications of acting as a surrogate sexual partner (see the US experience in Schultz, 1975). This will apply both to field and residential social workers.

Whatever factors affect the unpredictable birthrate, social work can expect to encounter the political strength of the women's movement demanding changes in traditional male/female roles in relation to the upbringing of children.

Social work will have to work out its relationship with the increasing militancy of minority groups who have their own consumerist definition of their problems, for example single parents, gays, foster parents, the elderly.

The further development of chemical and other treatments to change sexual behaviour will emphasize the need for a more specific ethical code of practice.

The increasing challenge to concepts of sexual fidelity, and exclusiveness to previously held notions of emotional health will have to be accounted for in social work theory, as will the considerations involved in child-free relationships.

If these examples of future concerns are added to the previous day-by-day problems of social work and sexual conduct, then obviously we need to consider the training requirements to fit the professional for such a task. It would be regrettable if social workers were unprepared to help their clients achieve equality in the enjoyment of their sexual lives. The areas covered in such teaching might be listed as follows:

A *Human sexual behaviour*
1 Psychological, sociological, biological, physiological and moral aspects of sex.
2 The varieties of sexual expression.
3 Cultural differences.
4 Lifespan and sexual expression.
5 Birth control.
6 Sex-related diseases.
B *The policy and politics of social work and sexual conduct*
1 Sexuality and emotional health.
2 Sex role.
3 Sex offenders.
4 Sexual minorities.
5 Under-age sexuality.
6 Future trends in sexuality.
C *Social work skills*
1 In relation to sexual dysfunctioning.
2 The advocacy of individual and group needs within
(a) communities, (b) social policy, national and local.
3 Educating about sexual behaviour with individuals within communities. Working with other community influences on sexual conduct—police, schools, church.

In an earlier discussion with a medical colleague on my plans for this book on sexual conduct, she accused me of putting the cart before the horse in emphasizing values rather than knowledge as being the prime area for discussion—'What social workers should *know* about birth control, the incidence of homosexuality' was the need, she thought. My intention has not been to discredit the value of such knowledge—rather to ask how is such knowledge obtained, why is it important and for what purpose, and within what kind of society is it used. In short, to explore its power. It is my view that such questioning and responses are essential to social work beyond the initial excitement of discussing sexuality.

Appendix

Some details of methodological experience in preparing this book

Initial considerations about gathering the material for this work set off for me immediate warning bells—sex is taboo, it is an area where social workers might feel under public criticism. Clients would probably be reluctant to discuss such intimate details with a stranger. From the beginning of the study, therefore, I was concerned to be as open as possible with participants as to the purpose of my questions and what I would do with their answers. Included in this was a promise that even though their own mothers might (or might not) recognize them, I would ensure that in the published work, their identities would not be revealed, although they might be recognizable to close friends.

I ruled out any attempts at questionnaire-type interviews. If people were to talk about often confused public and private conduct I would have to rely on a personal interview in which I used my skills to enable them to examine critically their own experience of social work help from the giving or receiving end. The text does give some indications of the occasions when I was successful and when I failed to achieve a rapport with someone. When the encounter worked, for example, a social worker was able to remember an increasing number of instances where sexual conduct was important in the relationship with a client; this may have been after initial denial of the frequency of such occurrences. On the other hand, some workers and clients were either not at ease with me or with the subject of our discussions and their answers were more restricted. I think that in such a personal area it is worth recording an example of how not to achieve the purpose of an interview.

Towards the end of our interview (see also pp. 157-8) Brian was discussing the social isolation which resulted in him being placed on probation for sexual behaviour in a public convenience. He was concerned to demonstrate to me these pressures and the fact that being on probation did not necessarily provide either a deterrent or an alternative to such activities; 'If you don't meet someone—let's face facts—I assume you are married?' I replied, 'No, I'm homosexual.' 'Oh, oh crikey, now you have stopped me now.' I asked him, 'What were you going to say?'

'Obviously that you want to meet someone and if you don't meet them in a gay pub or somewhere like that, you obviously go to a toilet. You have put me in a bit of a predicament now [laughs], I suppose when I came I didn't realise that a lecturer could be the same way as myself but I suppose there are homosexuals in all walks of life.'

I then asked about the possibility of having a probation officer who was homosexual: 'Well you would be having sex with them.' I asked, 'Do you think that *is* so?'

'Well obviously when you are on probation you are wary of going round town trying to pick someone up. If you have a probation officer who is homosexual obviously you will try. You are leading onto another matter I was going to embark on but obviously it's something you already know about. If you go to a public convenience and someone walks in, you have an inbuilt sense that they are homosexual—although I didn't know you were—I think the reason I didn't know was that when I came in you were introduced to me as a university lecturer and that went completely from my mind. . . .'

I asked, 'Would you want to know your probation officer was homosexual?'

'In one sense yes, in another no, because if I knew he was that way inclined I should probably let the sexual aspects come out and have homosexual relations with him. I would still expect help but it would certainly stop me [going to the public conveniences] for the period I was on probation—knowing that I had to come every week or fortnight and so knowing I would have sex with someone once a week instead of searching for it outside where I could not guarantee I'm going to find it. That still applies now. . . . If I didn't know I would expect a lot more help from him that by knowing. . . . It's difficult—I say that I would like him to be that way and have sex with him and yet—no, it's difficult.'

I suggested, 'There are parallel situations in male heterosexual probation officers seeing female clients. Presumably they get on all right without sexuality getting in the way?'

'Yes, obviously if the probation officer was married—he told me that—and I presumed he would be faithful to his wife and

not want to look at another woman. I didn't presume he would
be a homosexual.'

I commented, 'Well they exist, I assure you.' 'Do they? Well I
didn't think they did.'
The interview closed shortly afterwards. I would not want to
suggest the interview was without value. I include it to illustrate how
one's own needs, for recognition or political action can subvert a
task-centred approach in an interview.
Twenty-nine social workers and thirteen clients are involved in the
main section of the study. They are in no way random samples of
workers and clients. As I have indicated above, the approach to
obtain an interview was, in the main, on a personal basis, that is the
workers were known to me, or colleagues acted as intermediaries in
persuading the people of the propriety of my interest. The clients
were approached by their workers who then either set up the
interviews or indicated to me that I could directly approach the
clients.
I attempted to widen the net to include other social workers and
clients. I did this by means of letters to *Community Care, Social
Work Today* and *Gay News*, published during Spring/Summer
1977. I particularly hoped that the *Community Care* letter would
result in some non-fieldwork social workers offering to participate.
Happily the one response I received from that source was from those
workers in the children's home who are featured in the book. I had
one response from my letter in *Social Work Today*. From *Gay News*
I hoped for gay social workers and clients. I received two responses
from gay workers and none from clients. This letter was probably
not appropriate for both groups as it was written in 'professional
language'.
A further problem, perhaps of trusting a stranger, is emphasized
by my experience with the Paedophile Information Exchange. They
were kind enough to insert two notices in their magazine, of my
interest in meeting people who had been on the receiving end of
treatment for sexual behaviours, or of social workers who were
themselves paedophiles. I had no response from their membership,
which they claim contains people who are in the helping professions.
(However, I did have very useful discussions with their 'organizers'.)
In addition to these contacts, I wrote a number of letters to
organizations involved in the sexual counselling area and to
individuals connected with social work who had made public
statements about sexuality. Some of these people responded with
helpful comments. Others did not reply to my letter(s).
Overall then, I felt the response to my asking for help in
investigating social work and sexual conduct was disappointing in

quantity but in the event of actual interviews being achieved, the quality of people's responses was very satisfying. It may be that we should not view apparent reluctance to assist in the research as being due to the subject but to a more general wariness about investigations into social work's effectiveness.

A word is necessary about the interviews with clients. As I indicated in the study, the problem of self-definition of some sex offenders prevents direct discussion of sexual conduct with them. There is also the difficulty of isolating sexual problems within marital work and thereby defining such an area for specific investigation. This restricted the range of clients available for my interviews. Also, the clients who were made available by workers tended to be those with whom they were on good terms and possibly had known over a long period. On a few occasions workers promised to arrange for me to meet clients who then were overcome by personal problems and the interview was cancelled or the worker did not approach the client as promised. As far as I know, once approached by the worker, no client refused to meet me. My original intention to compare the responses of a group of clients of straight and gay workers was prevented by the difficulties in obtaining sufficient numbers and a wide enough range of clients of the first group and then realizing that permission would have to be sought within organizations to interview clients and that this might identify the gay workers.

True comparability between the two groups of workers was also negated by there being more social workers than probation officers in the gay group. This *might* also be a finding of some importance.

We are left with the question that if these are the responses of reasonably *open* gay and straight workers, what of those who would not be happy to discuss personal and political dimensions of social work and sexual conduct?

The approximately forty hours of tape were not, through cost rather than choice, transcribed fully but were repeatedly listened to by myself and then arranged in the categories. In terms of the data collected, it could be argued that the open-endedness of the questions and the presentation of the lengthy contributions of workers and clients are too imprecise. Although in some social science methods the data can sometimes be observed to have been manipulated to fit the design, in this study the data could be seen as being presented as too disorderly. I would, whilst acknowledging the tendency, defend the presentation in terms of doing justice to the people who took part in the study and the use of the richness of their contributions to begin to formulate a sufficient framework within which we can ask more valid questions and move towards some reliable answers about the policy and politics of social work.

Details of probation officers in the study

Probation Officer 1 is male, in his early 40s, heterosexually orientated. Had previously lived in a community of monks. He is a senior probation officer.

Probation Officer 2 is male, in his early 30s, heterosexually orientated. He is a senior probation officer with additional marriage guidance training.

Probation Officer 3 is female, in her mid 30s, heterosexually orientated. Previously she was a member of a religious community.

Probation Officer 4 is male, aged 30, heterosexually orientated.

Probation Officer 5 is male, in his mid 30s, heterosexually orientated.

Probation Officer 6 is male, in his early 30s, heterosexually orientated. He is a senior probation officer.

Probation Officer 7 is male, in his early 30s, heterosexually orientated.

Probation Officer 8 is male, in his mid 20s, heterosexually orientated. A member of a Christian Fundamentalist Evangelical Church.

Probation Officer 9 is male, aged 29, heterosexually orientated.

Probation Officer 10 is male, aged 30, homosexually orientated. He is a senior probation officer.

Probation Officer 11 is male, in his mid 20s, homosexually orientated.

Probation Officer 12 is female, in her early 30s, heterosexually orientated.

Probation Officer 13 is male, aged 29, heterosexually orientated.

Probation Officer 14 is female, in her late 40s, heterosexually orientated, a direct entrant to the service. With in-service training, she had specialized in marital work.

Probation Officer 15 is female, aged 29, heterosexually orientated.

Details of social workers in the study

Social Worker A is male, in his early 30s, homosexually orientated. Has just finished his CQSW course.

Social Worker B is male, aged 30, homosexually orientated. After several years of experience in local authority generic social work, is now specializing in intermediate treatment.

Social Worker C is male, in his early 30s, homosexually orientated. After some years of experience is now working in an emergency duty team.

Appendix

Social Worker D is female, aged 30, homosexually orientated. She works in a large psychiatric hospital.

Social Worker E is male, aged 30, homosexually orientated. He qualified one year ago and works in a large general hospital. He had been trained and ordained for the priesthood.

Social Worker F is male, aged 30, homosexually orientated. He is a team leader in an area office.

Social Worker G is male, in his early 50s, homosexually orientated. He worked in a psychiatric hospital as a principal social worker. He is an ordained priest of the Church of England.

Social Worker H is unqualified, in his early 30s, homosexually orientated. He has a degree in theology and trained for the priesthood. He works for a Church welfare agency.

Social Worker I is male, in his late 20s, homosexually orientated. He was about to join a CQSW course. Previously a professionally qualified residential worker.

Social Worker J is unqualified, in his mid 20s, homosexually orientated. He was trained as a teacher, now works in a residential setting.

Social Worker K is female, in her mid 40s, homosexually orientated. She has been in social work for over twenty years, beginning as a child care officer. She is now in charge of an area office.

Social Worker L is male, aged 27, homosexually orientated. He works in an intake team. He was born and brought up in Latin America.

For details of Residential Social Workers see p. 74.

It might be helpful if I give some details of the sort of questions I asked those involved in the study interviews. As will be seen from the text, sometimes the interview 'took off'—into areas I had not planned on discussing. I have included in this Appendix instance of where this process went wrong but this was an exception and usually I found it quite possible to achieve the purposes of the interview without diversion. I assured my respondents of confidentiality and tried to involve them in the process of data gathering by emphasising the uniqueness of their contribution and promising to keep them in touch with the book's progress. Contributing to the more effective training and operation of social workers was something with which apparently both clients and workers could identify. Some of the respondents mentioned after the interview how much they enjoyed the session and that the opportunity to conceptualize some of their social work practice was both rare and welcome. My decision not to use a more formal interview questionnaire is I think justified by the uniqueness of the responses.

Details of questions intended to outline the interviews with workers

The worker was asked to briefly outline all cases where sexual considerations were or could have been matters of concern on the present or recent past caseload. Frequently the response to this request was for the worker to declare s/he had only one or two cases but then to remember others during the course of the interview. Next the worker was asked to state aims in the case and how relevant were sexual conduct considerations to these aims. Questions then focused on whether tensions existed in the worker dealing with the sexual conduct. If they did I attempted to elicit the origins of these tensions; were they located in the expectations of 'society' or organizations that the worker should be controlling the behaviour of the client when, for example, prostitutes were placed on probation for soliciting—or the expectations from other family members that sexually aberrant behaviour should cease (see, for example, pp. 22-3). Did the tensions arise from the worker's lack of knowledge about certain types of sexual expression or dysfunction? Was the conflict close to the actual encounter with the client because of the client's or the worker's attitude and response to discussion of sexual behaviour or interests?

In these aspects of work with clients what moral evaluation was the worker placing on the client's behaviour, and whence came these evaluations—personal factors, religious beliefs, political ideologies, legal or organizational constraints, public opinion, the client's own view of his/her behaviour? Were there additional factors, for example a belief in the goodness or otherwise of family life?

How often was the sexual conduct not discussed with a client even though the worker assessed it as being of significance?

Did the worker believe s/he held any stereotypes of sexual offenders?

How did the worker rate the importance of his/her own sexual gender, response, experience, and interests in working with clients?

What role did training and/or experience, age, supervision, play in how the worker assessed his/her competence in dealing with matters of sexual conduct?

I finished each interview by asking respondents if they thought I had omitted any questions relevant to sexual conduct in social work.

Details of questions intended to outline the interviews with clients

What part did sexual conduct play in your contact with the probation officer/social worker?

What did you think the worker thought of your behaviour?

Appendix

What did s/he think of your sexual interests/orientation?
Did s/he want to change these?
Could you talk about them to the worker? If not, to whom could you talk?
What were your expectations of the worker's attitude? How far were these confirmed?
Did you feel able to be yourself with the worker?
How helpful was s/he? Reasons for this.
How important was the worker's sex/personality/orientation?
How do you see the origins of your sexual conduct?
Are you alone in behaving like this/having these interests?
Were there any other areas you feel I should have asked about?

Further sources

Sex education

A film that the author has found useful is an American one, *Sexuality and Communication*. This provides basic sexual instruction suitable for a wide age-range of audience. The more sophisticated can note the sexism implicit in the role-play between a wife and husband medical team illustrating sexual communication in the doctor/patient relationship and the husband/wife relationship. The emphasis is on heterosexual and emotionally committed relationships. Available for hire and sale from Ortho Pharmaceutical Ltd, P.O. Box 79, Saunderton, High Wycombe, Buckinghamshire HP14 4HJ. This company also has *family planning* educational material available free of charge.

Free literature is also available on such topics as family planning and venereal diseases from the Health Education Council, 78 New Oxford Street, London WC1A 1AH; 01-637 1881.

Refer also to

The Association of Sexual and Marital Therapists, 79 Harley Street, London, W1.

Standing Conference for the Advancement of Counselling, acting for the British Association for Counselling; concerned with personal marital/sexual/family counselling; 1a Little Church Street, Rugby CV21 3AP. A directory of agencies offering therapy, counselling and support entitled *Psycho-sexual Problems* is available for sale.

Committee on Sexual Problems of the Disabled, 49 Victoria Street, London SW1; advisory leaflets, information, education and counselling.

National Marriage Guidance Council, Herbert Gray College, Little Church Street, Rugby CV21 3AP.

Further sources

Self-help groups

The problem with these are that they sometimes have a short life or new ones are always being formed. An excellent way of obtaining up to date information is from the regular supplement in *Gay News* (fortnightly), 1A Normand Gardens, Greyhound Road, London W14 9SB.

Additionally

Albany Trust, 16/18 Strutton Ground, London SW1P 2HP, tel. 01-222 0701.
Gay Legal Advice, c/o Friend, 274 Upper Street, London, N1, or direct contact on 01-262 2892, 7-12 p.m.
Rape Crisis Centre, P.O. Box 42, London N6 5BU.

Literature

The Department of Health and Social Security Library are producing useful Selected References on social work topics including aspects of sexuality. These have included: *Selected References on Sex and the Physically Handicapped*, August 1976 (Bibliography Series No. 1356); *Selected References on Incest*, June 1976 (Bibliography Series No. 1351); *Selected References on Paedophilia and Sexual Offences against Children*, December 1977 (Bibliography Series 1391). Obtainable from the Librarian, Department of Health and Social Security, Alexander Fleming House, Elephant and Castle, London SE1 6B7 (01-407 5522).
    Sex Information and Education Council of the United States (Siecus) 137-155, North Franklin Street, Hempstead, New York, 11550. Publications available from Librusa Ltd, 3 Henrietta Street, London WC1 8LU.
    Parker, W., *Homosexuality Bibliography*, Supplement 1970-5 contains every significant publication during this period. This supplements the earlier *Homosexuality: A Selective Bibliography* (1971). Both books are published by Scarecrow Press, available from Bailey Bros & Swinfen Ltd, Warner House, Folkestone, Kent.

Some other selected references

Bancroft, J. (1978), 'The Prevention of Sexual Offenses', in Qualls, C. B., Wincze, J. P. Barlow, D. H. (eds), *The Prevention of Sexual Disorders*, Plenum, New York.
Berger, R. M. (1977), 'An Advocate Model for Intervention with Homosexuals', *Social Work (USA)*, vol. 22, no. 4, pp. 280-3.
Brown, P. and Faulder, C. (1978), *Treat Yourself to Sex*, Dent, London.

Central Council for Education and Training in Social Work (1976),
Paper 13: Social Work Curriculum Study: Values in Social Work,
A discussion paper produced by the working party on the teaching
of the value bases of social work.

Cheetham, J. (1976), 'Pregnancy in the Unmarried: The Continuing
Dilemmas for Social Policy and Social Work', in Halsey, A. H.
(ed.), *Traditions of Social Policy: Essays in Honour of Violet
Butler*, Blackwell, Oxford.

Chetwynd, J. and Hartnett, O. (eds) (1978), *The Sex Role System:
Psychological and Sociological Perspectives*, Routledge & Kegan
Paul, London.

Craft, M. and A. (1978), *Sex and the Mentally Handicapped*,
Routledge & Kegan Paul, London.

Christopher, E. (1975), 'Should Social Workers be Involved in
Family Planning?', *Social Work Today*, vol. 5, no. 20, pp. 611-16.

Davis, L. (1978), 'In Residence: Sex Behind Bars', *Social Work
Today*, vol. 9, no. 37, p. 28.

DHSS Health Circular (1977), *Health Services Development,
Arrangements for Counselling of Patients Seeking Abortion*,
HC(77)26, July.

Felstein, I. (1970), *Sex and the Longer Life*, Allen Lane, The
Penguin Press, Harmondsworth.

Films produced by Orchard Films for British Pregnancy Advisory
Service, Ansty Manor, Wootton Wawen, Solihull, West Midlands
B95 6DA: *A Question of Understanding; The Abortion Obstacle
Game; Abortion—A Tale of Two Cities; The Counselling
Approach*. (Available for sale and hire through Concord Films
Council, Ipswich, Suffolk IP10 OJ2. Phone 0473 76012.)

Fitzjohn, J. (1974), 'An Interactionist View of the Social Work
Interview', *British Journal of Social Work*, vol. 4, no. 4, pp.
425-33.

Gagnon, J. H. (1977), *Human Sexualities*, Scott Foresman, Illinois;
available from Eurospan Ltd, Kershaw House, 3 Henrietta Street,
London.

Gagnon, J. W. and Simon, W. (eds) (1967), *Sexual Deviance*,
Harper & Row, New York.

Greengross, W. (1976), *Entitled to Love: The Sexual and Emotional
Needs of the Handicapped*, Malaby, in association with the
National Fund for Research into Crippling Diseases.

Harris, G. and Wagner, N. (1973), 'Treatment of Sexual Dysfunction: Casework Techniques', *Clinical Social Work,* **vol. 1**
(Winter), pp. 244-50.

Hart, J. (1978), 'V.D.—The Need for a New Response', *Community
Care*, 28 September, vol. 181, pp. 18-19.

Honoré, T. (1978), *Sex Law,* Duckworth, London.

Further sources

Kahn, A. J. (1976), 'Men in a Women's Profession', *Social Work (USA)*, vol. 21, no. 6, pp. 440-7.

Kaplan, H. S. (1974), *The New Sex Therapy*, Baillière Tindall, London.

Keith-Lucas, A. (1975), 'An Alliance for Power', *Social Work (USA)*, vol. 20, March, pp. 93-7.

Lees, R. (1972), *Politics and Social Work*, Routledge & Kegan Paul, London.

Levy, C. S. (1976), *Social Work Ethics*, Human Sciences Press, New York.

Libby, R. W. and Whitehurst, R. N. (1977), *Marriage and Alternatives: Exploring Intimate Relationships*, Scott Foresman, Illinois; available from Eurospan Ltd, Kershaw House, 3 Henrietta Street, London.

Lowenthal, M. F. and Haven, C. (1968), 'Interactions and adaptation: Intimacy as a Critical Variable', *American Sociological Review*, vol. 33, February, pp. 20-30.

Manning, M. (1977), 'Should we Pity the Paedophiles?', *Community Care*, 19 October, no. 184, pp. 17-20.

Manning, M. (1978), 'When it's an "Unhappy Event". Describing Counselling on Abortion and Pregnancy', *Community Care*, 8 February, no. 199, pp. 22-4.

Middleman, R. R. and Goldberg, G. (1974), *Social Service Delivery: A Structural Approach to Social Work Practice*, Columbia University Press.

Morrison, E. S. and Price, M. U. (1974), *Values in Sexuality*, Hart, New York.

Pearce, F. and Roberts, A. (1973), 'The Social Regulation of Sexual Behaviour and the Development of Industrial Capitalism in Britain', in Bailey, R. and Young, J. (eds), *Contemporary Social Problems in Britain*, Saxon House, London.

Peters, J. J. and Roether, H. A. (1971), 'Group Psychotherapy for Probationed Sex Offenders', *International Psychiatric Clinics*, vol. 8, pp. 69-80.

Rainwater, L. (ed.) (1974), *Social Problems and Public Policy: Deviance and Liberty*, Aldine, Chicago.

Resnick, H. (1975), 'The Professional—Pro-Active Decision Making in the Organisation', speech to BASW Conference, edited version in *Social Work Today*, vol. 6, no. 15, pp. 462-7.

Rosebury, T. (1971), *Microbes and Morals* (on venereal diseases), Viking Press, New York.

Rubinstein, E. A., Green, R. and Brecher, E. (eds) (1976), *New Directions in Sex Research*, Plenum, New York and London.

Samuels, A. (1977), 'Confidentiality and the Law', *Social Service Quarterly*, vol. 21, no. 1, pp. 14-16.

196

Schur, E. M. (1965), *Crimes without Victims, Deviant Behaviour and Public Policy*, Prentice-Hall, Englewood Cliffs, New Jersey.

Supplementary Benefits Commission, Department of Health and Social Security (1976), *Living Together as Husband and Wife*, Report by the Supplementary Benefits Commission to the Secretary of State for Social Services, HMSO, London.

Taylor, B. (1976), 'Motives for Guilt—Free Paederasty: Some Literary Considerations', *Sociological Review*, vol. 24, no. 1, pp. 97-114.

Taylor, T. (1977), 'The Heterosexual Transvestite in Australia', *Australian Social Work*, vol. 30, no. 1, pp. 29-33.

Walker, M. (1977), *Men Loving Men: A Gay Sex Guide and Consciousness Book*, Gay Sunshine Press, San Francisco.

Weissman, H. (1973), *Overcoming Mismanagement in the Human Service Professions*, Jossey-Bass, San Francisco.

West, D. J., Roy, C. and Nichols, F. L. (1978), *Understanding Sexual Attacks*, Heinemann, London.

Wicks, L. K. (1977), 'Transsexualism: A Social Work Approach', *Health and Social Work* (New York), vol. 2, no. 1, February, pp. 179-93.

Wyland, F. (1977), *Motherhood, Lesbianism and Child Custody*, Wages Due Lesbians, Toronto and Falling Wall Press; 40p, available from Wages Due Lesbians, Staverton Road, London, NW2.

References

Archer, J. (1976), 'Biological Explanations of Psychological Sex Differences', in Lloyd, B. and Archer, J. (eds), *Exploring Sex Differences*, Academic Press, London.

Babuscio, J. (1976), *'We Speak for Ourselves': Experiences in Homosexual Counselling*, Society for Promoting Christian Knowledge, London.

Bailey, D. S. (ed.) (1956), *Sexual Offenders and Social Punishment*, The Church Information Board.

Bailey, R. and Brake, M. (eds) (1975), *Radical Social Work*, Edward Arnold, London.

Bakwin, H. (1968), 'Deviant Gender-Role Behaviour in Children', *Pediatrics*, vol. 41, pp. 620-9.

Bancroft, J. (1974), *Deviant Sexual Behaviour: Modification and Assessment*, Oxford University Press, London.

Bannister, K. and Pincus, L. (1965), *Shared Phantasy in Marital Problems: Therapy in a Four Person Relationship*, Institute of Marital Studies, London.

Bean, P. (1976), *Rehabilitation and Deviance*, Routledge & Kegan Paul, London.

Brongersma, E. (1977), reported in *Childhood Rights*, vol. 1, no. 2, Paedophile Information Exchange, P.O. Box 318, London SE3 8QD.

Broverman, I. K., Broverman, D. M., Clarkson, F. E., Rosenkrantz, P. S. and Vogel, S. R. (1970), 'Sex-Roles Stereotypes and Clinical Judgements of Mental Health', *Journal of Consulting and Clinical Psychology*, vol. 34, no. 1, pp. 341-7.

Brown, A. (1977), 'Worker Style in Social Work', *Social Work Today*, vol. 8, no. 29, pp. 13-14.

Burton, L. (1968), *Vulnerable Children*, Routledge & Kegan Paul, London.

Campaign for Homosexual Equality (1975), *Sexual Offences Bill*, P.O. Box 427, 69 Corporation Street, Manchester M60 2EL.

Cohen, S. (1976), 'It's Alright for You to Talk: Political and Sociological Manifestos for Social (Work) Action', in Bailey, R. and Brake, M. (eds), *Radical Social Work*, Edward Arnold, London.

Connell, N. and Wilson, C. (eds) (1974), *Rape Speak Out: The First Sourcebook for Women*, New York Radical Feminists, New American Library.

198

Davies, M. (1977), 'Impact on Probation', *Community Care,* 12 January, no. 144.

Davis, L. F. (1975), 'Touch, Sexuality and Power in Residential Settings', *British Journal of Social Work*, vol. 5, no. 4, pp. 397-411.

Davis, N. J. (1971), 'The Prostitute: Developing a Deviant Identity', in Henslin, J. M. (ed.), *Studies in the Sociology of Sex*, Appleton-Century-Crofts, New York.

DeMause, L. (1975), 'Our Forebears Made Childhood a Nightmare', *Psychology Today* (New York), vol. 8, pp. 85-8.

Denzin, N. K. (1970), 'Rules of Conduct and the Study of Deviant Behaviour', in Douglas, J. D. (ed.), *Deviance and Respectability: The Social Construction of Moral Meanings*, Basic Books, New York and London.

Douglas, J. D. (ed.) (1970), *Deviance and Respectability: The Social Construction of Moral Meanings*, Basic Books, New York and London.

Douglas, J. D. (1971), *American Social Order: Social Rules in a Pluralistic Society*, Free Press, New York, Collier Macmillan, London.

Elstein, M., Gordon, A. D. G. and Buckingham, M. S. (1977), 'Sexual Knowledge and Attitudes of General Practitioners in Wessex', *British Medical Journal*, vol. 1, pp. 369-71.

Eysenck, H. J. (1976), *Sex and Personality*, Open Books, London.

Foren, R. and Bailey, R. (1968), *Authority in Social Casework*, Pergamon Press, London.

Freud, S. (1917), *The Standard Edition XVII of the Complete Psychological Works of Sigmund Freud*, 24 vols, 1955 edn, Hogarth Press and the Institute of Psychoanalysis, London.

Friedman, A. S. *et al.* (1971), *Therapy with Families of Sexually Acting Out Girls*, Springer, New York.

Gagnon, J. H. and Simon, W. (1974), *Sexual Conduct: The Social Sources of Human Sexuality*, Hutchinson, London.

Gebhard, P. H., Gagnon, J. H., Pomeroy, W. B. and Christenson, C. V. (1965), *Sex Offenders: An Analysis of Types*, Heinemann, London.

Geis, G. (1977), Seminar to Law Faculty, University of Sheffield. (Prof. Geis of the University of California Irvine was at that time Visiting Fellow, Institute of Criminology, Cambridge.) 9 June.

Gibbens, T. C. N. (1977), 'More Facts about Rape', *New Society*, vol. 38, no. 749, pp. 275-6.

Glastonbury, B., Burdett, M. and Austin, R. (1972), 'Community Perceptions and the Personal Social Services', *Policy and Politics*, vol. 1, no. 3, pp. 191-211.

Gochros, H. L. and Schultz, L. G. (eds) (1972), *Human Sexuality and Social Work*, Association Press, New York.

Goldberg, S. (1974), *The Inevitability of Patriarchy*, Morrow, New York.

The Gospel According to St Matthew, Chapter 27, Verses 65-66 (Authorized Version).

Green, R. (1969), 'Childhood Cross-Gender Identification', in Green, R. and Money, J. (eds), *Transsexualism and Sex Reassignment*, Johns Hopkins University Press, Baltimore.

References

Green, R. (1978), 'Intervention and Prevention: The Child with Cross-Sex Identity', in Qualis, C. B., Wincze, J. P. and Barlow, D. M. (eds), *The Prevention of Sexual Disorders*, Plenum Press, New York and London.

Green, R. and Fuller, M. (1973), 'Group Therapy with Feminine Boys and their Parents', *International Journal of Group Therapy*, vol. 23, pp. 54-68.

Green, R. and Money, J. (eds) (1969), *Transsexualism and Sex Reassignment*, Johns Hopkins University Press, Baltimore.

Halmos, P. (1965), *The Faith of the Counsellors*, Constable, London.

Hardiker, P. (1977), 'Social Work Ideologies in the Probation Service', *British Journal of Social Work*, vol. 7, no. 2, pp. 131-54.

Hardy, K. R. (1971), 'An Appetitional Theory of Sexual Motivation', in Leiberman, B. (ed.), *Human Sexual Behaviour: A Book of Readings*, Wiley, New York.

Harris, D. (1977), 'Seven Models of Residential Care', *Social Work Today*, vol. 9, no. 1, pp. 19-20.

Hart, J. (1978), 'Integration of Social Work Education in the United States', *Social Work Today*, vol. 9, no. 21, pp. 12-13.

Humphreys, L. (1970), *Tearoom Trade: Impersonal Sex in Public Places*, Aldine, Chicago.

Hutt, C. (1972), *Males and Females*, Penguin, Harmondsworth.

Jones, E. (1955), *The Life and Work of Sigmund Freud*, Basic Books, New York.

Jordan, B. (1977), 'Against the Unitary Approach to Social Work', *New Society*, vol. 40, no. 765, pp. 448-50.

Joseph, Sir Keith (1974), Speech reported in *The Times*, Monday 21 October.

Kagan, J. and Moss, H. A. (1962), *Birth to Maturity*, Wiley, New York and London.

Kinsey, A. C., Pomeroy, W. B. and Martin, C. E. (1948), *Sexual Behaviour in the Human Male*, Saunders, Philadelphia.

Kirkham, G. L. (1971), 'Homosexuality in Prison', in Henslin, J. M. (ed.), *Studies in the Sociology of Sex*, Appleton-Century-Crofts, New York.

Laschet, U. (1973), 'Antiandrogen in the Treatment of Sex Offenders: Mode of Action and Therapeutic Outcome', in Zubin, J. and Money, J. (eds), *Contemporary Sexual Behaviour; Critical Issues in the 1970's*, Johns Hopkins University Press, Baltimore.

Leonard, P. (1976), 'The Function of Social Work in Society: A Preliminary Exploration', in Timms, N. and Watson, D. (eds), *Talking about Welfare: Readings in Philosophy and Social Policy*, Routledge & Kegan Paul, London.

Lloyd, B. (1976), 'Social Responsibility and Research on Sex Differences', in Lloyd, B. and Archer, J. (eds), *Exploring Sex Differences*, Academic Press, London.

McGrath, P. G. (1976), 'Sexual Offenders', in Milne, H. and Hardy, S. J. (eds), *Psycho-Sexual Problems. Proceedings of the Congress held at the University of Bradford, 1974*, University of Bradford Press.

Mackay, D. (1976), 'Modification of Sexual Behaviour', in Crown, S. (ed.), *Psychosexual Problems, Psychotherapy, Counselling and Behavioural Modification*, Academic Press, London.

Masters, W. H. and Johnson, V. E. (1966), *Human Sexual Response*, Little, Brown, Boston.

Mayer, J. E. and Timms, N. (1970), *The Client Speaks*, Routledge & Kegan Paul, London.

Money, J. (1970), 'Sexual Dimorphism and Homosexual Gender Identity', *Psychological Bulletin*, vol. 74, pp. 425-40.

Money, J. and Ehrhardt, A. A. (1972), *Man and Woman, Boy and Girl*. Johns Hopkins University Press, Baltimore.

Morris, T. (1976), *Deviance and Control: The Secular Heresy*, Hutchinson, London.

Munro, A. and McCulloch, W. (1969), *Psychiatry for Social Workers*, Pergamon Press, London.

National Council for Civil Liberties (1977), *Homosexuality and the Social Services: The Report of an NCCL Survey of Local Authority Social Service Committees*, NCCL, 186 Kings Cross Road, London WC1 9DE.

North, M. and Toates, F. (1977), 'Is Adultery Biological?', *New Society*, vol. 41, no. 772, pp. 125-6.

O'Hare, J. (1960), 'The Road to Promiscuity', *British Journal of Venereal Diseases*, vol. 36, pp. 122-4.

Paedophile Information Exchange (1975), *Evidence on the Law Relating to the Penalties for Certain Sexual Offences Involving Children*, for the Home Office Criminal Law Revision Committee. See also their *Survey of Members*, August 1976. P.O. Box 318, London SE3 8QD.

Paintin, D. B. (1976), 'The Physiology of Sex', in Milne, H. and Hardy, S. J. (eds), *Psycho-Sexual Problems*, Bradford University Press.

Parkinson, G. (1977), 'Probation by Stealth', *New Society*, vol. 39, no. 756, pp. 655-6.

Pearson, G. (1975), *The Deviant Imagination: Psychiatry, Social Work and Social Change*, McMillan, London.

Pearson, M. (1972), *The Age of Consent: Victorian Prostitution and its Enemies*, David & Charles, Newton Abbot.

Perlman, H. H. (1971), *Perspectives on Social Casework*, Temple University Press, Philadelphia.

Personal Social Services Council (1977), *Residential Care Reviewed*, PSSC, London.

Petrie, G. (1971), *A Singular Iniquity: The Campaigns of Josephine Butler*, McMillan, London.

Piaget, J. (1932), *The Moral Judgement of the Child*, Routledge & Kegan Paul, London.

Pincus, L. (1960), *Marriage: Studies in Emotional Conflict and Growth*, Family Discussion Bureau Publications, Methuen, London.

Plant, R. (1970), *Social and Moral Theory in Casework*, Routledge & Kegan Paul, London.

Plummer, K. (1975), *Sexual Stigma: an Interactionist Account*, Routledge & Kegan Paul, London.

References

Quinn, J. T., Harbison, J. M. and McAllister, H. (1970), 'An Attempt to Shape Human Penile Responses', *Behaviour Research and Therapy*, vol. 8, pp. 213-16.

Read, G. and Millard, D. (1977), in Letters, *New Society*, vol. 40, no. 761 (refers to 'Parkinson Case').

Reed, E. (1975), *Women's Evolution: from Matriarchal Clan to Patriarchal Family*, Pathfinder Press, New York, Toronto and London.

Reiner, B., Simcox and Kaufman, I. (1959), *Character Disorders in Parents of Delinquents*, Family Service Association of America, New York.

Richan, W. C. (1972), 'A Common Language for Social Work', *Social Work (USA)*, vol. 17, pp. 14-22.

Richmond, M. (1917), *Social Diagnosis*, Russell Sage Foundation, New York.

Rieff, P. (1960), *Freud: the Mind of the Moralist*, Gollancz, London.

Righton, P. (1977), 'Sex and the Residential Social Worker', *Social Work Today*, vol. 8, no. 19, p. 12.

Rogers, L. (1976), 'Male Hormones and Behaviour', in Lloyd, B. and Archer, J. (eds), *Exploring Sex Differences*, Academic Press, London.

Rooth, G. (1973), 'Exhibitionism, Sexual Violence and Paedophilia', *British Journal of Psychiatry*, vol. 122, no. 571, pp. 705-10.

Russell, S. (1960) 'Morals and the Social Worker', *Report of Conference held at Oxford, September 1959*, Association of Social Workers, London.

Rutter, M. (1971), 'Normal Psychosexual Development', *Journal of Child Psychology and Psychiatry*, vol. 11, no. 4, pp. 259-83.

Ryan, A. (1975), 'Two Kinds of Morality', *New Society*, vol. 52, no. 652, pp. 24-6.

Sainsbury, E. (1977), Unpublished Research, University of Sheffield, Department of Sociological Studies.

Schofield, M. (1965a), *Sociological Aspects of Homosexuality: A Comparative Study of Three Types of Homosexuals*, Longmans, London.

Schofield, M. (1965b), *The Sexual Behaviour of Young People*, Longmans, London.

Schofield, M. (1973), *The Sexual Behaviour of Young Adults*, Allen Lane, London.

Schofield, M. (1976), *Promiscuity*, Gollancz, London.

Schultz, L. G. (1975), 'Ethical Issues in Treating Sexual Dysfunction', *Social Work (USA)*, vol. 20, no. 2, pp. 126-8.

Seemanová, E. (1971), 'A Study of Children of Incestuous Matings', *Human Heredity*, vol. 21, pp. 108-28.

Smart, C. (1977), *Women, Crime and Criminology: A Feminist Critique*, Routledge & Kegan Paul, London.

Soothill, K. and Jack, A. (1975), 'How Rape is Reported', *New Society*, vol. 32, no. 663, pp. 702-4.

Storr, A. (1964), *Sexual Deviation*, Penguin, Harmondsworth.

Taylor, L. (1972), 'The Significance and Interpretation of Replies to Motivational Questions: The Case of Sex Offenders', *Sociology*, vol. 6, no. 1, pp. 23-39.

Timms, N. (1964), *Psychiatric Social Work in Great Britain (1939-1962)*, Routledge & Kegan Paul, London.

Toffler, A. (1971), *Future Shock*, Pan Books, London.

Weinberg, G. (1973), *Society and the Healthy Homosexual*, Doubleday, New York.

Weinberg, M. S. and Williams, C. J. (1974), *Male Homosexuals, Their Problems and Adaptations*, Oxford University Press, New York.

Whalin, R. E. (1971), 'Sexual Motivation', in Leiberman, B. (ed.), *Human Sexual Behaviour: A Book of Readings*, Wiley, New York.

Whittaker, J. K. (1976), 'Treatment of Choice . . . or Chance?', in Olsen, M. R. (ed.), *Differential Approaches in Social Work with the Mentally Disordered*, British Association of Social Workers, London.

Whittington, C. (1977), 'Social Workers' Orientations: An Action Perspective', *British Journal of Social Work*, vol. 7, no. 1, pp. 73-95.

Wilson, E. (1977), *Women and the Welfare State*, Tavistock, London.

Wilson, G. T. and Davison, G. C. (1974), 'Behaviour Therapy and Homosexuality: A Critical Perspective', *Behaviour Therapy*, vol. 5, pp. 16-28.

Zuger, B. (1966), 'Effeminate Behaviour Present in Boys from Early Childhood: 1. The Clinical Syndrome and Follow-up Studies', *Journal of Paediatrics*, vol. 69, pp. 1098-107.

Zurcher, L. A. and Kirkpatrick, R. G. (1976), *Citizens for Decency: Antipornography Crusaders as Status Defense*, University of Texas Press, Austin.

Index